LEGENDARY
COMICS

P R E S E N T S

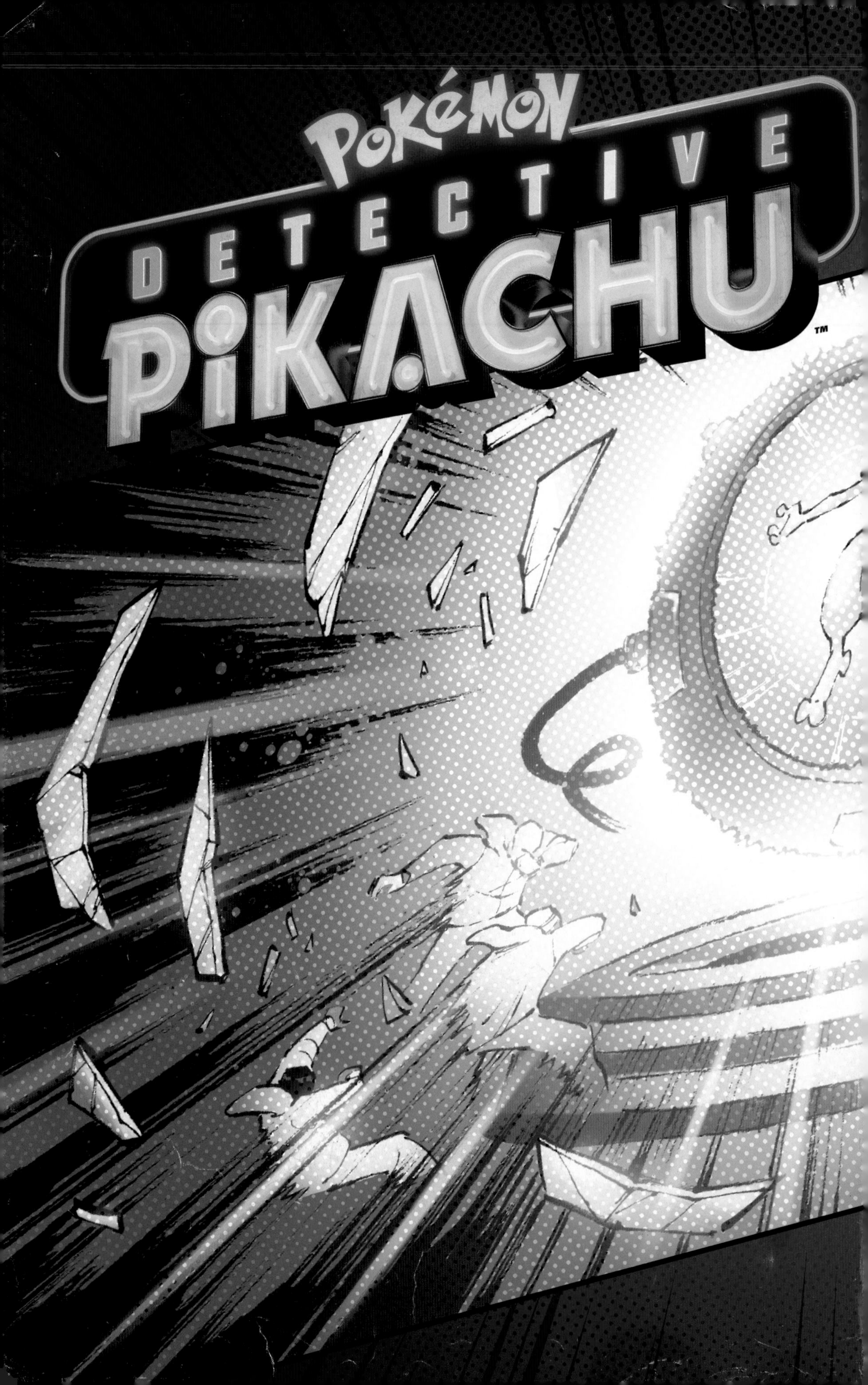
POKéMON
DETECTIVE
PIKACHU™

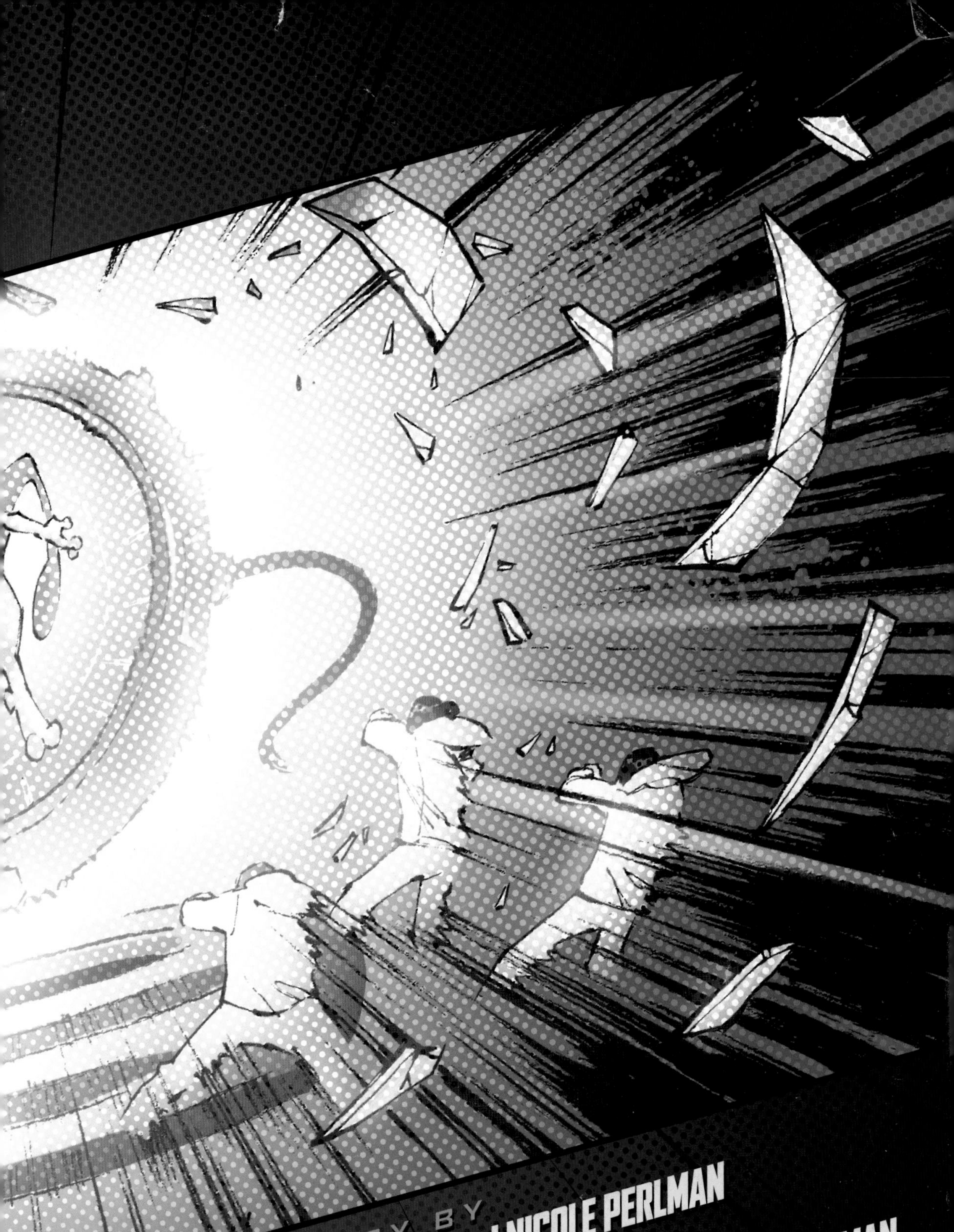

STORY BY
DAN HERNANDEZ & BENJI SAMIT and NICOLE PERLMAN
SCREENPLAY BY
DAN HERNANDEZ & BENJI SAMIT and ROB LETTERMAN
and DEREK CONNOLY
DIRECTED BY
ROB LETTERMAN

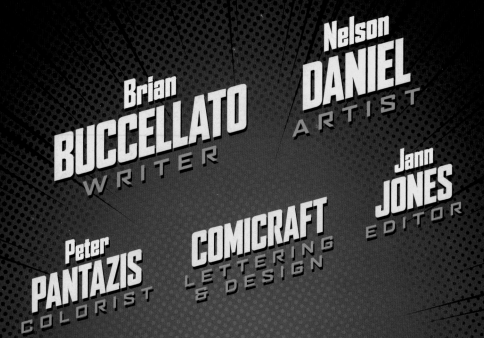

Brian **BUCCELLATO**
WRITER

Nelson **DANIEL**
ARTIST

Peter **PANTAZIS**
COLORIST

COMICRAFT
LETTERING & DESIGN

Jann **JONES**
EDITOR

LEGENDARY

JOSHUA GRODE
Chief Executive Officer

MARY PARENT
Vice Chairman of Worldwide Production

NICK PEPPER
President Of Legendary Television & Digital Studios

RONALD HOHAUSER
Chief Financial Officer

BARNABY LEGG
SVP, Creative Strategy

MIKE ROSS
EVP, Business & Legal Affairs

KRISTINA HOLLIMAN
VP, Business & Legal Affairs

DAN FEINBERG
SVP, Corporate Counsel

BAYAN LAIRD
SVP, Business & Legal Affairs

LEGENDARY COMICS

ROBERT NAPTON
SVP, Publishing

NIKITA KANNEKANTI
Editor

JANN JONES
Manager, Brand Development & Publishing Operations

Special Thanks To:
HEATHER DALGLEISH, EMILY LEWIS, KARI YANAI & EOIN SANDERS

FIRST PRINTING: FEBRUARY 2020

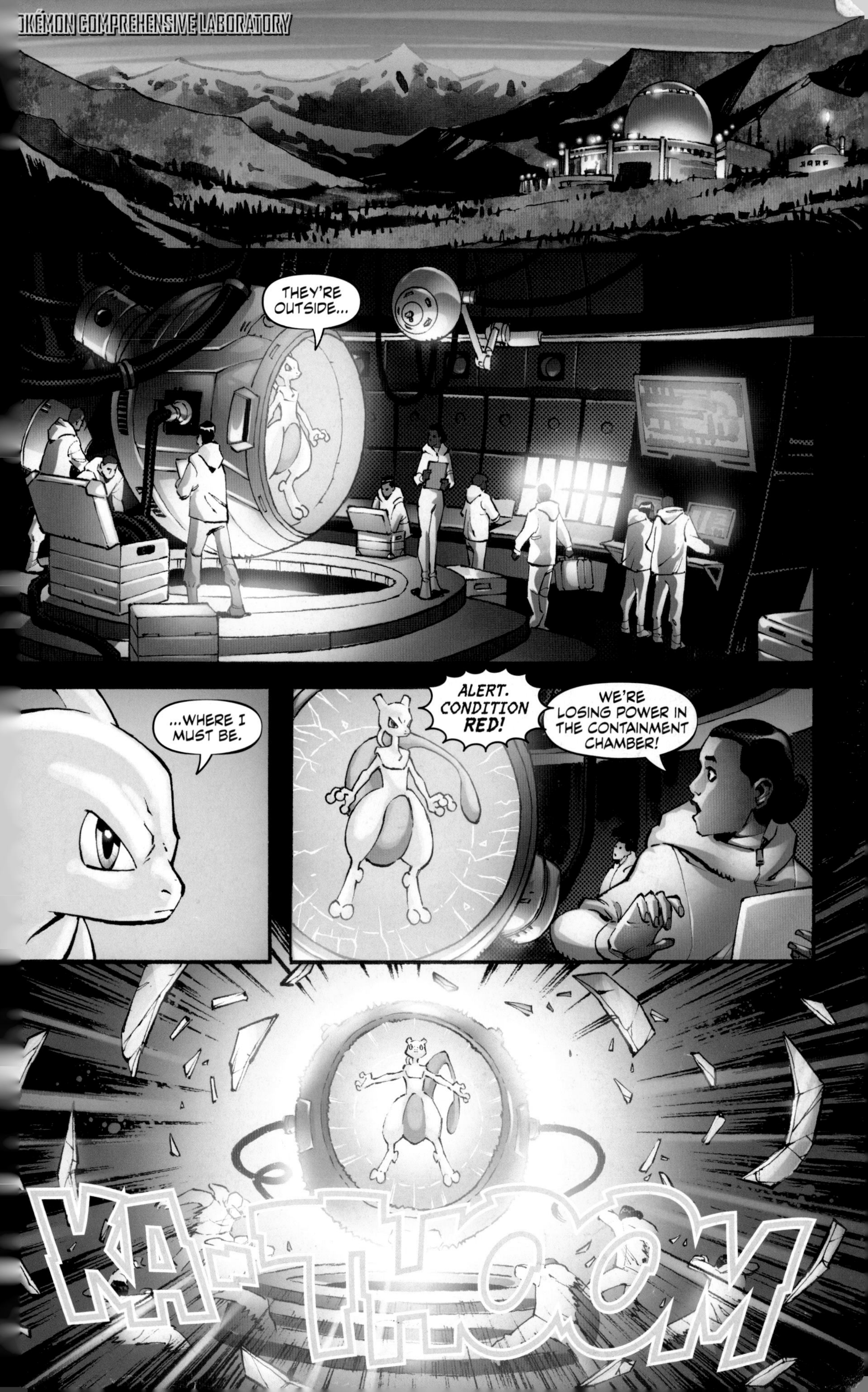
OKÉMON COMPREHENSIVE LABORATORY
THEY'RE OUTSIDE...
...WHERE I MUST BE.
ALERT. CONDITION RED!
WE'RE LOSING POWER IN THE CONTAINMENT CHAMBER!
KA-THOOM

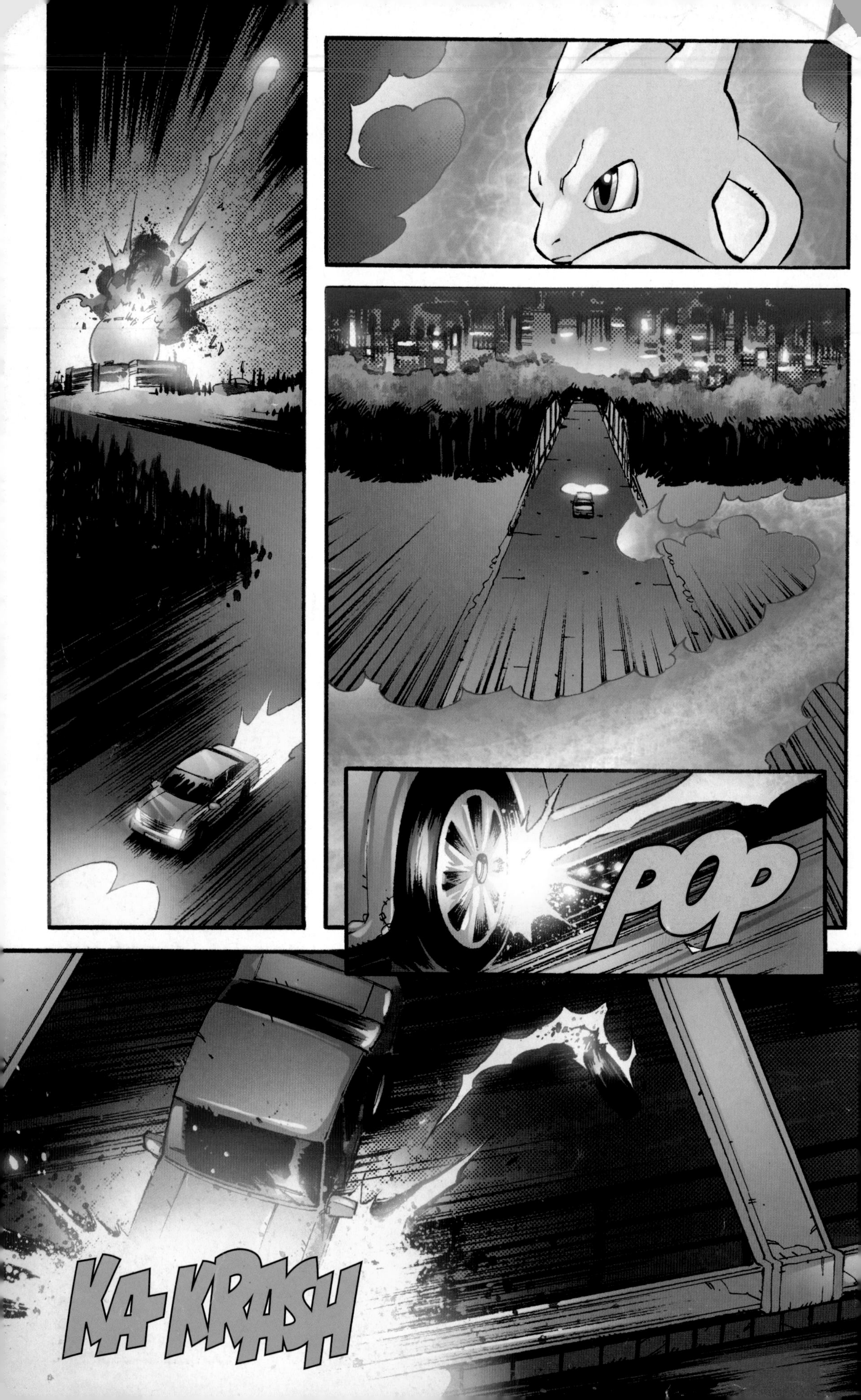
POP
KA-KRASH

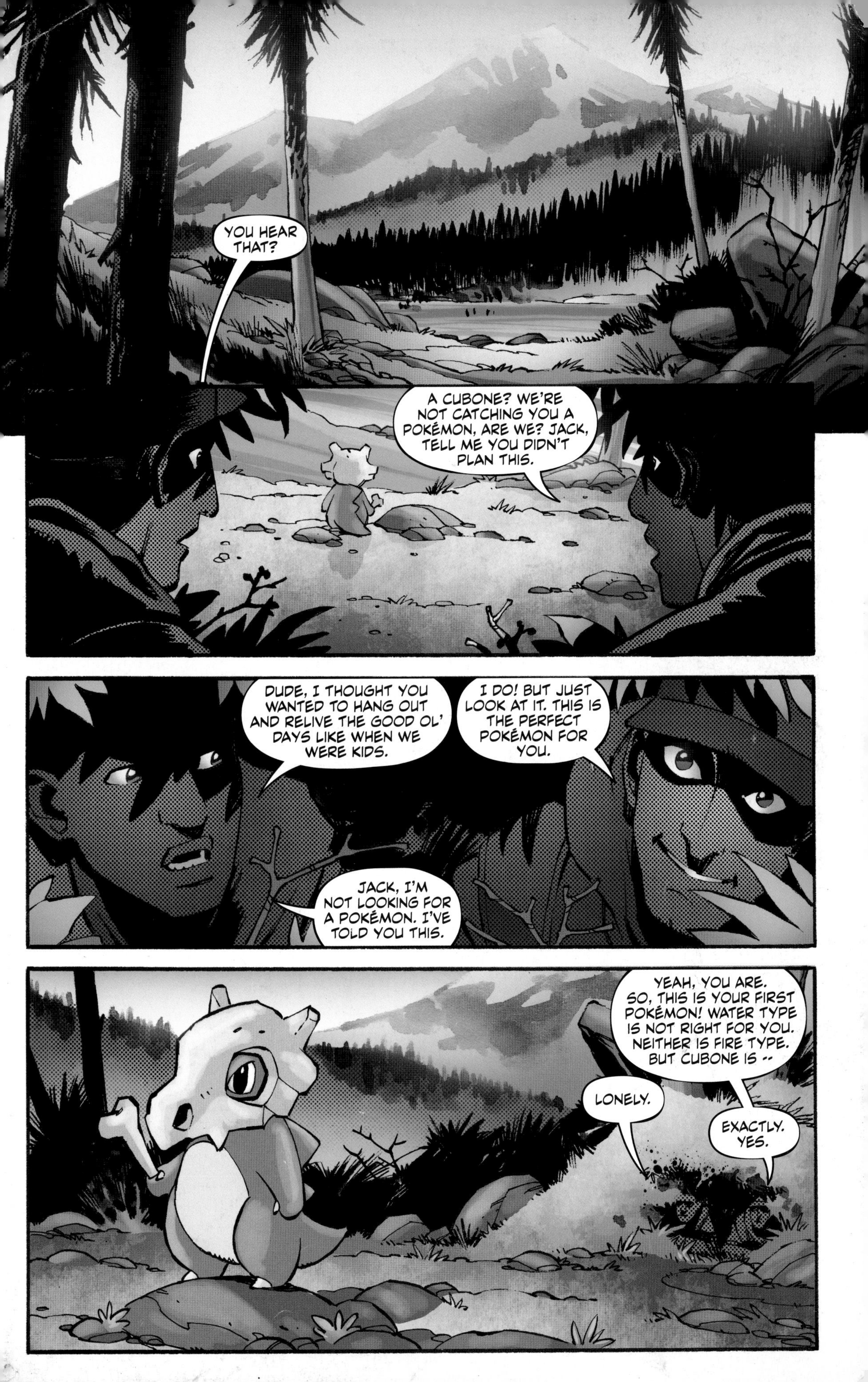
YOU HEAR THAT?
A CUBONE? WE'RE NOT CATCHING YOU A POKÉMON, ARE WE? JACK, TELL ME YOU DIDN'T PLAN THIS.
DUDE, I THOUGHT YOU WANTED TO HANG OUT AND RELIVE THE GOOD OL' DAYS LIKE WHEN WE WERE KIDS.
I DO! BUT JUST LOOK AT IT. THIS IS THE PERFECT POKÉMON FOR YOU.
JACK, I'M NOT LOOKING FOR A POKÉMON. I'VE TOLD YOU THIS.
YEAH, YOU ARE. SO, THIS IS YOUR FIRST POKÉMON! WATER TYPE IS NOT RIGHT FOR YOU. NEITHER IS FIRE TYPE. BUT CUBONE IS --
LONELY.
EXACTLY. YES.

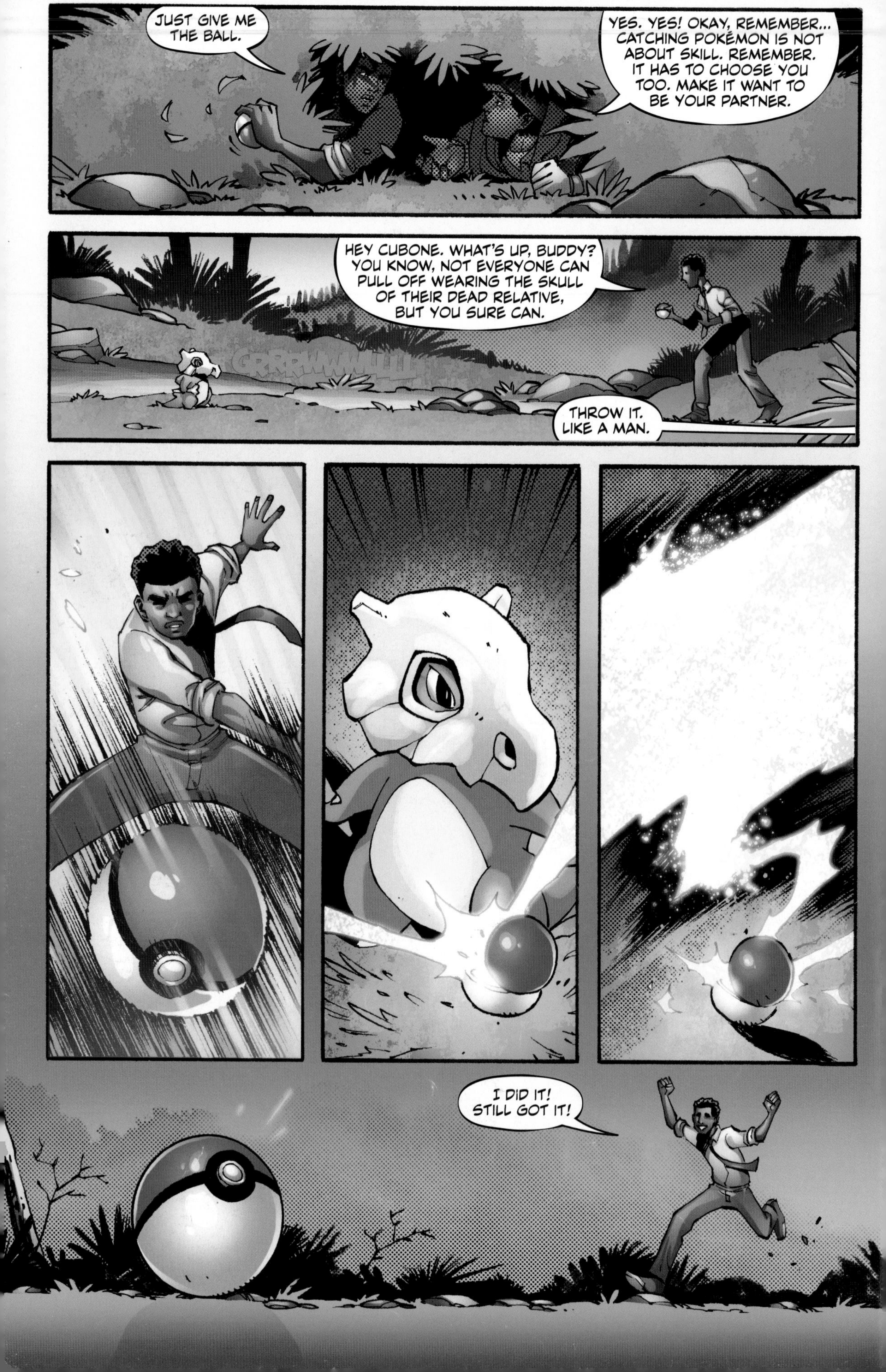
JUST GIVE ME THE BALL.
YES. YES! OKAY, REMEMBER... CATCHING POKÉMON IS NOT ABOUT SKILL. REMEMBER. IT HAS TO CHOOSE YOU TOO. MAKE IT WANT TO BE YOUR PARTNER.
HEY CUBONE. WHAT'S UP, BUDDY? YOU KNOW, NOT EVERYONE CAN PULL OFF WEARING THE SKULL OF THEIR DEAD RELATIVE, BUT YOU SURE CAN.
GRRRWWWLLL!
THROW IT. LIKE A MAN.
I DID IT! STILL GOT IT!

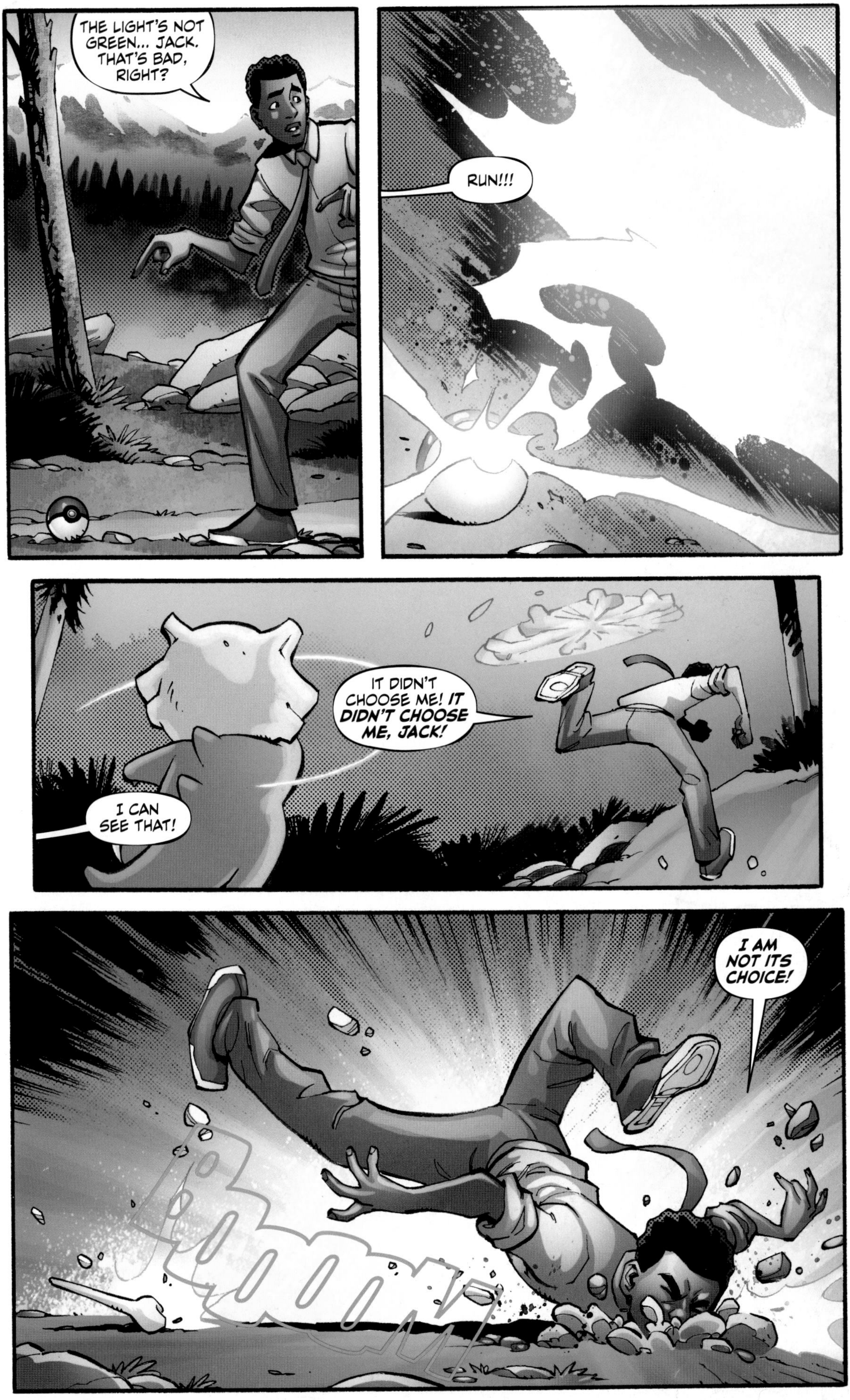
THE LIGHT'S NOT GREEN... JACK. THAT'S BAD, RIGHT?
RUN!!!
IT DIDN'T CHOOSE ME! *IT DIDN'T CHOOSE ME, JACK!*
I CAN SEE THAT!
I AM NOT ITS CHOICE!
BOOM

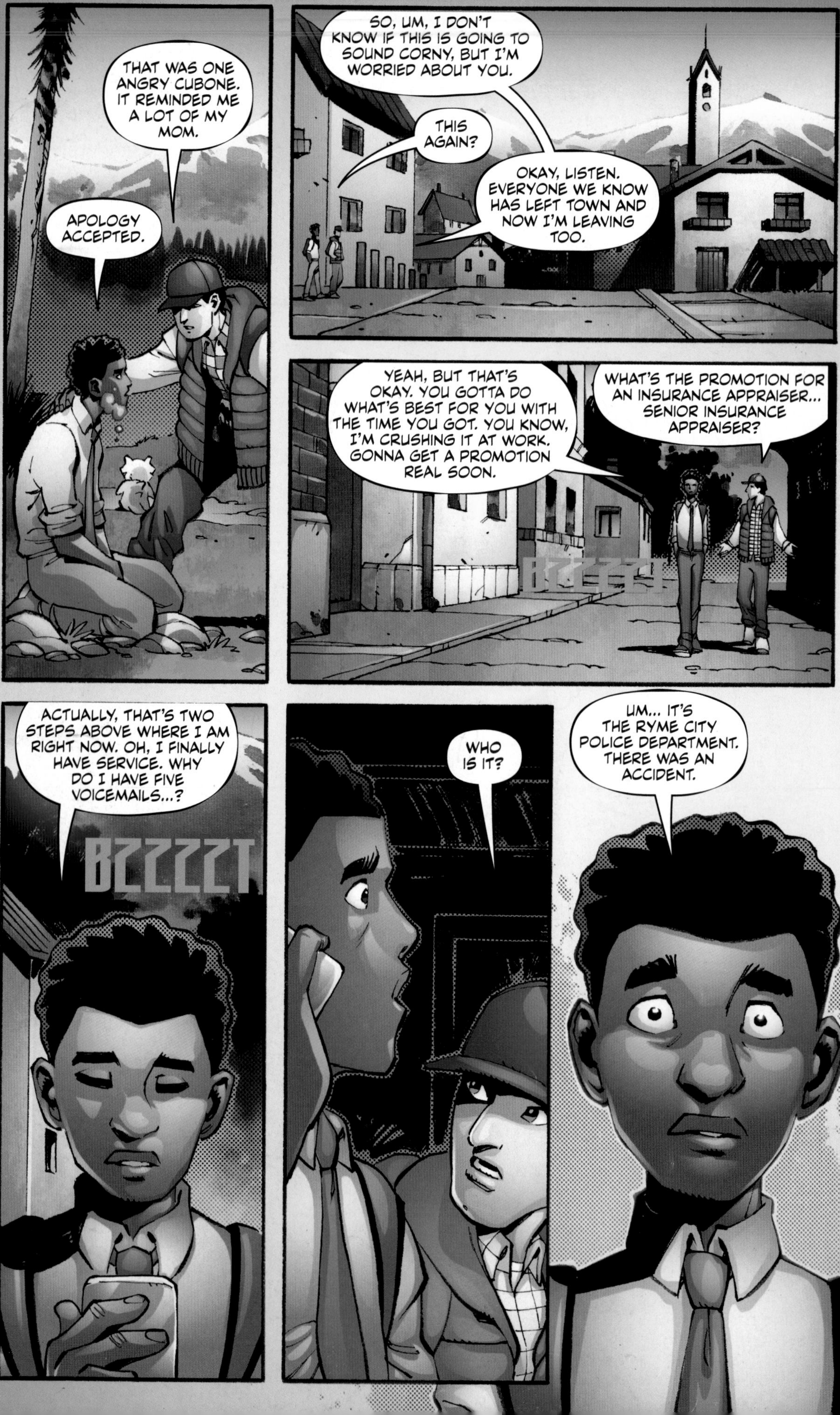
THAT WAS ONE ANGRY CUBONE. IT REMINDED ME A LOT OF MY MOM.
APOLOGY ACCEPTED.
SO, UM, I DON'T KNOW IF THIS IS GOING TO SOUND CORNY, BUT I'M WORRIED ABOUT YOU.
THIS AGAIN?
OKAY, LISTEN. EVERYONE WE KNOW HAS LEFT TOWN AND NOW I'M LEAVING TOO.
YEAH, BUT THAT'S OKAY. YOU GOTTA DO WHAT'S BEST FOR YOU WITH THE TIME YOU GOT. YOU KNOW, I'M CRUSHING IT AT WORK. GONNA GET A PROMOTION REAL SOON.
WHAT'S THE PROMOTION FOR AN INSURANCE APPRAISER... SENIOR INSURANCE APPRAISER?
BZZZZT
ACTUALLY, THAT'S TWO STEPS ABOVE WHERE I AM RIGHT NOW. OH, I FINALLY HAVE SERVICE. WHY DO I HAVE FIVE VOICEMAILS...?
BZZZZT
WHO IS IT?
UM... IT'S THE RYME CITY POLICE DEPARTMENT. THERE WAS AN ACCIDENT.

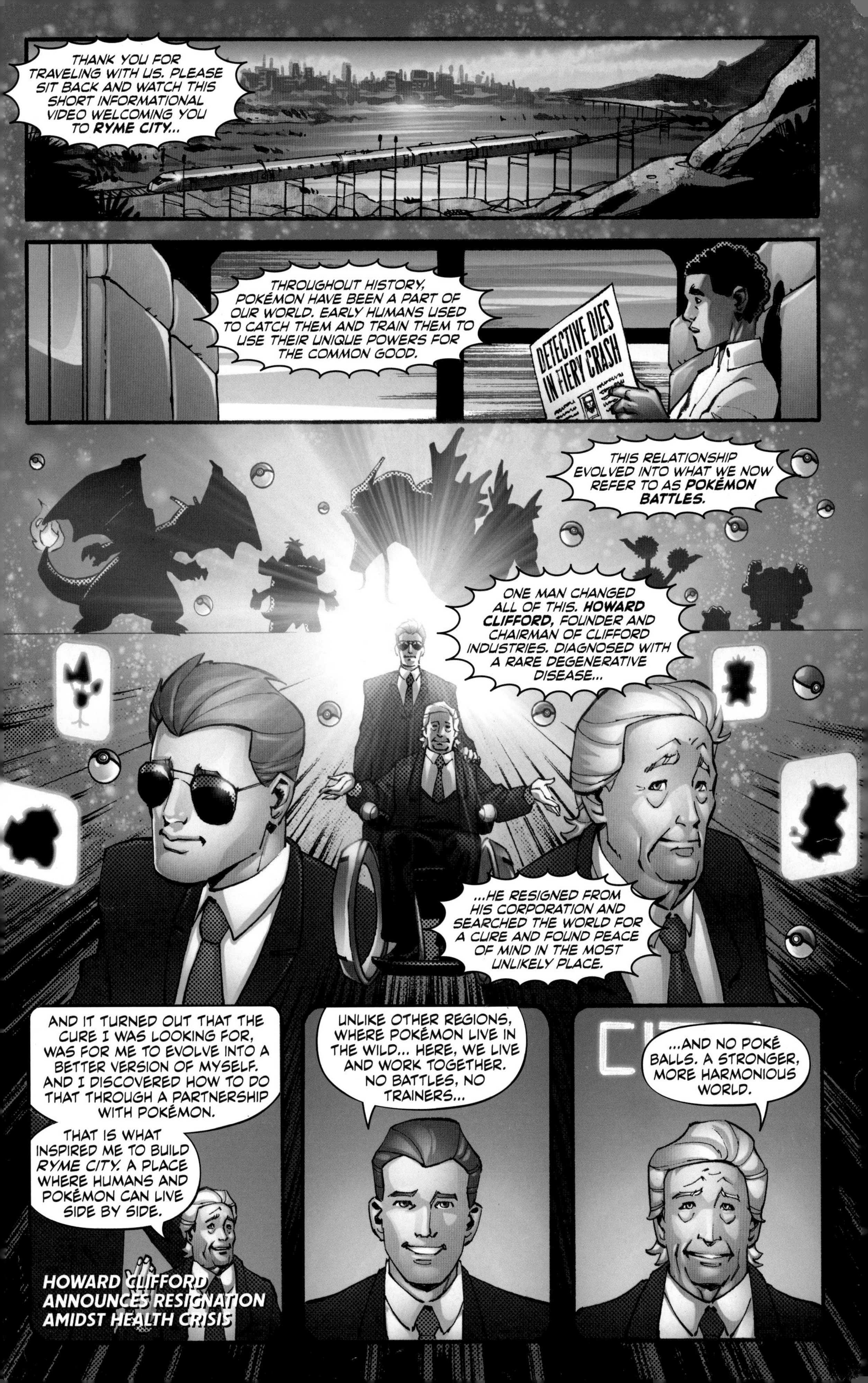

THANK YOU FOR TRAVELING WITH US. PLEASE SIT BACK AND WATCH THIS SHORT INFORMATIONAL VIDEO WELCOMING YOU TO **RYME CITY**...
THROUGHOUT HISTORY, POKÉMON HAVE BEEN A PART OF OUR WORLD. EARLY HUMANS USED TO CATCH THEM AND TRAIN THEM TO USE THEIR UNIQUE POWERS FOR THE COMMON GOOD.
DETECTIVE DIES IN FIERY CRASH
THIS RELATIONSHIP EVOLVED INTO WHAT WE NOW REFER TO AS **POKÉMON BATTLES.**
ONE MAN CHANGED ALL OF THIS. **HOWARD CLIFFORD,** FOUNDER AND CHAIRMAN OF CLIFFORD INDUSTRIES. DIAGNOSED WITH A RARE DEGENERATIVE DISEASE...
...HE RESIGNED FROM HIS CORPORATION AND SEARCHED THE WORLD FOR A CURE AND FOUND PEACE OF MIND IN THE MOST UNLIKELY PLACE.
AND IT TURNED OUT THAT THE CURE I WAS LOOKING FOR, WAS FOR ME TO EVOLVE INTO A BETTER VERSION OF MYSELF. AND I DISCOVERED HOW TO DO THAT THROUGH A PARTNERSHIP WITH POKÉMON.
THAT IS WHAT INSPIRED ME TO BUILD *RYME CITY*. A PLACE WHERE HUMANS AND POKÉMON CAN LIVE SIDE BY SIDE.
HOWARD CLIFFORD ANNOUNCES RESIGNATION AMIDST HEALTH CRISIS
UNLIKE OTHER REGIONS, WHERE POKÉMON LIVE IN THE WILD... HERE, WE LIVE AND WORK TOGETHER. NO BATTLES, NO TRAINERS...
...AND NO POKÉ BALLS. A STRONGER, MORE HARMONIOUS WORLD.

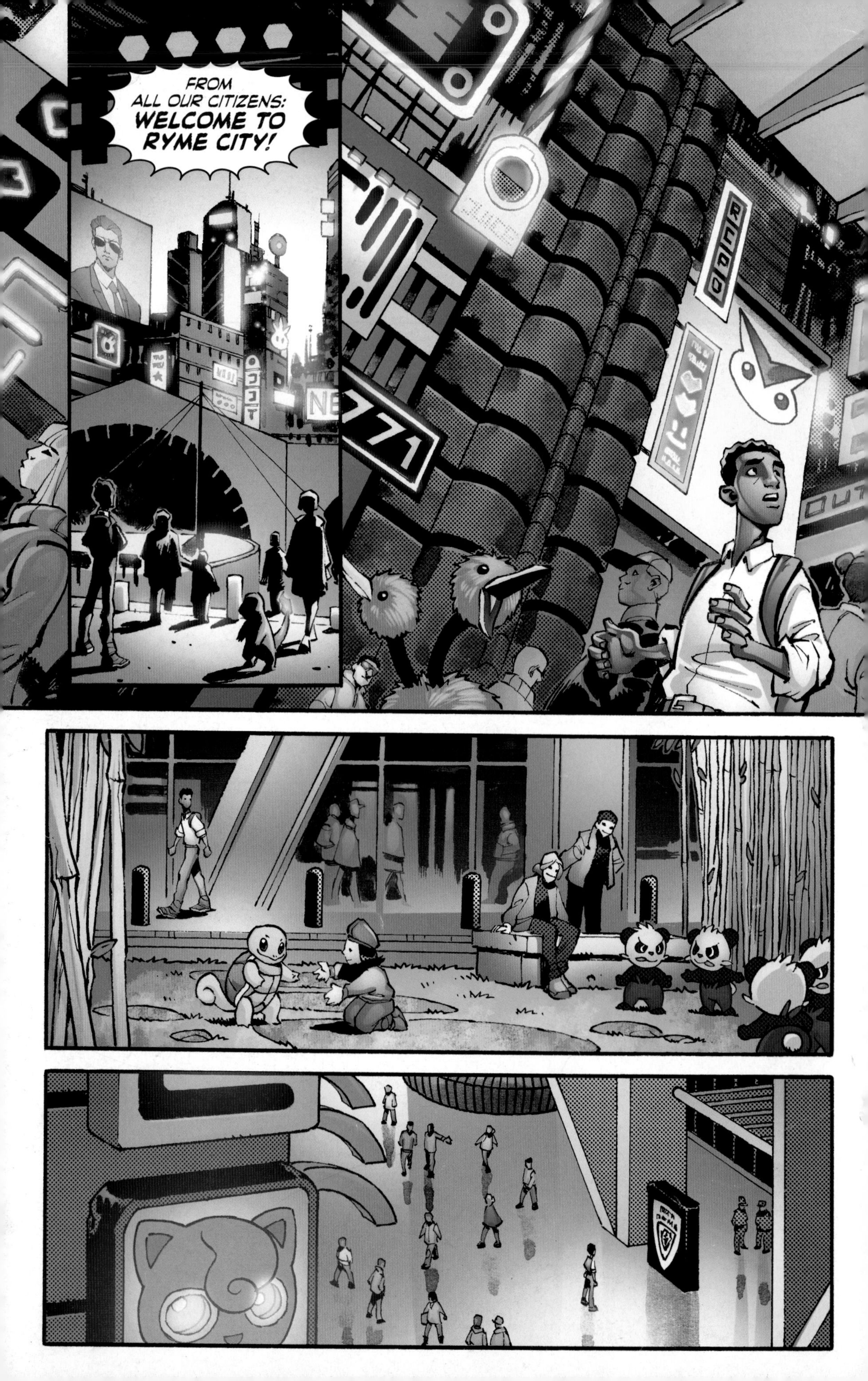
FROM ALL OUR CITIZENS: WELCOME TO RYME CITY!
JUICE
771

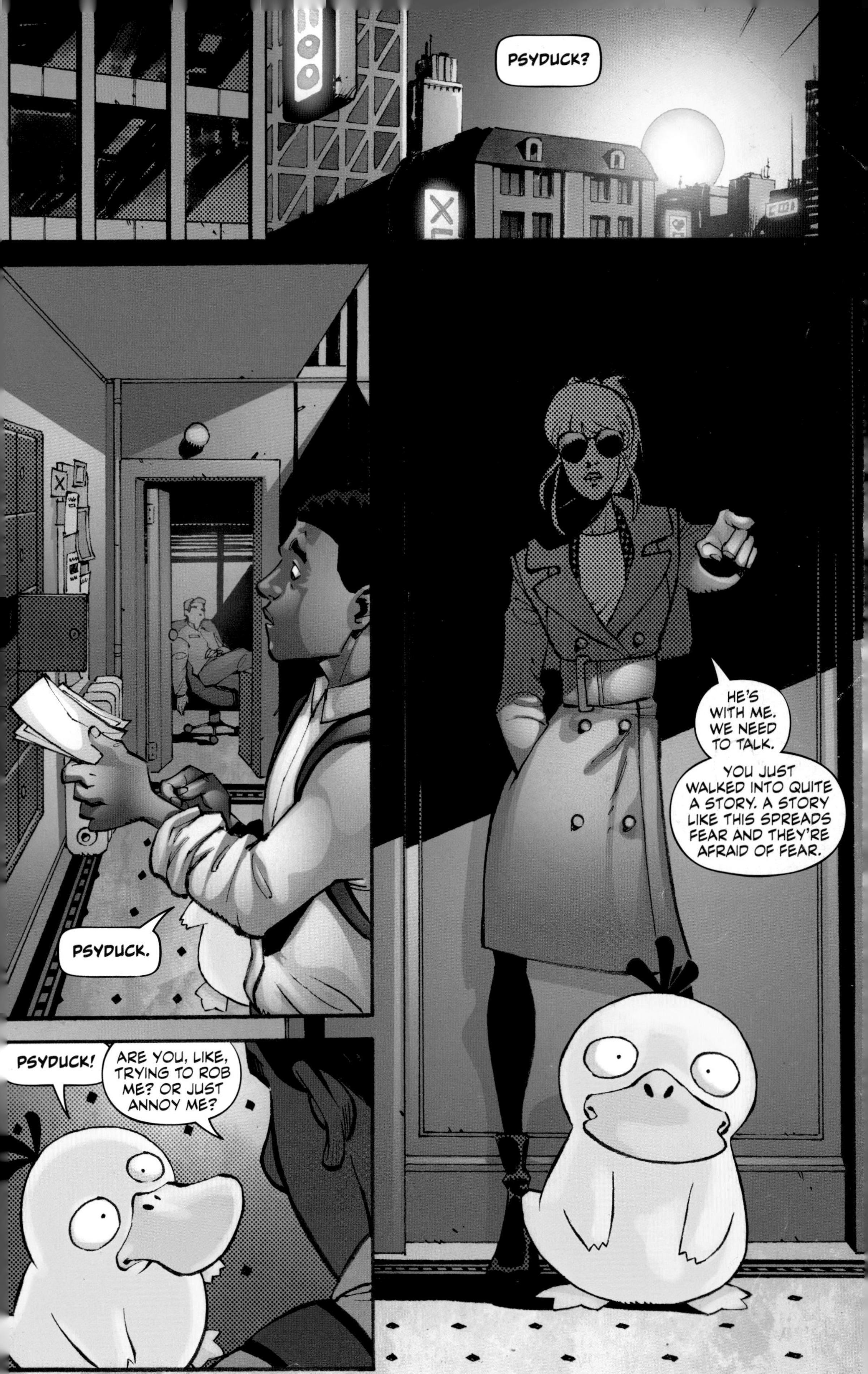

PSYDUCK?
PSYDUCK.
HE'S WITH ME. WE NEED TO TALK.
YOU JUST WALKED INTO QUITE A STORY. A STORY LIKE THIS SPREADS FEAR AND THEY'RE AFRAID OF FEAR.
PSYDUCK!
ARE YOU, LIKE, TRYING TO ROB ME? OR JUST ANNOY ME?

BUT I DON'T FEAR FEAR. I WALK THE WALK AND I TALK THE TALK AND I'M WILLING TO DO WHATEVER IT TAKES TO GET THE HONEST SCOOP AND THAT'S THE HARD TRUTH.

I'M SORRY, WHO ARE YOU?

LUCY STEVENS, REPORTER FOR CNM.

YOU SEEM KINDA YOUNG FOR THAT.

I'M A JUNIOR REPORTER. I WORK FOR THE CNM BLOG MAKING POKÉMON LISTICLES ALL DAY, OKAY? *TOP TEN CUTEST POKÉMON.*

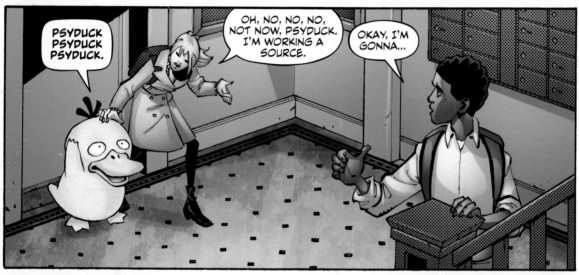

PSYDUCK PSYDUCK PSYDUCK.

OH, NO, NO, NO, NOT NOW, PSYDUCK. I'M WORKING A SOURCE.

OKAY, I'M GONNA...

I'M GONNA NEED YOU TO GO ON THE RECORD AND TELL ME EVERYTHING YOU KNOW ABOUT HARRY GOODMAN.

WAIT... WHAT?

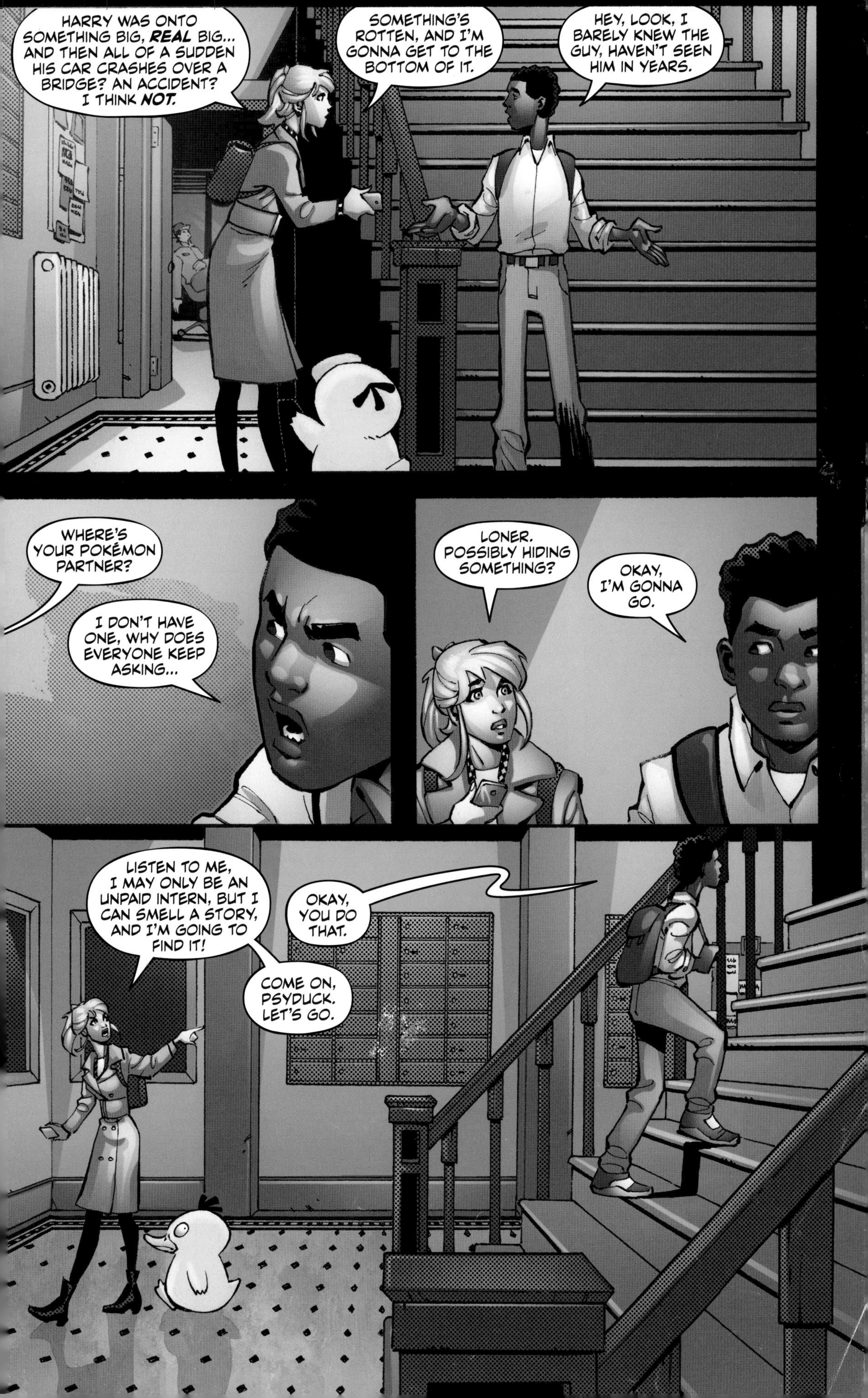
HARRY WAS ONTO SOMETHING BIG, **REAL** BIG... AND THEN ALL OF A SUDDEN HIS CAR CRASHES OVER A BRIDGE? AN ACCIDENT? I THINK **NOT.**
SOMETHING'S ROTTEN, AND I'M GONNA GET TO THE BOTTOM OF IT.
HEY, LOOK, I BARELY KNEW THE GUY, HAVEN'T SEEN HIM IN YEARS.
WHERE'S YOUR POKÉMON PARTNER?
I DON'T HAVE ONE, WHY DOES EVERYONE KEEP ASKING...
LONER. POSSIBLY HIDING SOMETHING?
OKAY, I'M GONNA GO.
LISTEN TO ME, I MAY ONLY BE AN UNPAID INTERN, BUT I CAN SMELL A STORY, AND I'M GOING TO FIND IT!
OKAY, YOU DO THAT.
COME ON, PSYDUCK. LET'S GO.

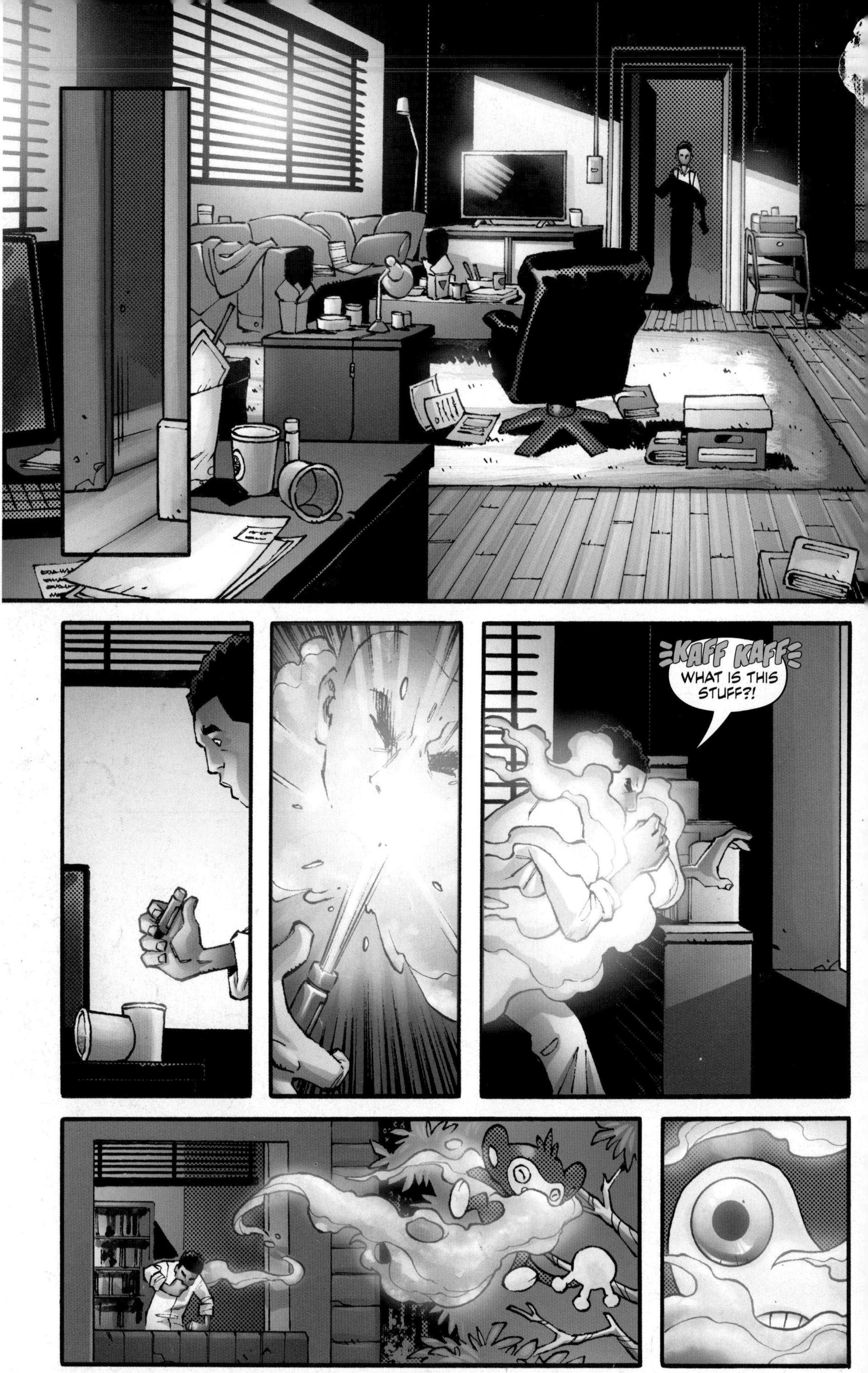
KAFF KAFF
WHAT IS THIS STUFF?!

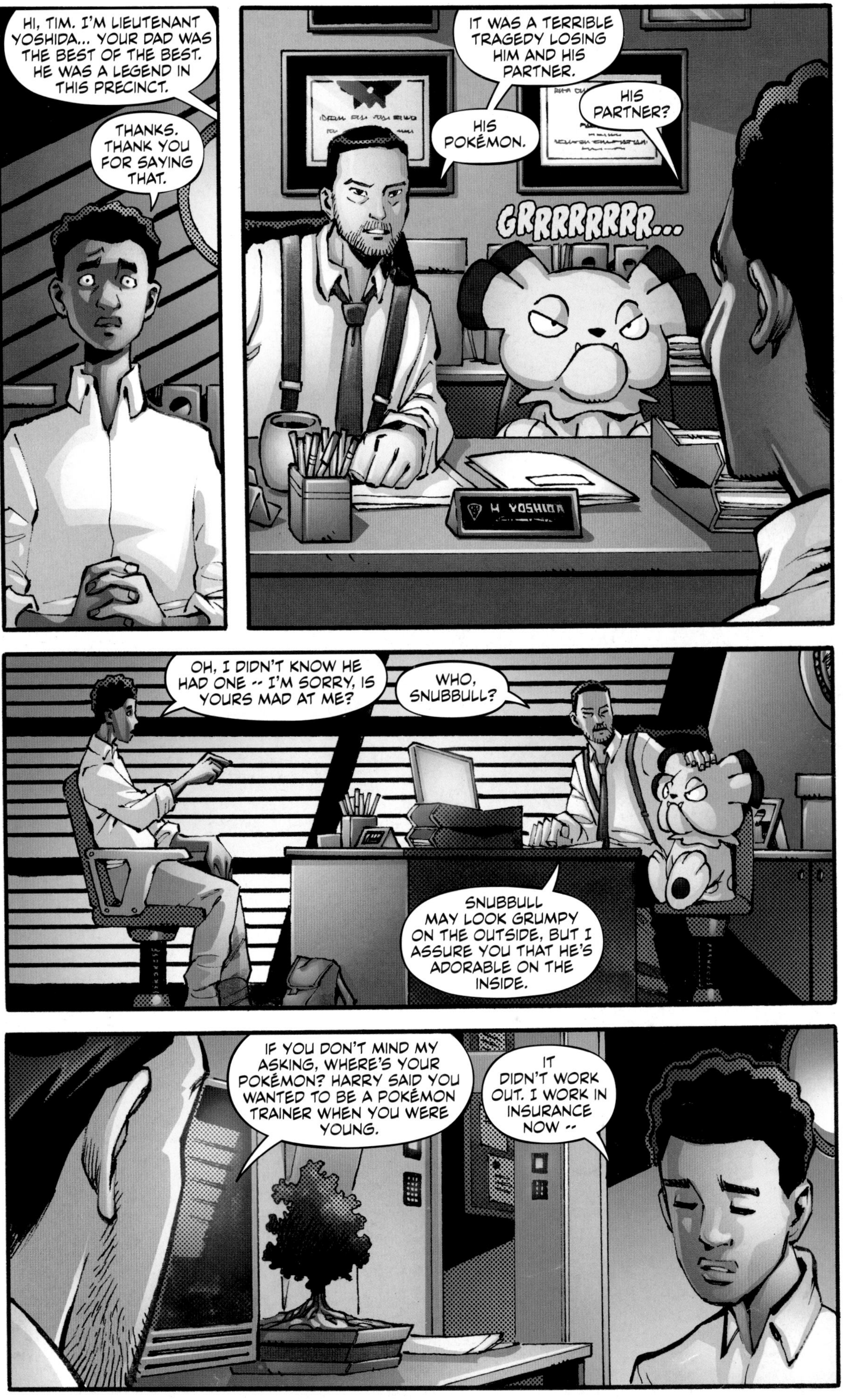
HI, TIM. I'M LIEUTENANT YOSHIDA... YOUR DAD WAS THE BEST OF THE BEST. HE WAS A LEGEND IN THIS PRECINCT.
THANKS. THANK YOU FOR SAYING THAT.
IT WAS A TERRIBLE TRAGEDY LOSING HIM AND HIS PARTNER.
HIS PARTNER?
HIS POKÉMON.
GRRRRRRRR...
H. YOSHIDA
OH, I DIDN'T KNOW HE HAD ONE -- I'M SORRY, IS YOURS MAD AT ME?
WHO, SNUBBULL?
SNUBBULL MAY LOOK GRUMPY ON THE OUTSIDE, BUT I ASSURE YOU THAT HE'S ADORABLE ON THE INSIDE.
IF YOU DON'T MIND MY ASKING, WHERE'S YOUR POKÉMON? HARRY SAID YOU WANTED TO BE A POKÉMON TRAINER WHEN YOU WERE YOUNG.
IT DIDN'T WORK OUT. I WORK IN INSURANCE NOW --

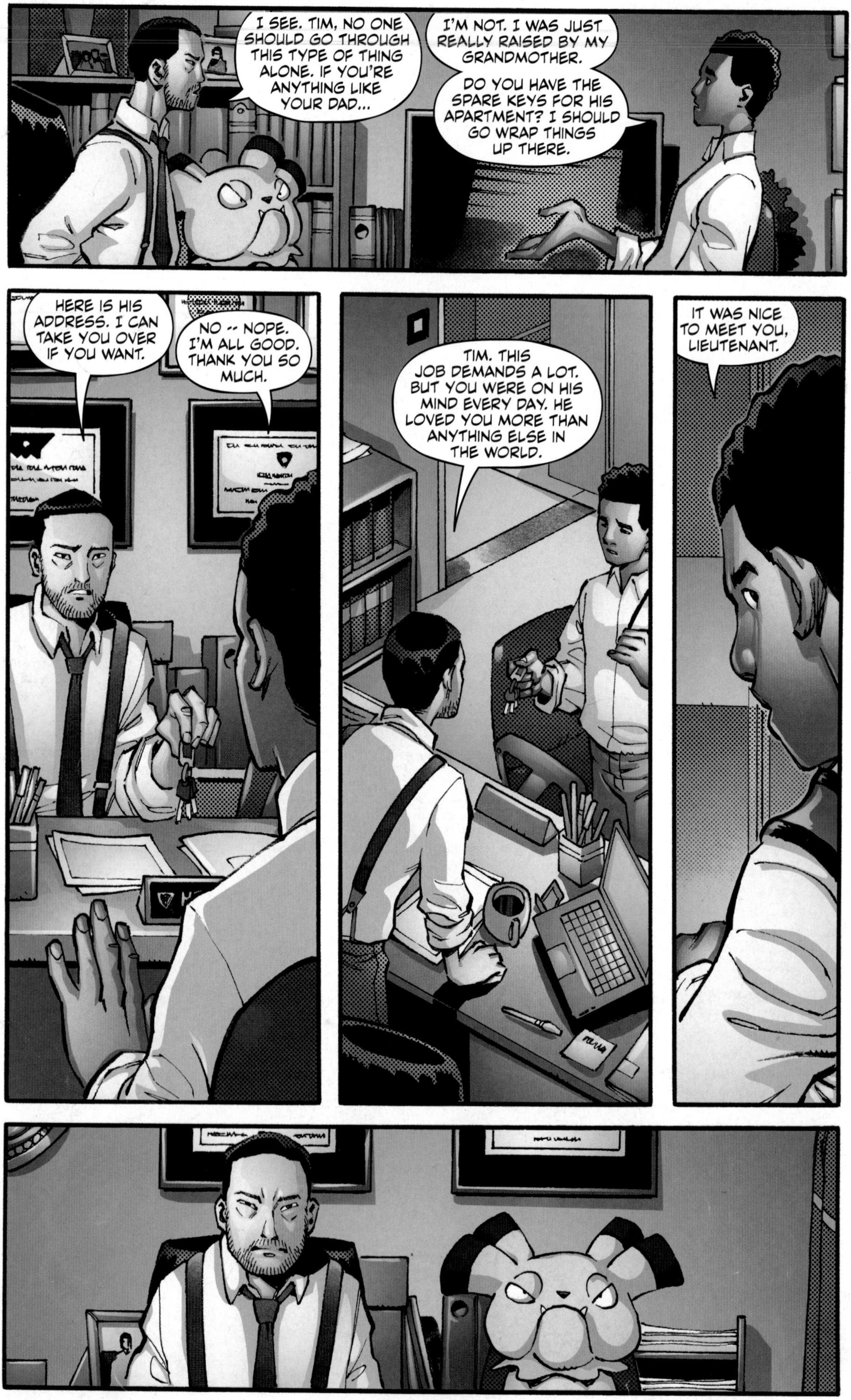
I SEE. TIM, NO ONE SHOULD GO THROUGH THIS TYPE OF THING ALONE. IF YOU'RE ANYTHING LIKE YOUR DAD...
I'M NOT. I WAS JUST REALLY RAISED BY MY GRANDMOTHER.
DO YOU HAVE THE SPARE KEYS FOR HIS APARTMENT? I SHOULD GO WRAP THINGS UP THERE.
HERE IS HIS ADDRESS. I CAN TAKE YOU OVER IF YOU WANT.
NO -- NOPE. I'M ALL GOOD. THANK YOU SO MUCH.
TIM. THIS JOB DEMANDS A LOT. BUT YOU WERE ON HIS MIND EVERY DAY. HE LOVED YOU MORE THAN ANYTHING ELSE IN THE WORLD.
IT WAS NICE TO MEET YOU, LIEUTENANT.

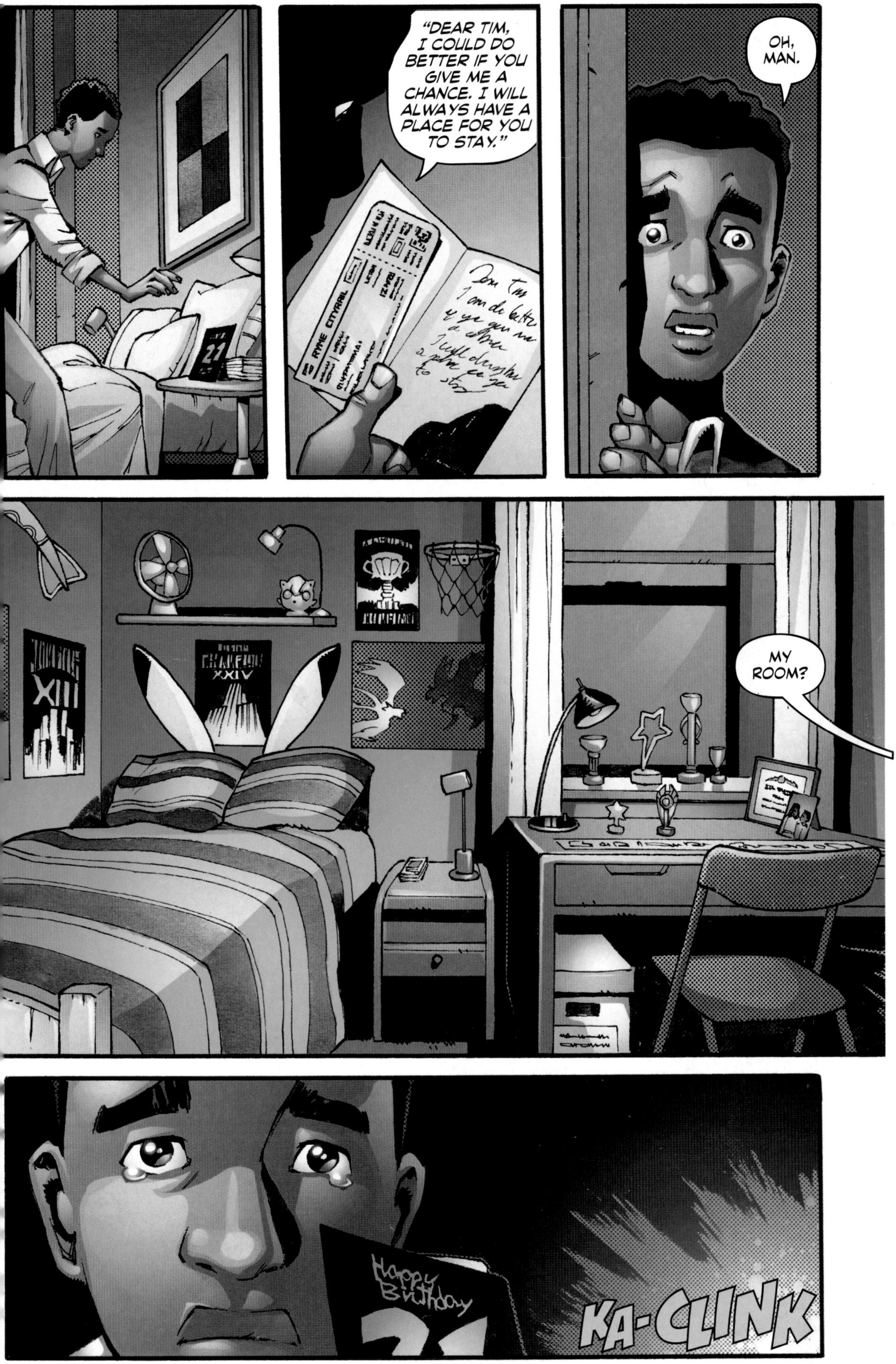

"DEAR TIM, I COULD DO BETTER IF YOU GIVE ME A CHANCE. I WILL ALWAYS HAVE A PLACE FOR YOU TO STAY."
OH, MAN.
MY ROOM?
Happy Birthday
KA-CLINK

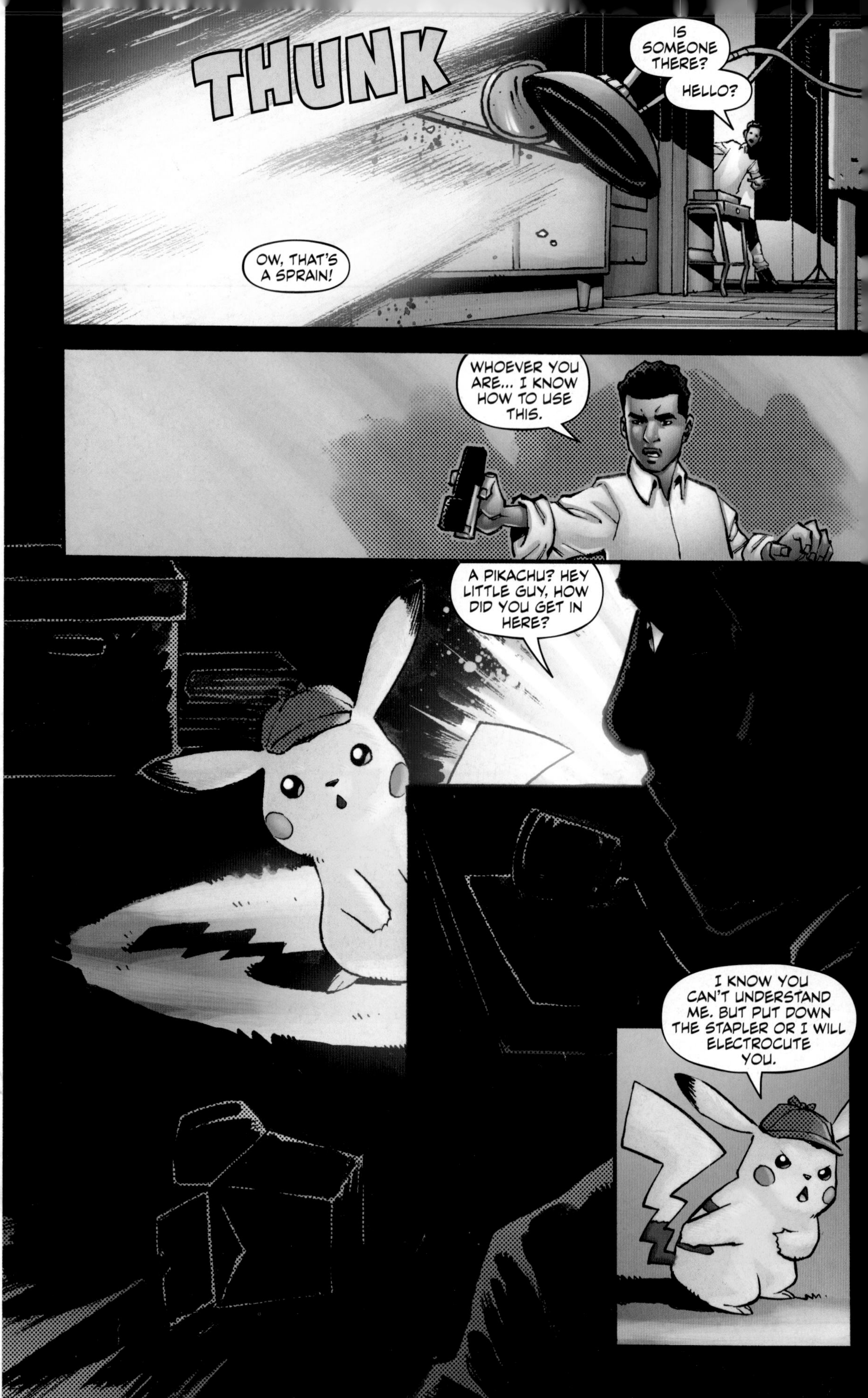
THUNK
IS SOMEONE THERE?
HELLO?
OW, THAT'S A SPRAIN!
WHOEVER YOU ARE... I KNOW HOW TO USE THIS.
A PIKACHU? HEY LITTLE GUY, HOW DID YOU GET IN HERE?
I KNOW YOU CAN'T UNDERSTAND ME. BUT PUT DOWN THE STAPLER OR I WILL ELECTROCUTE YOU.

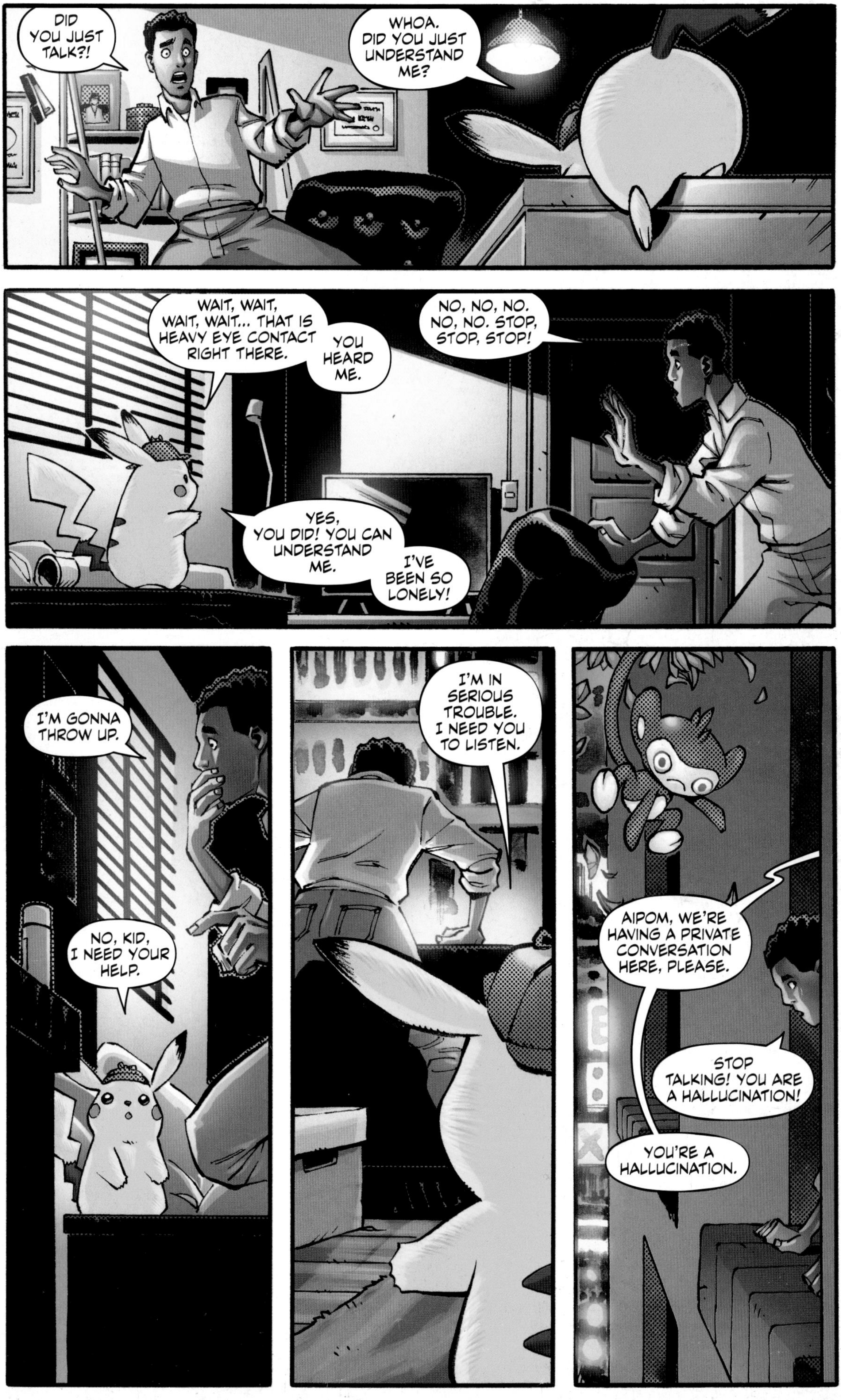

DID YOU JUST TALK?!
WHOA. DID YOU JUST UNDERSTAND ME?
WAIT, WAIT, WAIT, WAIT... THAT IS HEAVY EYE CONTACT RIGHT THERE.
YOU HEARD ME.
NO, NO, NO. NO, NO. STOP, STOP, STOP!
YES, YOU DID! YOU CAN UNDERSTAND ME.
I'VE BEEN SO LONELY!
I'M GONNA THROW UP.
NO, KID, I NEED YOUR HELP.
I'M IN SERIOUS TROUBLE. I NEED YOU TO LISTEN.
AIPOM, WE'RE HAVING A PRIVATE CONVERSATION HERE, PLEASE.
STOP TALKING! YOU ARE A HALLUCINATION!
YOU'RE A HALLUCINATION.

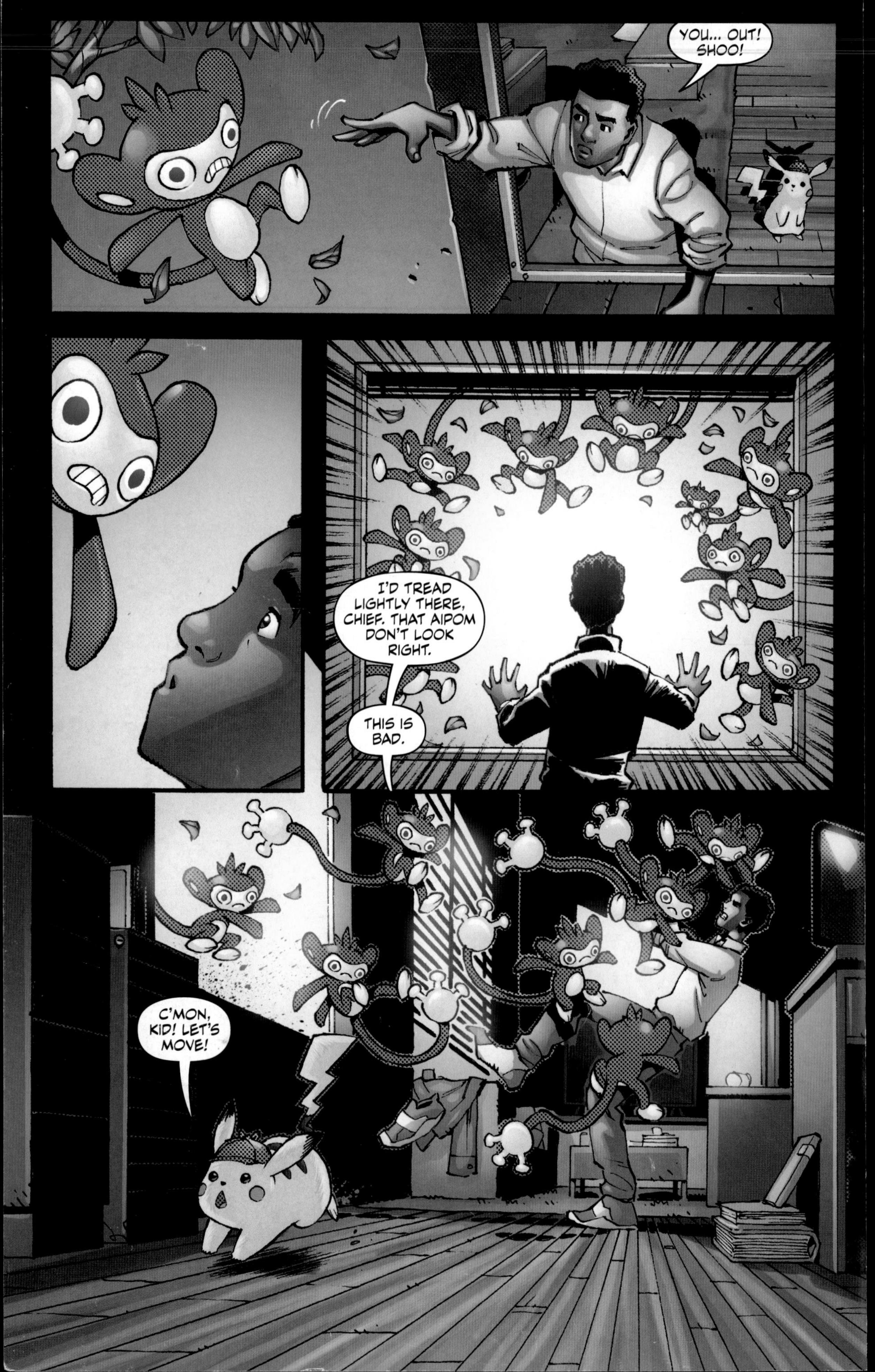
YOU... OUT! SHOO!
I'D TREAD LIGHTLY THERE, CHIEF. THAT AIPOM DON'T LOOK RIGHT.
THIS IS BAD.
C'MON, KID! LET'S MOVE!

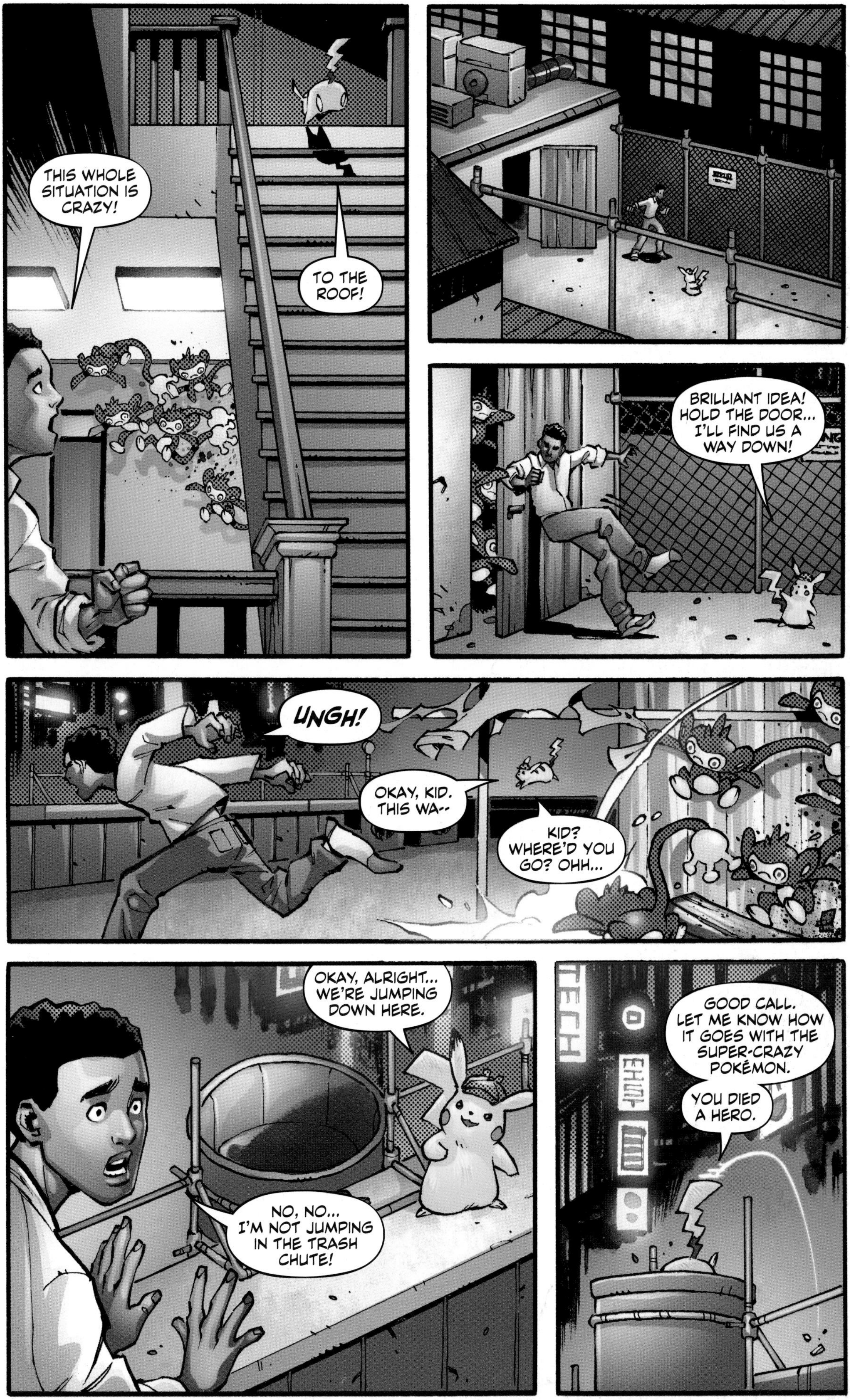
THIS WHOLE SITUATION IS CRAZY!
TO THE ROOF!
BRILLIANT IDEA! HOLD THE DOOR... I'LL FIND US A WAY DOWN!
UNGH!
OKAY, KID. THIS WA--
KID? WHERE'D YOU GO? OHH...
OKAY, ALRIGHT... WE'RE JUMPING DOWN HERE.
NO, NO... I'M NOT JUMPING IN THE TRASH CHUTE!
GOOD CALL. LET ME KNOW HOW IT GOES WITH THE SUPER-CRAZY POKÉMON.
YOU DIED A HERO.

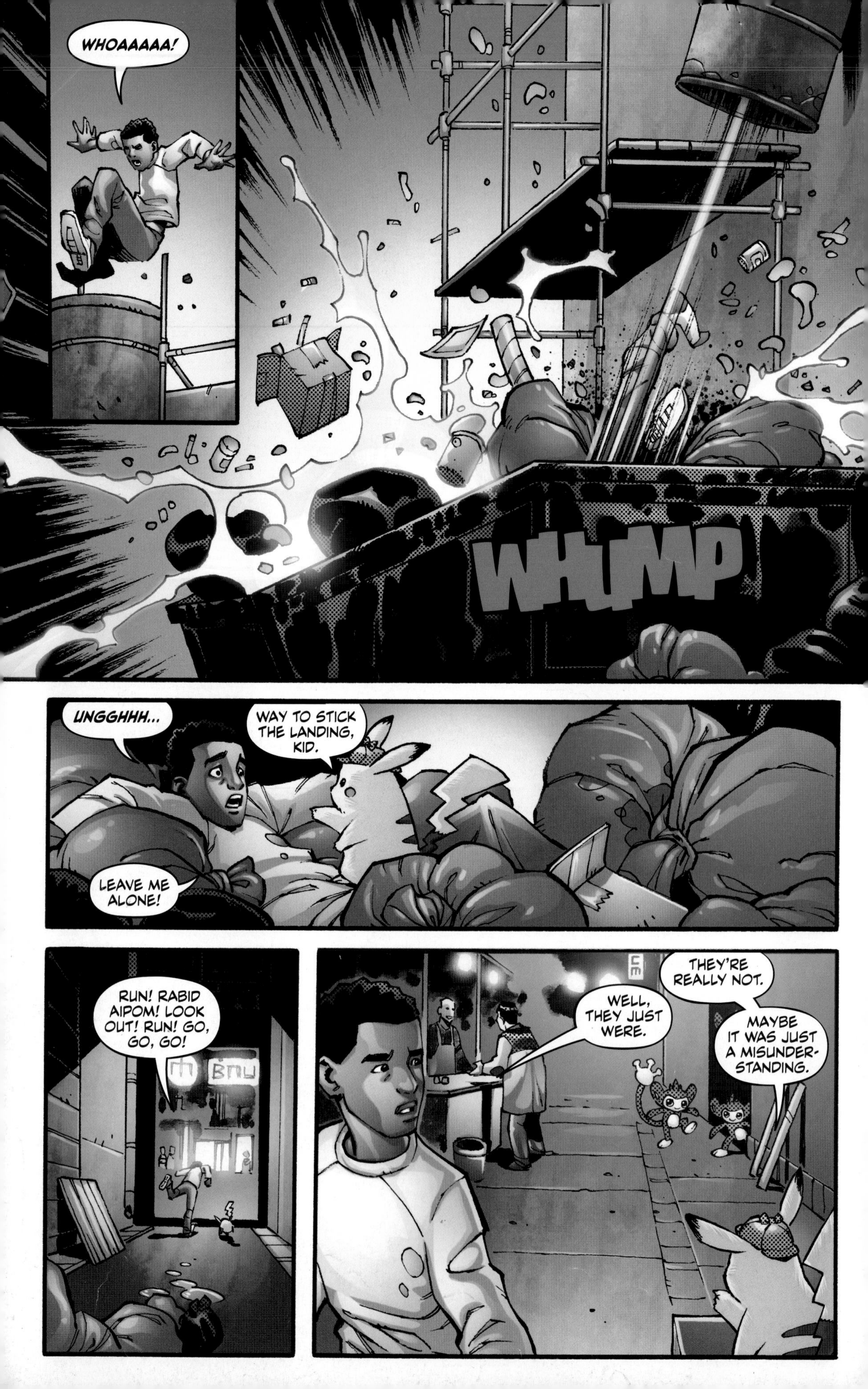
WHOAAAAA!
WHUMP
UNGGHHH...
WAY TO STICK THE LANDING, KID.
LEAVE ME ALONE!
RUN! RABID AIPOM! LOOK OUT! RUN! GO, GO, GO!
THEY'RE REALLY NOT.
WELL, THEY JUST WERE.
MAYBE IT WAS JUST A MISUNDERSTANDING.

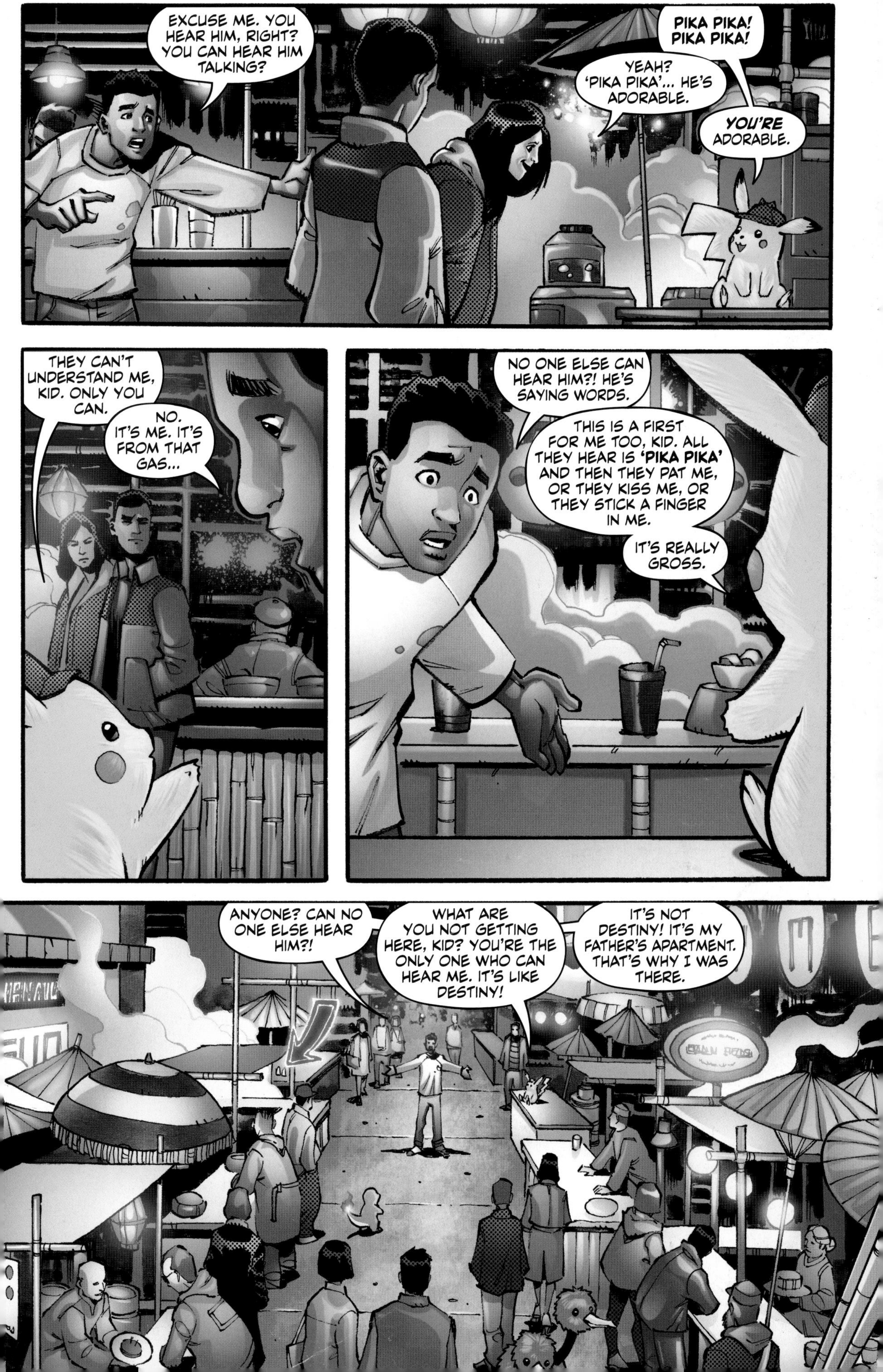
EXCUSE ME. YOU HEAR HIM, RIGHT? YOU CAN HEAR HIM TALKING?
PIKA PIKA! PIKA PIKA!
YEAH? 'PIKA PIKA'... HE'S ADORABLE.
YOU'RE ADORABLE.
THEY CAN'T UNDERSTAND ME, KID. ONLY YOU CAN.
NO. IT'S ME. IT'S FROM THAT GAS...
NO ONE ELSE CAN HEAR HIM?! HE'S SAYING WORDS.
THIS IS A FIRST FOR ME TOO, KID. ALL THEY HEAR IS **'PIKA PIKA'** AND THEN THEY PAT ME, OR THEY KISS ME, OR THEY STICK A FINGER IN ME.
IT'S REALLY GROSS.
ANYONE? CAN NO ONE ELSE HEAR HIM?!
WHAT ARE YOU NOT GETTING HERE, KID? YOU'RE THE ONLY ONE WHO CAN HEAR ME. IT'S LIKE DESTINY!
IT'S NOT DESTINY! IT'S MY FATHER'S APARTMENT. THAT'S WHY I WAS THERE.

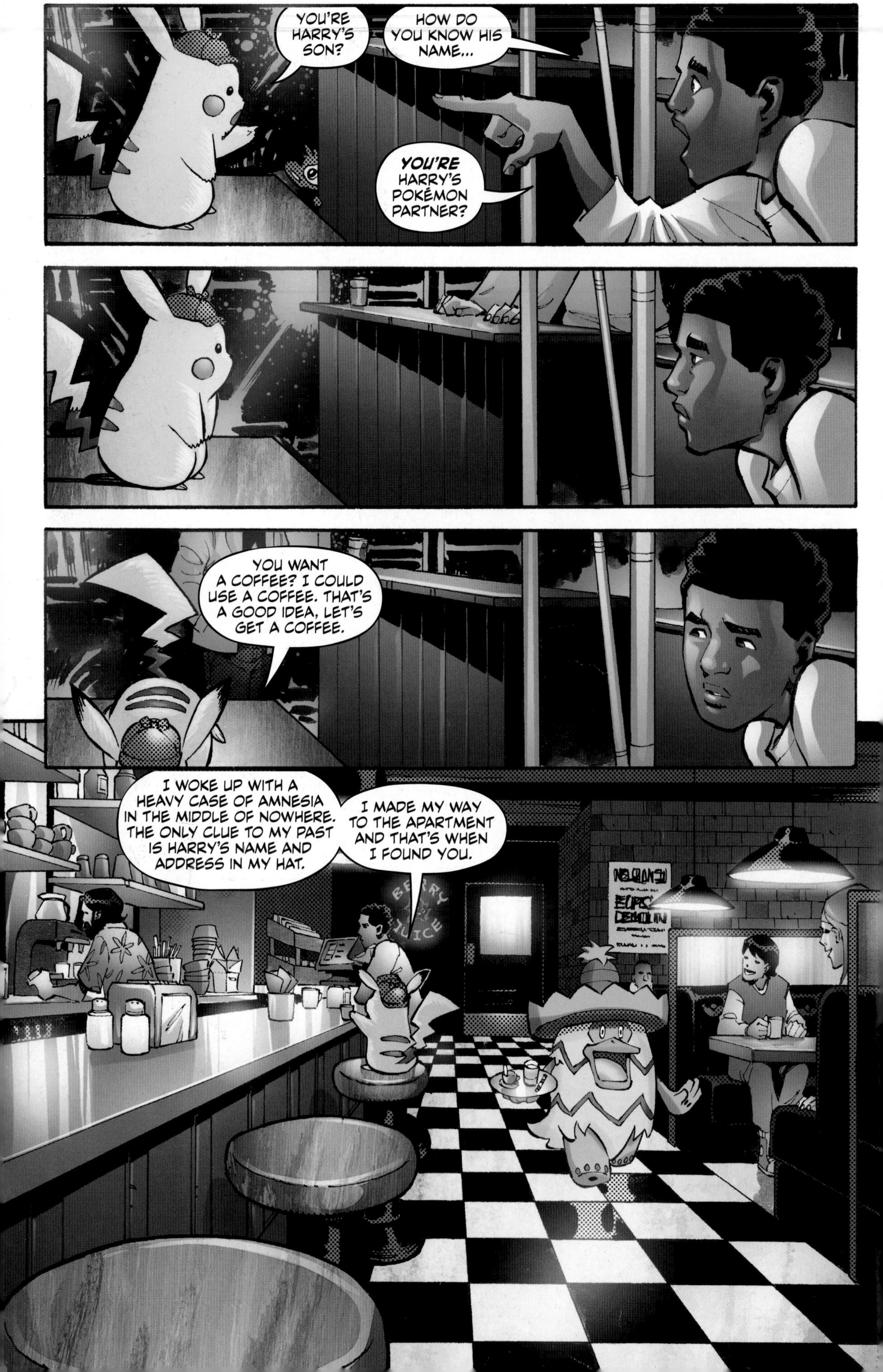
YOU'RE HARRY'S SON?
HOW DO YOU KNOW HIS NAME...
YOU'RE HARRY'S POKÉMON PARTNER?
YOU WANT A COFFEE? I COULD USE A COFFEE. THAT'S A GOOD IDEA, LET'S GET A COFFEE.
I WOKE UP WITH A HEAVY CASE OF AMNESIA IN THE MIDDLE OF NOWHERE. THE ONLY CLUE TO MY PAST IS HARRY'S NAME AND ADDRESS IN MY HAT.
I MADE MY WAY TO THE APARTMENT AND THAT'S WHEN I FOUND YOU.
BERRY JUICE

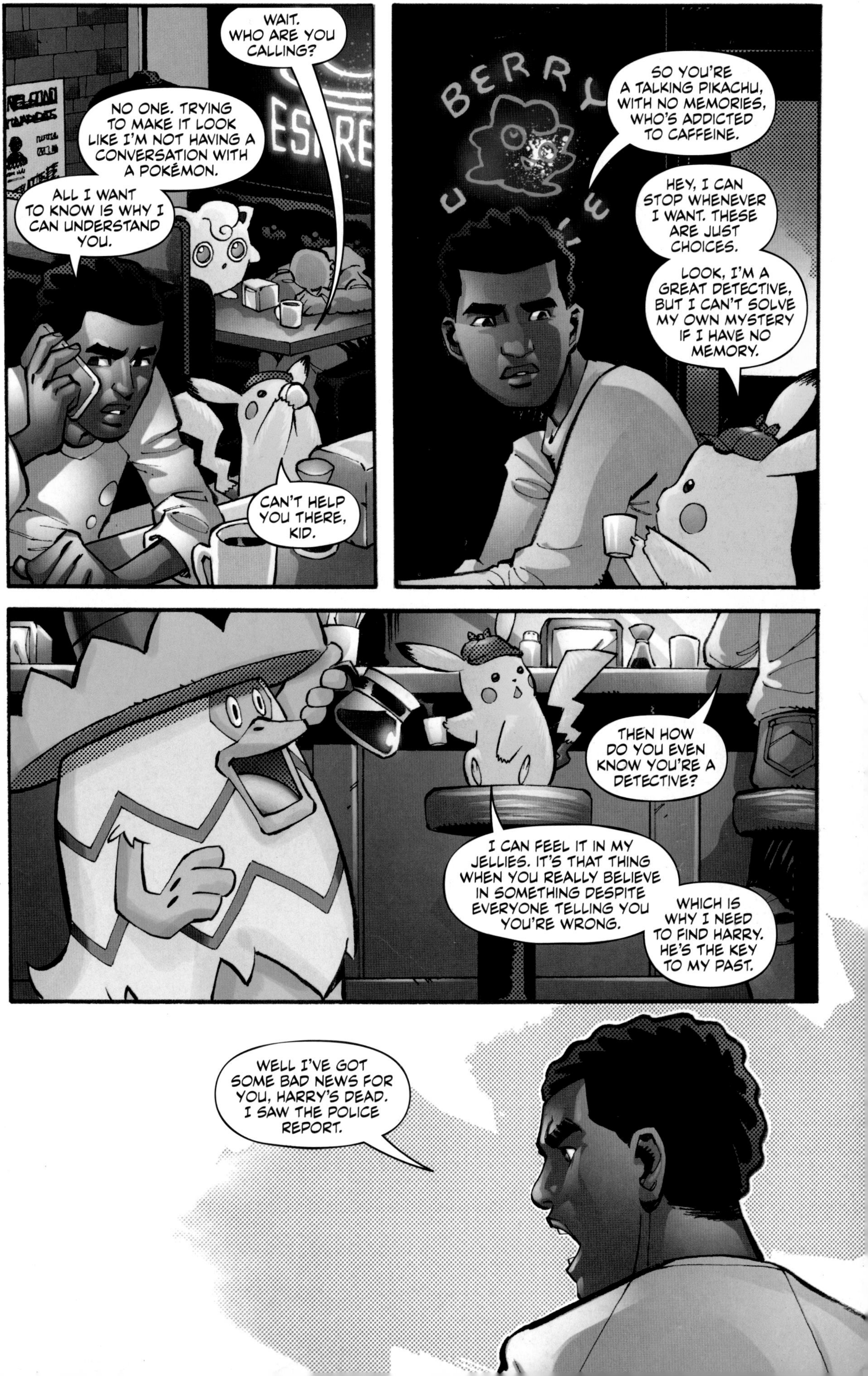

WAIT. WHO ARE YOU CALLING?
NO ONE. TRYING TO MAKE IT LOOK LIKE I'M NOT HAVING A CONVERSATION WITH A POKÉMON.
ALL I WANT TO KNOW IS WHY I CAN UNDERSTAND YOU.
CAN'T HELP YOU THERE, KID.
BERRY
SO YOU'RE A TALKING PIKACHU, WITH NO MEMORIES, WHO'S ADDICTED TO CAFFEINE.
HEY, I CAN STOP WHENEVER I WANT. THESE ARE JUST CHOICES.
LOOK, I'M A GREAT DETECTIVE, BUT I CAN'T SOLVE MY OWN MYSTERY IF I HAVE NO MEMORY.
THEN HOW DO YOU EVEN KNOW YOU'RE A DETECTIVE?
I CAN FEEL IT IN MY JELLIES. IT'S THAT THING WHEN YOU REALLY BELIEVE IN SOMETHING DESPITE EVERYONE TELLING YOU YOU'RE WRONG.
WHICH IS WHY I NEED TO FIND HARRY. HE'S THE KEY TO MY PAST.
WELL I'VE GOT SOME BAD NEWS FOR YOU, HARRY'S DEAD. I SAW THE POLICE REPORT.

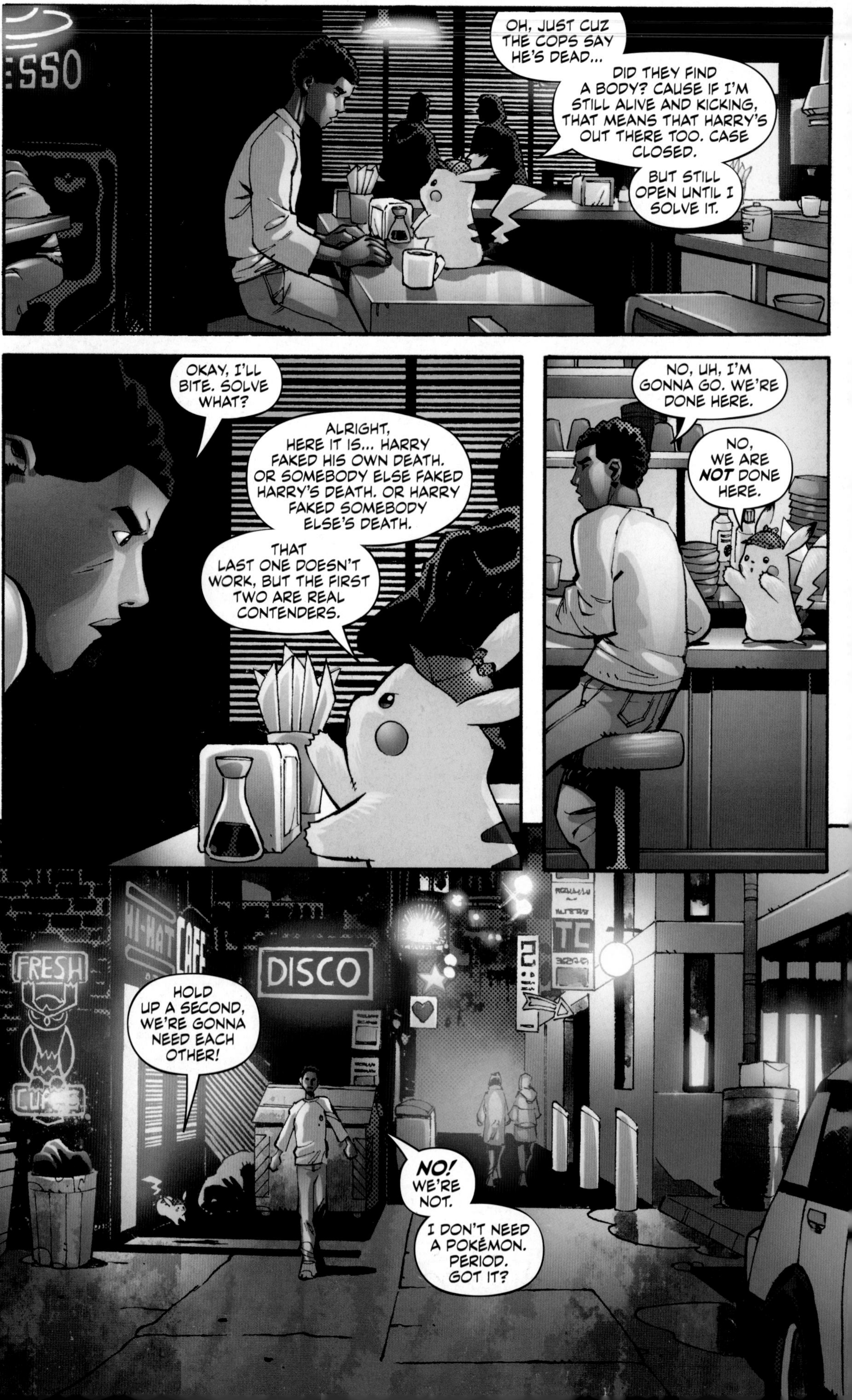
ESSO
OH, JUST CUZ THE COPS SAY HE'S DEAD...
DID THEY FIND A BODY? CAUSE IF I'M STILL ALIVE AND KICKING, THAT MEANS THAT HARRY'S OUT THERE TOO. CASE CLOSED.
BUT STILL OPEN UNTIL I SOLVE IT.
OKAY, I'LL BITE. SOLVE WHAT?
ALRIGHT, HERE IT IS... HARRY FAKED HIS OWN DEATH. OR SOMEBODY ELSE FAKED HARRY'S DEATH. OR HARRY FAKED SOMEBODY ELSE'S DEATH.
THAT LAST ONE DOESN'T WORK, BUT THE FIRST TWO ARE REAL CONTENDERS.
NO, UH, I'M GONNA GO. WE'RE DONE HERE.
NO, WE ARE ***NOT*** DONE HERE.
HI-HAT
CAFE
FRESH
DISCO
TC
HOLD UP A SECOND, WE'RE GONNA NEED EACH OTHER!
NO! WE'RE NOT.
I DON'T NEED A POKÉMON. PERIOD. GOT IT?

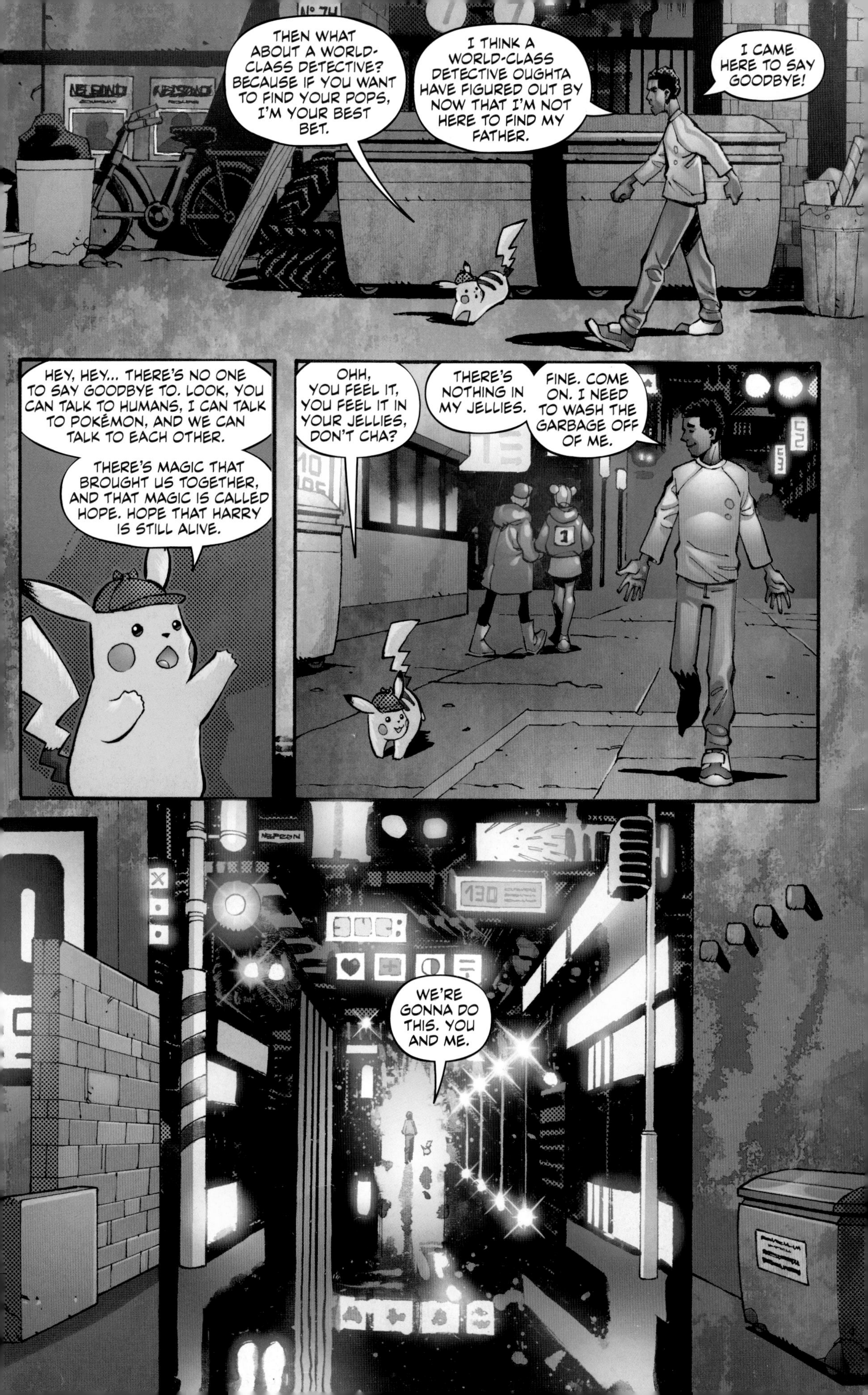
THEN WHAT ABOUT A WORLD-CLASS DETECTIVE? BECAUSE IF YOU WANT TO FIND YOUR POPS, I'M YOUR BEST BET.
I THINK A WORLD-CLASS DETECTIVE OUGHTA HAVE FIGURED OUT BY NOW THAT I'M NOT HERE TO FIND MY FATHER.
I CAME HERE TO SAY GOODBYE!
HEY, HEY... THERE'S NO ONE TO SAY GOODBYE TO. LOOK, YOU CAN TALK TO HUMANS, I CAN TALK TO POKÉMON, AND WE CAN TALK TO EACH OTHER.
THERE'S MAGIC THAT BROUGHT US TOGETHER, AND THAT MAGIC IS CALLED HOPE. HOPE THAT HARRY IS STILL ALIVE.
OHH, YOU FEEL IT, YOU FEEL IT IN YOUR JELLIES, DON'T CHA?
THERE'S NOTHING IN MY JELLIES.
FINE. COME ON. I NEED TO WASH THE GARBAGE OFF OF ME.
WE'RE GONNA DO THIS. YOU AND ME.

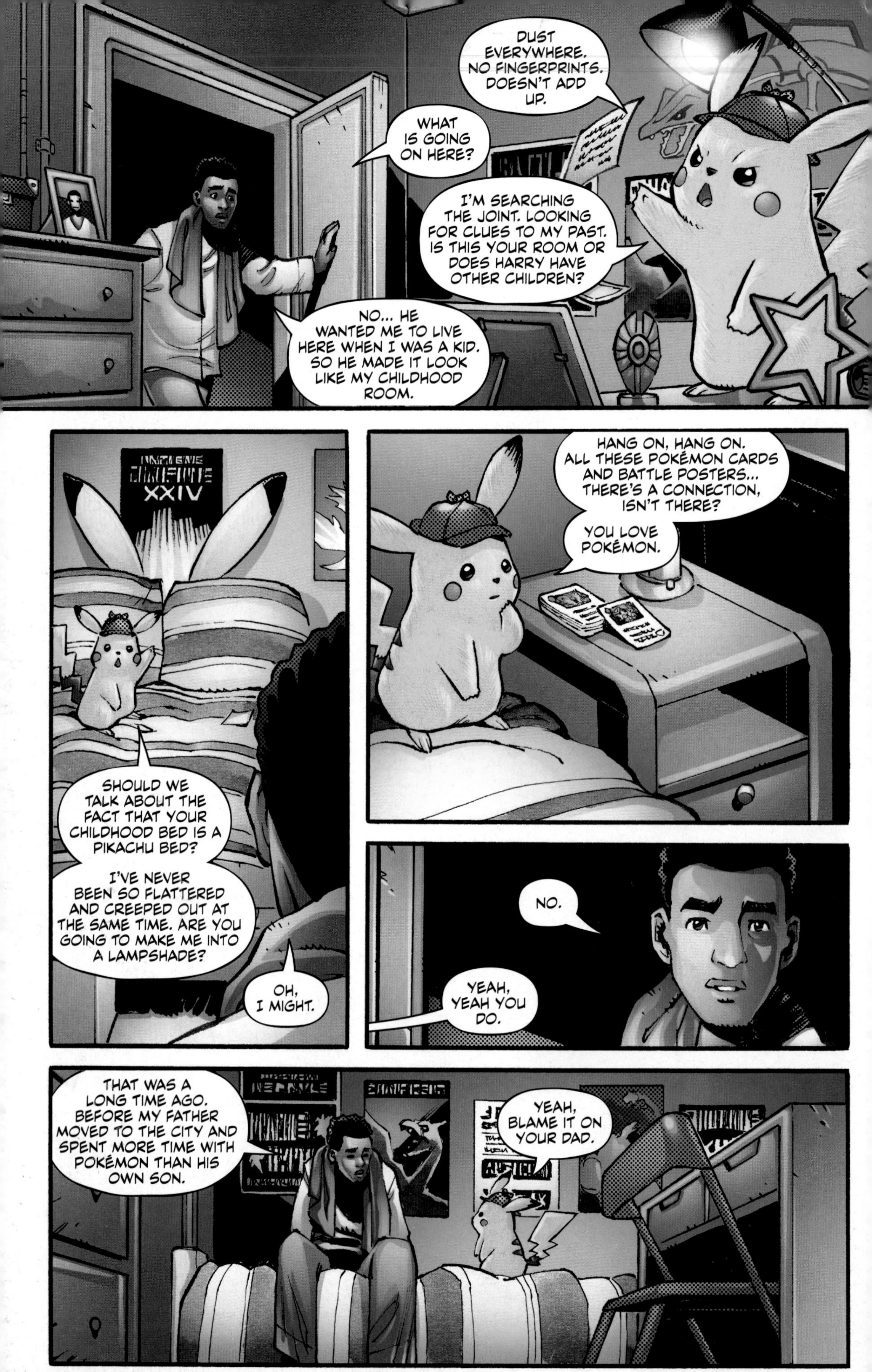
DUST EVERYWHERE. NO FINGERPRINTS. DOESN'T ADD UP.
WHAT IS GOING ON HERE?
I'M SEARCHING THE JOINT. LOOKING FOR CLUES TO MY PAST. IS THIS YOUR ROOM OR DOES HARRY HAVE OTHER CHILDREN?
NO... HE WANTED ME TO LIVE HERE WHEN I WAS A KID. SO HE MADE IT LOOK LIKE MY CHILDHOOD ROOM.
XXIV
SHOULD WE TALK ABOUT THE FACT THAT YOUR CHILDHOOD BED IS A PIKACHU BED?
I'VE NEVER BEEN SO FLATTERED AND CREEPED OUT AT THE SAME TIME. ARE YOU GOING TO MAKE ME INTO A LAMPSHADE?
OH, I MIGHT.
HANG ON, HANG ON. ALL THESE POKÉMON CARDS AND BATTLE POSTERS... THERE'S A CONNECTION, ISN'T THERE?
YOU LOVE POKÉMON.
NO.
YEAH, YEAH YOU DO.
THAT WAS A LONG TIME AGO. BEFORE MY FATHER MOVED TO THE CITY AND SPENT MORE TIME WITH POKÉMON THAN HIS OWN SON.
YEAH, BLAME IT ON YOUR DAD.

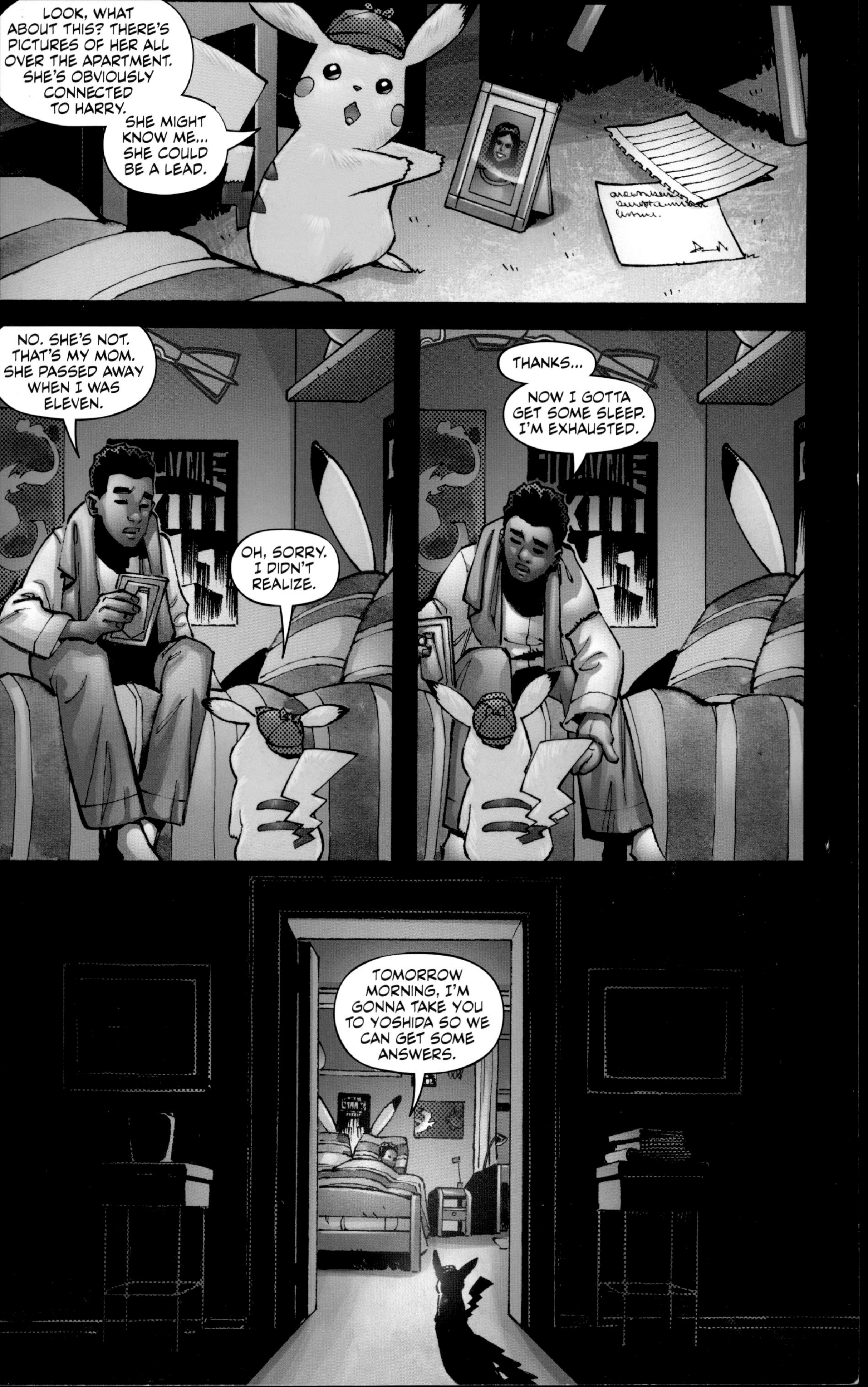
LOOK, WHAT ABOUT THIS? THERE'S PICTURES OF HER ALL OVER THE APARTMENT. SHE'S OBVIOUSLY CONNECTED TO HARRY.
SHE MIGHT KNOW ME... SHE COULD BE A LEAD.
NO. SHE'S NOT. THAT'S MY MOM. SHE PASSED AWAY WHEN I WAS ELEVEN.
OH, SORRY. I DIDN'T REALIZE.
THANKS...
NOW I GOTTA GET SOME SLEEP. I'M EXHAUSTED.
TOMORROW MORNING, I'M GONNA TAKE YOU TO YOSHIDA SO WE CAN GET SOME ANSWERS.

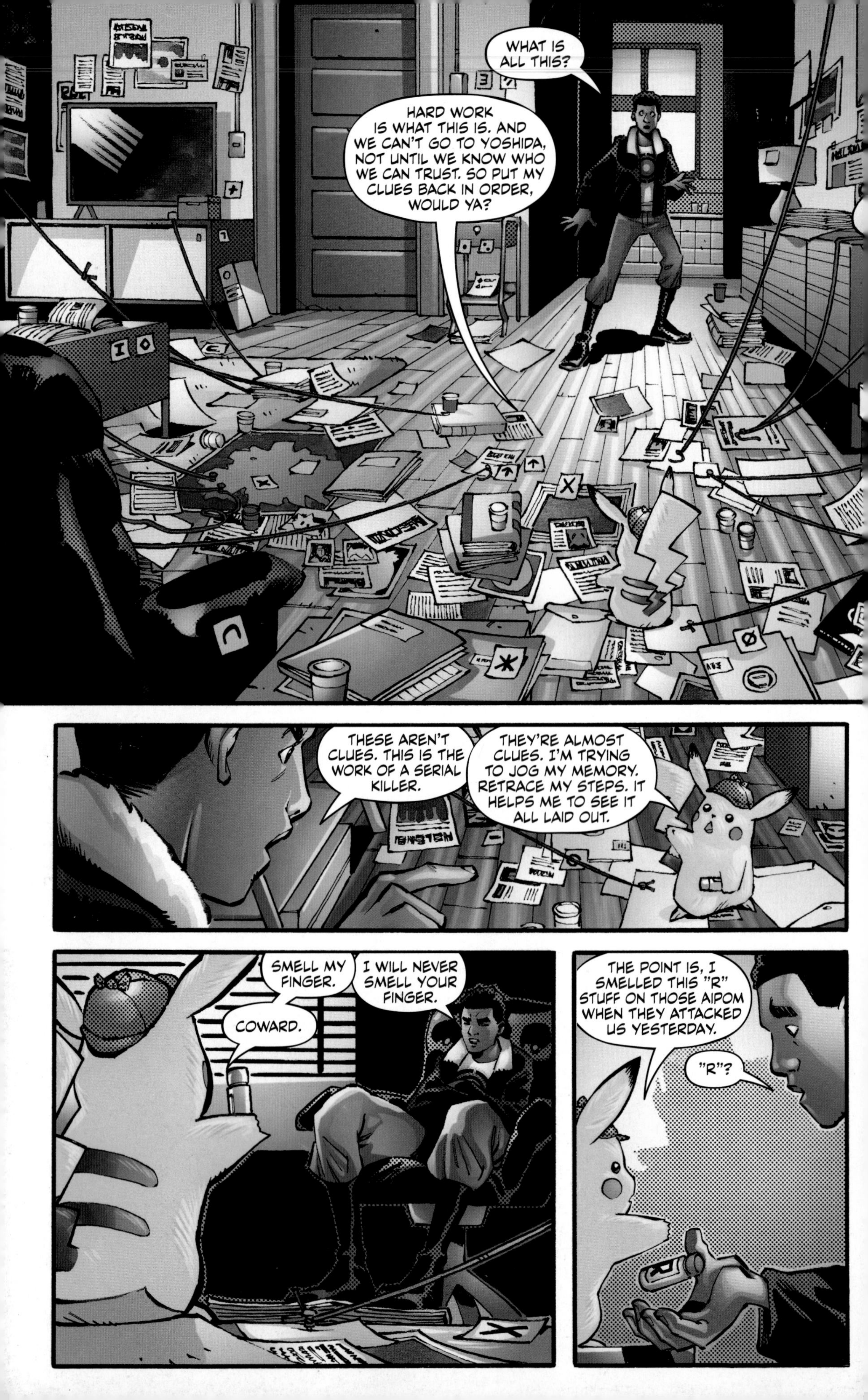
WHAT IS ALL THIS?
HARD WORK IS WHAT THIS IS. AND WE CAN'T GO TO YOSHIDA, NOT UNTIL WE KNOW WHO WE CAN TRUST. SO PUT MY CLUES BACK IN ORDER, WOULD YA?
THESE AREN'T CLUES. THIS IS THE WORK OF A SERIAL KILLER.
THEY'RE ALMOST CLUES. I'M TRYING TO JOG MY MEMORY. RETRACE MY STEPS. IT HELPS ME TO SEE IT ALL LAID OUT.
SMELL MY FINGER.
I WILL NEVER SMELL YOUR FINGER.
COWARD.
THE POINT IS, I SMELLED THIS "R" STUFF ON THOSE AIPOM WHEN THEY ATTACKED US YESTERDAY.
"R"?

OR *HER-SELF.*

SO WHAT IS THE WAY IN, HUH? THE ANSWER IS IN THIS ROOM.

THIS ISN'T A ROOM, THIS IS A FIRE HAZARD. THIS IS JUST JUNK AND PAPERS...

...AND NEWSPAPERS.

BINGO. SEE, I'M THINKING HARRY CAUGHT A BREAK IN THE CASE, FORCING OUR SHADOWY KINGPIN TO SEND OUT HIRED GOONS TO DELIVER THE BIG...

...HUSH-HUSH. WE NEED TO RETRACE HARRY'S STEPS, EITHER SOLVE THE CASE OURSELVES OR GET FAR ENOUGH ALONG THAT THIS A-NUMBER-ONE BAD GUY HAS TO REVEAL HIMSELF...

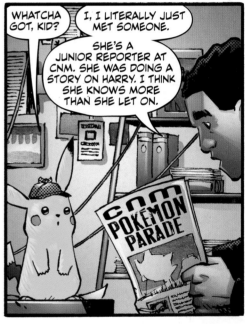

WHATCHA GOT, KID?

I, I LITERALLY JUST MET SOMEONE.

SHE'S A JUNIOR REPORTER AT CNM. SHE WAS DOING A STORY ON HARRY. I THINK SHE KNOWS MORE THAN SHE LET ON.

POKÉMON PARADE

A-HAH! THE SMART ONES ALWAYS DO. WE GOTTA GO DOWN TO HER WORK AND PRESS HER. THAT'S A METAPHOR.

YEAH, I KNOW WHAT A METAPHOR IS...

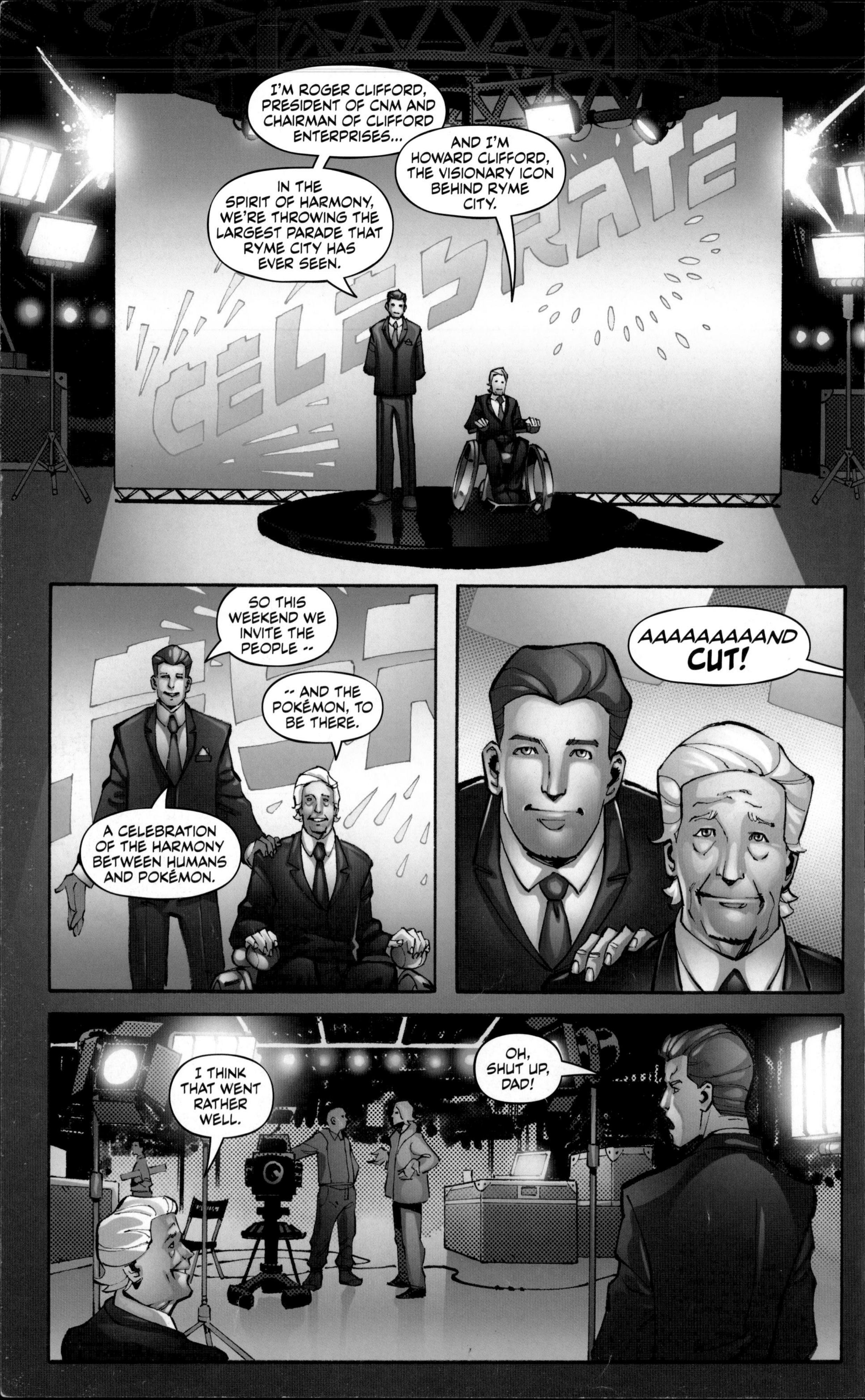
I'M ROGER CLIFFORD, PRESIDENT OF CNM AND CHAIRMAN OF CLIFFORD ENTERPRISES...
IN THE SPIRIT OF HARMONY, WE'RE THROWING THE LARGEST PARADE THAT RYME CITY HAS EVER SEEN.
AND I'M HOWARD CLIFFORD, THE VISIONARY ICON BEHIND RYME CITY.
CELEBRATE
SO THIS WEEKEND WE INVITE THE PEOPLE --
-- AND THE POKÉMON, TO BE THERE.
A CELEBRATION OF THE HARMONY BETWEEN HUMANS AND POKÉMON.
AAAAAAAAAND CUT!
I THINK THAT WENT RATHER WELL.
OH, SHUT UP, DAD!

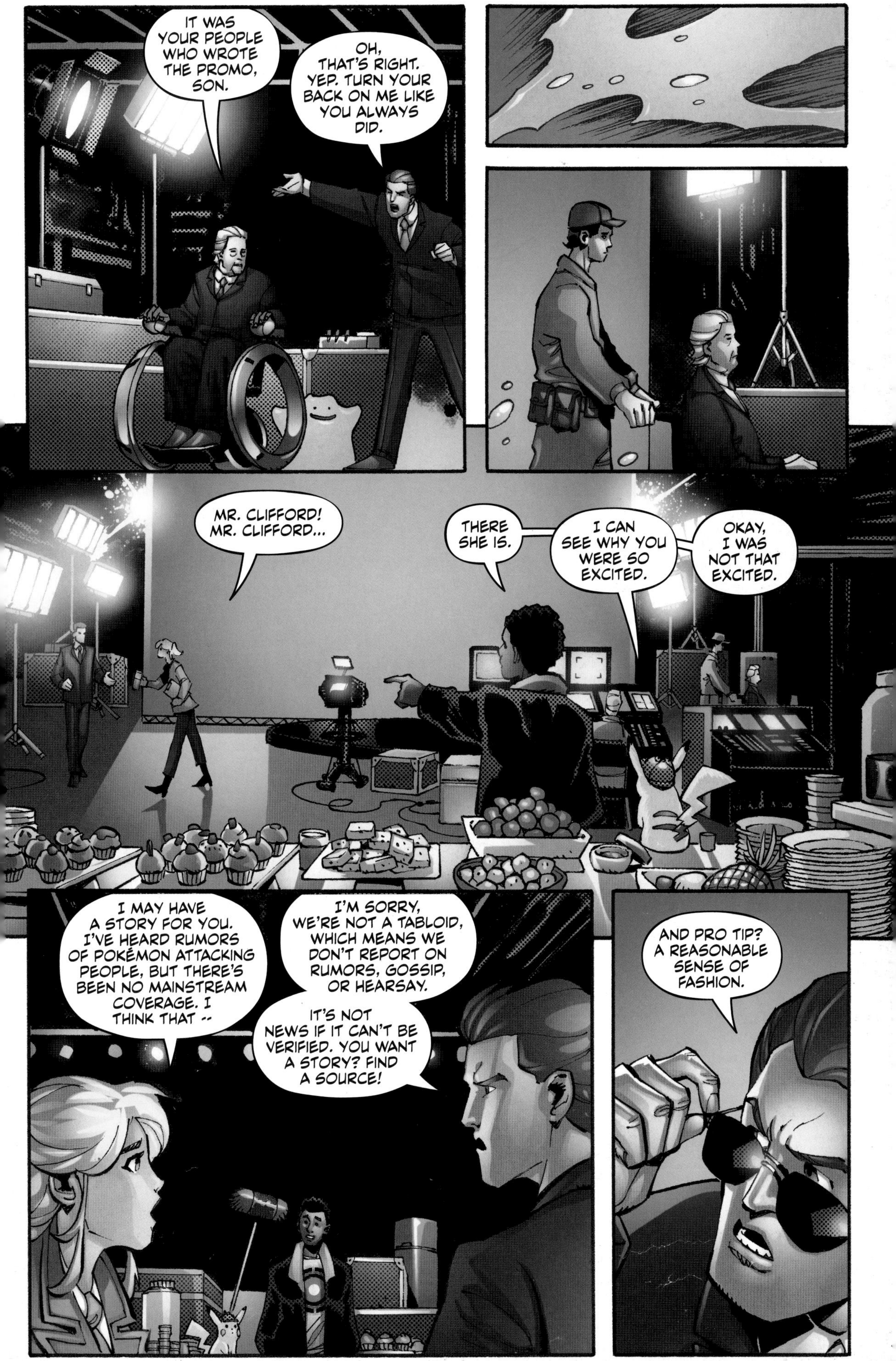
IT WAS YOUR PEOPLE WHO WROTE THE PROMO, SON.
OH, THAT'S RIGHT. YEP. TURN YOUR BACK ON ME LIKE YOU ALWAYS DID.
MR. CLIFFORD! MR. CLIFFORD...
THERE SHE IS.
I CAN SEE WHY YOU WERE SO EXCITED.
OKAY, I WAS NOT THAT EXCITED.
I MAY HAVE A STORY FOR YOU. I'VE HEARD RUMORS OF POKÉMON ATTACKING PEOPLE, BUT THERE'S BEEN NO MAINSTREAM COVERAGE. I THINK THAT --
I'M SORRY, WE'RE NOT A TABLOID, WHICH MEANS WE DON'T REPORT ON RUMORS, GOSSIP, OR HEARSAY.
IT'S NOT NEWS IF IT CAN'T BE VERIFIED. YOU WANT A STORY? FIND A SOURCE!
AND PRO TIP? A REASONABLE SENSE OF FASHION.

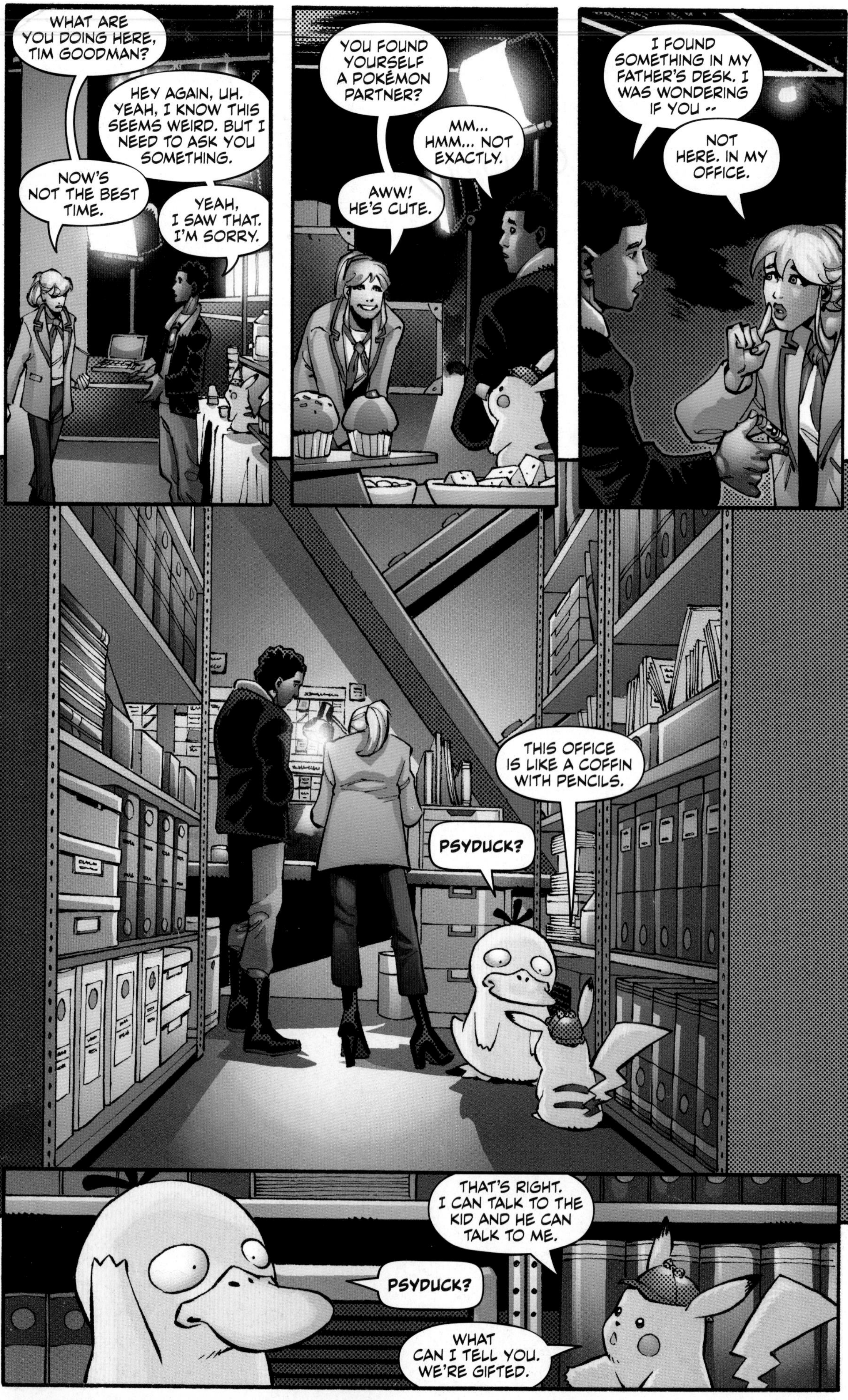
WHAT ARE YOU DOING HERE, TIM GOODMAN?
HEY AGAIN, UH. YEAH, I KNOW THIS SEEMS WEIRD. BUT I NEED TO ASK YOU SOMETHING.
NOW'S NOT THE BEST TIME.
YEAH, I SAW THAT. I'M SORRY.
YOU FOUND YOURSELF A POKÉMON PARTNER?
MM... HMM... NOT EXACTLY.
AWW! HE'S CUTE.
I FOUND SOMETHING IN MY FATHER'S DESK. I WAS WONDERING IF YOU --
NOT HERE. IN MY OFFICE.
THIS OFFICE IS LIKE A COFFIN WITH PENCILS.
PSYDUCK?
THAT'S RIGHT. I CAN TALK TO THE KID AND HE CAN TALK TO ME.
PSYDUCK?
WHAT CAN I TELL YOU. WE'RE GIFTED.

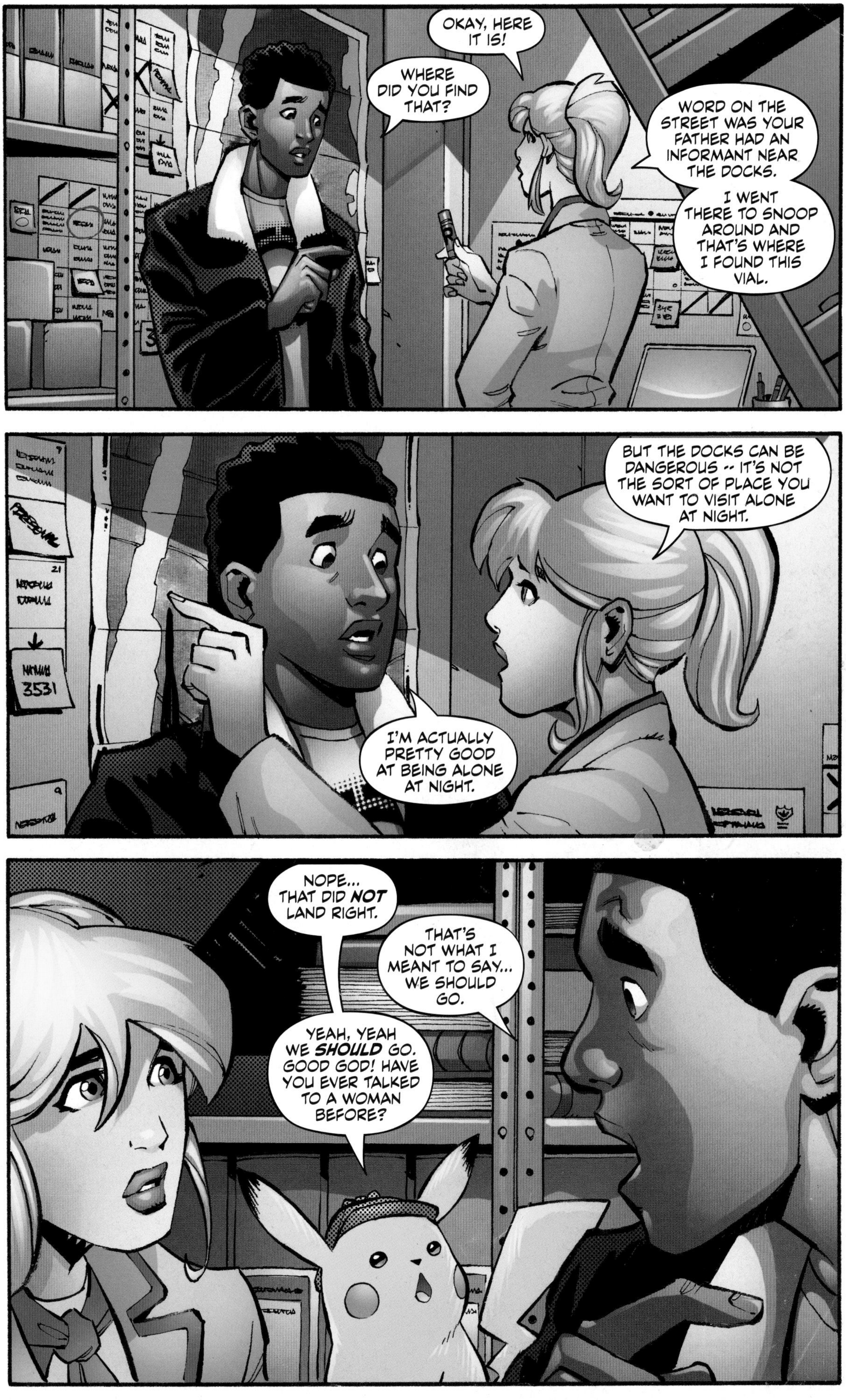
OKAY, HERE IT IS!
WHERE DID YOU FIND THAT?
WORD ON THE STREET WAS YOUR FATHER HAD AN INFORMANT NEAR THE DOCKS.
I WENT THERE TO SNOOP AROUND AND THAT'S WHERE I FOUND THIS VIAL.
BUT THE DOCKS CAN BE DANGEROUS -- IT'S NOT THE SORT OF PLACE YOU WANT TO VISIT ALONE AT NIGHT.
I'M ACTUALLY PRETTY GOOD AT BEING ALONE AT NIGHT.
NOPE... THAT DID ***NOT*** LAND RIGHT.
THAT'S NOT WHAT I MEANT TO SAY... WE SHOULD GO.
YEAH, YEAH WE ***SHOULD*** GO. GOOD GOD! HAVE YOU EVER TALKED TO A WOMAN BEFORE?

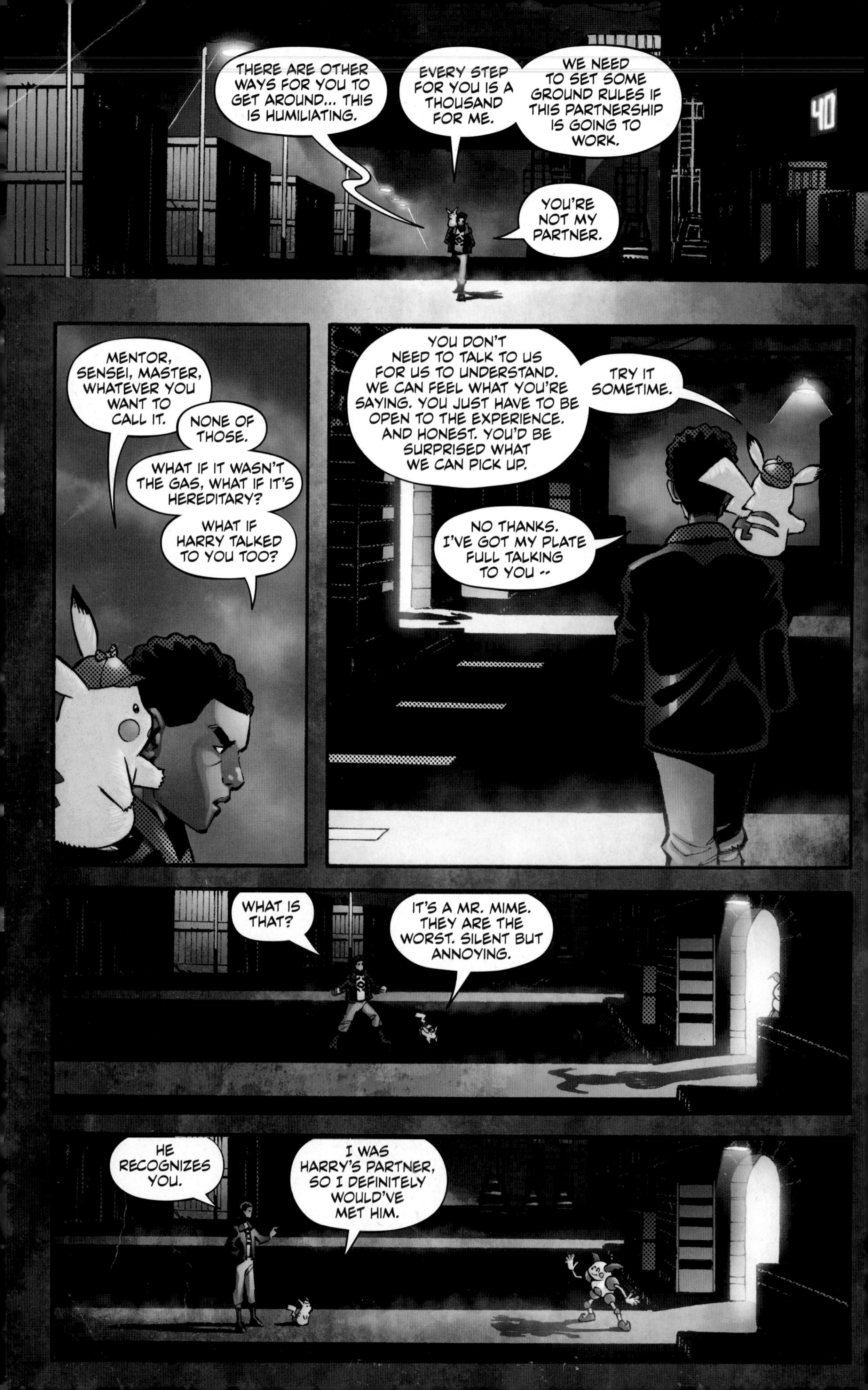
THERE ARE OTHER WAYS FOR YOU TO GET AROUND... THIS IS HUMILIATING.
EVERY STEP FOR YOU IS A THOUSAND FOR ME.
WE NEED TO SET SOME GROUND RULES IF THIS PARTNERSHIP IS GOING TO WORK.
YOU'RE NOT MY PARTNER.
MENTOR, SENSEI, MASTER, WHATEVER YOU WANT TO CALL IT.
NONE OF THOSE.
WHAT IF IT WASN'T THE GAS, WHAT IF IT'S HEREDITARY?
WHAT IF HARRY TALKED TO YOU TOO?
YOU DON'T NEED TO TALK TO US FOR US TO UNDERSTAND. WE CAN FEEL WHAT YOU'RE SAYING. YOU JUST HAVE TO BE OPEN TO THE EXPERIENCE. AND HONEST. YOU'D BE SURPRISED WHAT WE CAN PICK UP.
TRY IT SOMETIME.
NO THANKS. I'VE GOT MY PLATE FULL TALKING TO YOU --
WHAT IS THAT?
IT'S A MR. MIME. THEY ARE THE WORST. SILENT BUT ANNOYING.
HE RECOGNIZES YOU.
I WAS HARRY'S PARTNER, SO I DEFINITELY WOULD'VE MET HIM.

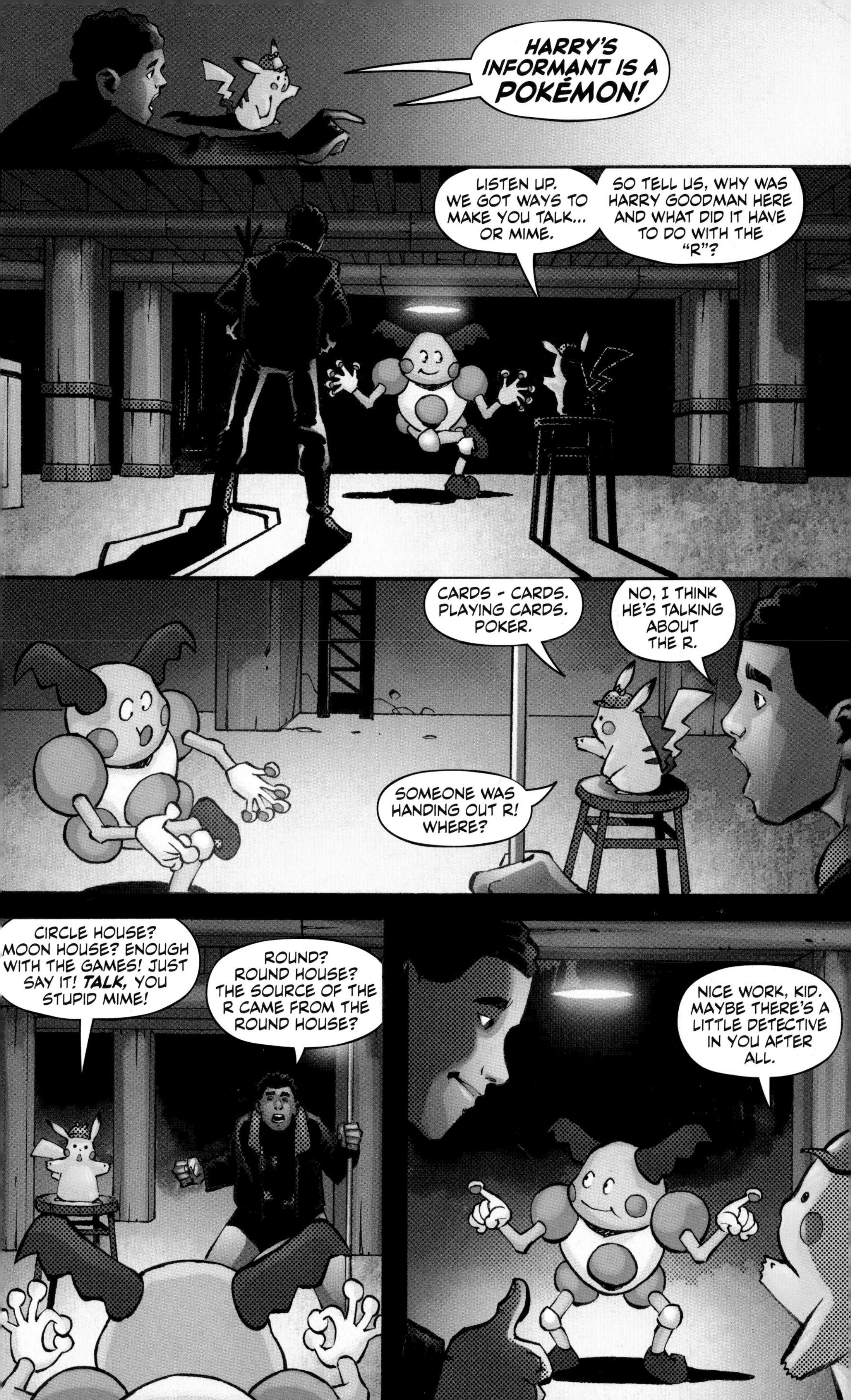
HARRY'S INFORMANT IS A POKÉMON!
LISTEN UP. WE GOT WAYS TO MAKE YOU TALK... OR MIME.
SO TELL US, WHY WAS HARRY GOODMAN HERE AND WHAT DID IT HAVE TO DO WITH THE "R"?
CARDS - CARDS. PLAYING CARDS. POKER.
NO, I THINK HE'S TALKING ABOUT THE R.
SOMEONE WAS HANDING OUT R! WHERE?
CIRCLE HOUSE? MOON HOUSE? ENOUGH WITH THE GAMES! JUST SAY IT! TALK, YOU STUPID MIME!
ROUND? ROUND HOUSE? THE SOURCE OF THE R CAME FROM THE ROUND HOUSE?
NICE WORK, KID. MAYBE THERE'S A LITTLE DETECTIVE IN YOU AFTER ALL.

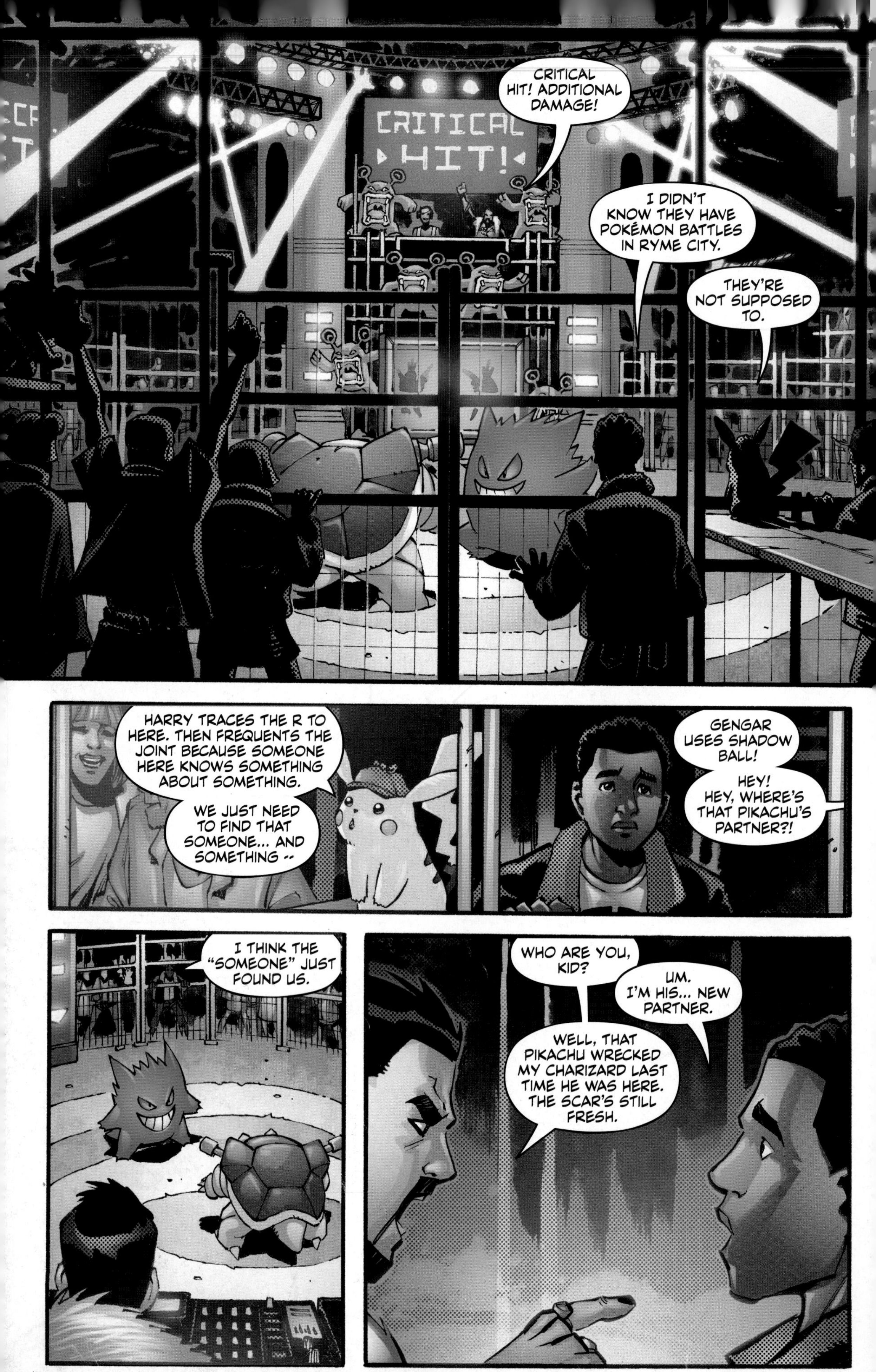
CRITICAL HIT! ADDITIONAL DAMAGE!
CRITICAL HIT!
I DIDN'T KNOW THEY HAVE POKÉMON BATTLES IN RYME CITY.
THEY'RE NOT SUPPOSED TO.
HARRY TRACES THE R TO HERE. THEN FREQUENTS THE JOINT BECAUSE SOMEONE HERE KNOWS SOMETHING ABOUT SOMETHING.
WE JUST NEED TO FIND THAT SOMEONE... AND SOMETHING --
GENGAR USES SHADOW BALL!
HEY! HEY, WHERE'S THAT PIKACHU'S PARTNER?!
I THINK THE "SOMEONE" JUST FOUND US.
WHO ARE YOU, KID?
UM. I'M HIS... NEW PARTNER.
WELL, THAT PIKACHU WRECKED MY CHARIZARD LAST TIME HE WAS HERE. THE SCAR'S STILL FRESH.

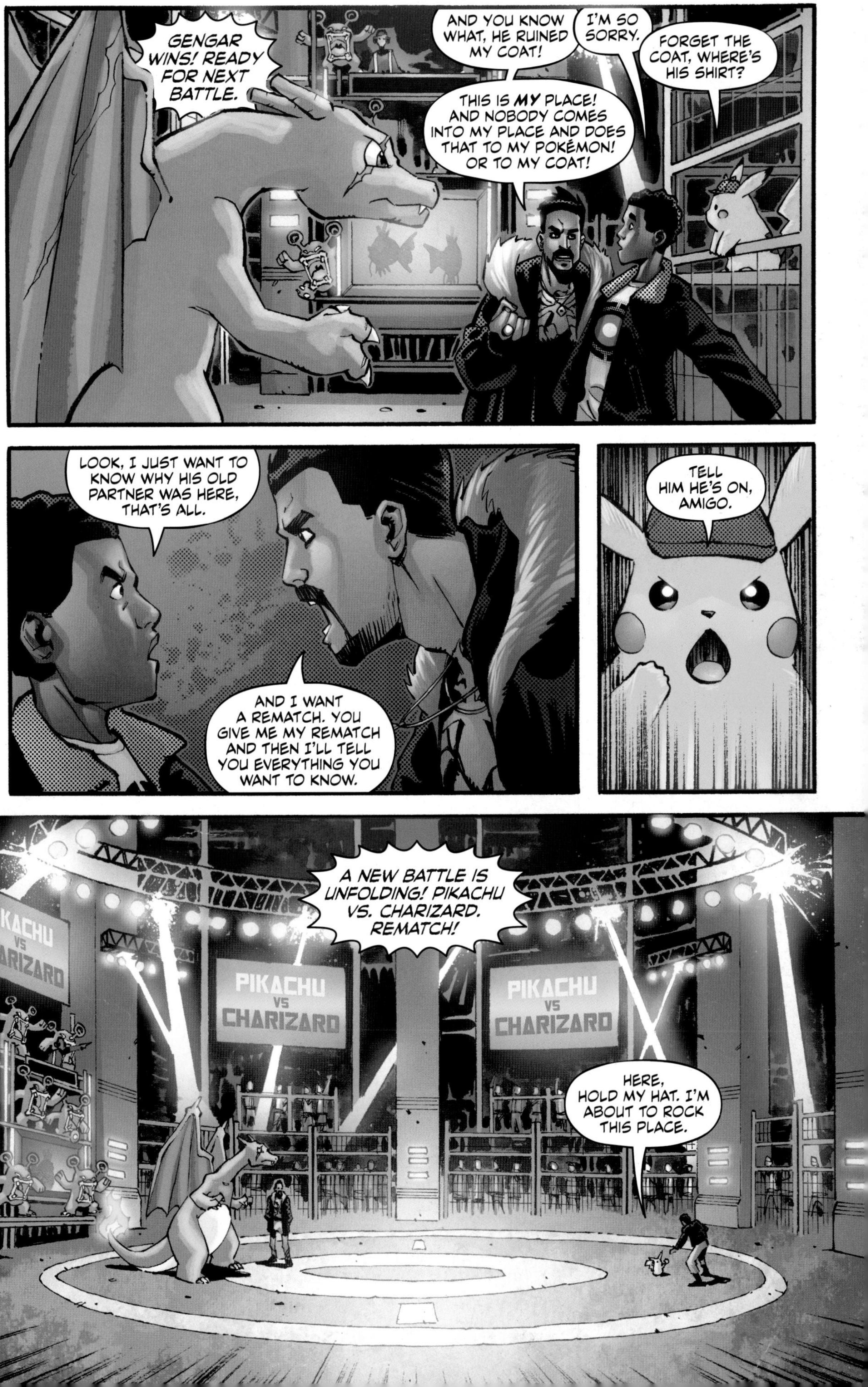
GENGAR WINS! READY FOR NEXT BATTLE.
AND YOU KNOW WHAT, HE RUINED MY COAT!
THIS IS **MY** PLACE! AND NOBODY COMES INTO MY PLACE AND DOES THAT TO MY POKÉMON! OR TO MY COAT!
I'M SO SORRY.
FORGET THE COAT, WHERE'S HIS SHIRT?
LOOK, I JUST WANT TO KNOW WHY HIS OLD PARTNER WAS HERE, THAT'S ALL.
AND I WANT A REMATCH. YOU GIVE ME MY REMATCH AND THEN I'LL TELL YOU EVERYTHING YOU WANT TO KNOW.
TELL HIM HE'S ON, AMIGO.
A NEW BATTLE IS UNFOLDING! PIKACHU VS. CHARIZARD. REMATCH!
PIKACHU VS CHARIZARD
PIKACHU VS CHARIZARD
PIKACHU VS CHARIZARD
HERE, HOLD MY HAT. I'M ABOUT TO ROCK THIS PLACE.

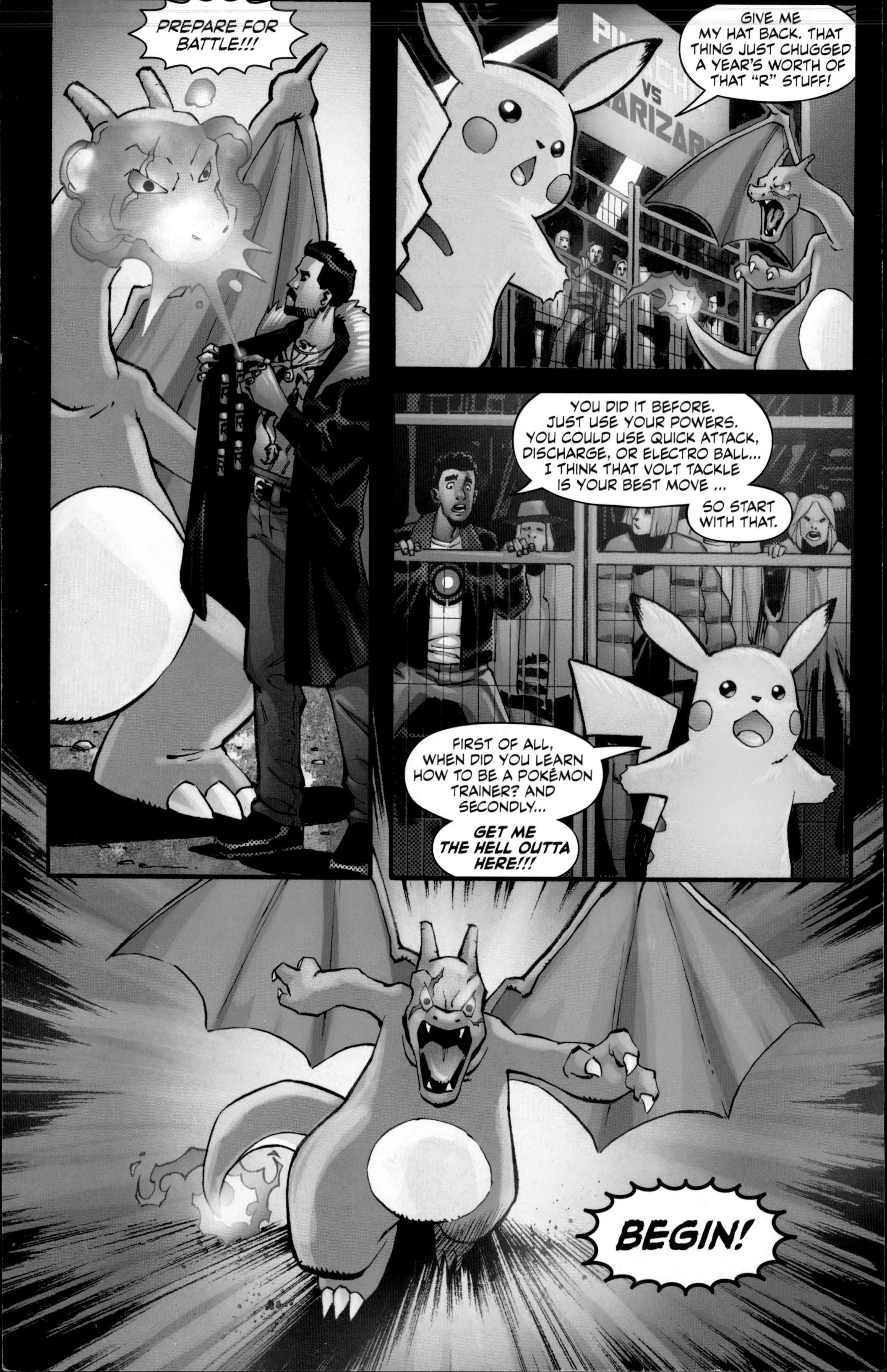
PREPARE FOR BATTLE!!!
GIVE ME MY HAT BACK. THAT THING JUST CHUGGED A YEAR'S WORTH OF THAT "R" STUFF!
PIKACHU VS CHARIZARD
YOU DID IT BEFORE. JUST USE YOUR POWERS. YOU COULD USE QUICK ATTACK, DISCHARGE, OR ELECTRO BALL... I THINK THAT VOLT TACKLE IS YOUR BEST MOVE ...
SO START WITH THAT.
FIRST OF ALL, WHEN DID YOU LEARN HOW TO BE A POKÉMON TRAINER? AND SECONDLY...
GET ME THE HELL OUTTA HERE!!!
BEGIN!

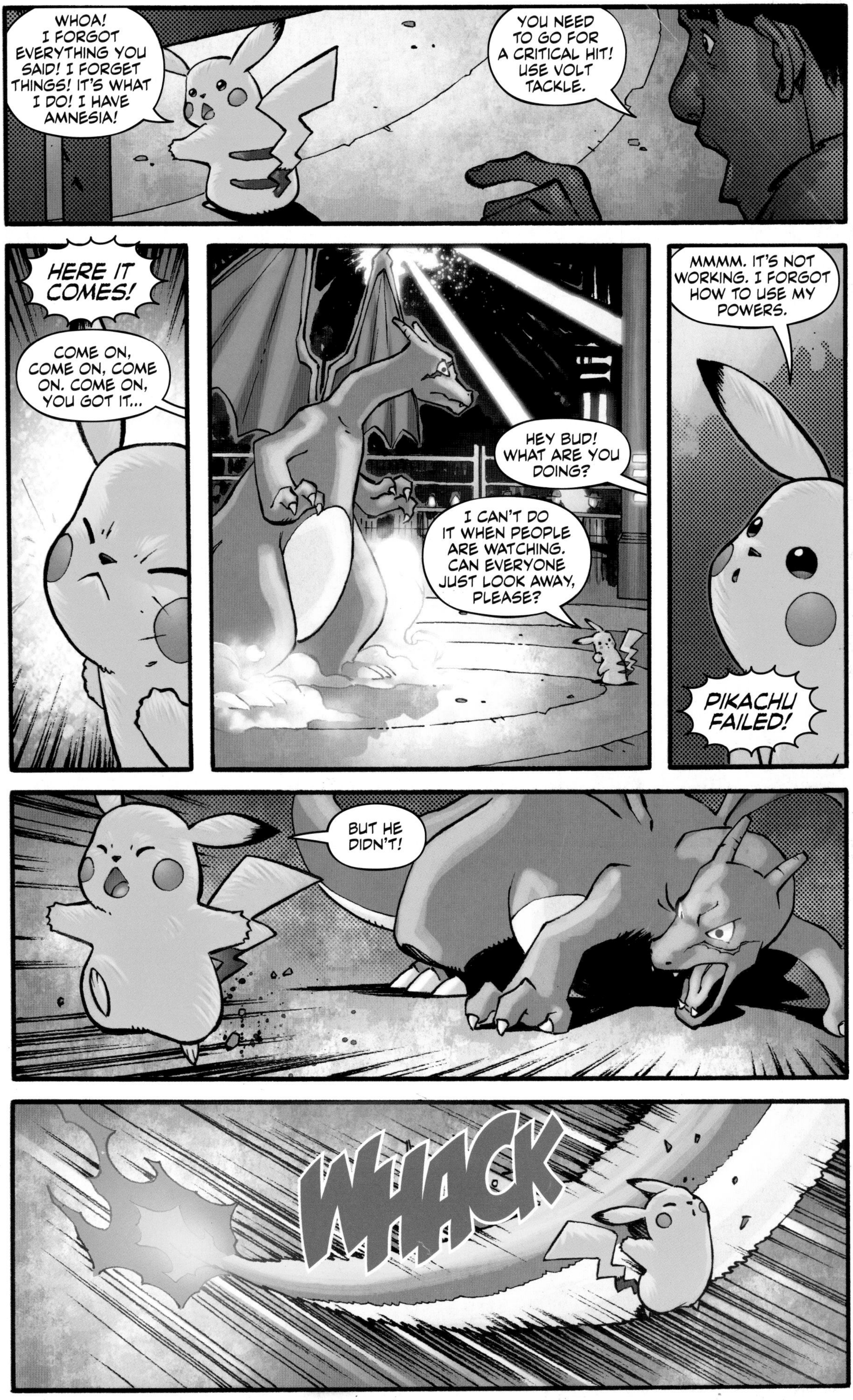
WHOA! I FORGOT EVERYTHING YOU SAID! I FORGET THINGS! IT'S WHAT I DO! I HAVE AMNESIA!
YOU NEED TO GO FOR A CRITICAL HIT! USE VOLT TACKLE.
HERE IT COMES!
COME ON, COME ON, COME ON. COME ON, YOU GOT IT...
HEY BUD! WHAT ARE YOU DOING?
I CAN'T DO IT WHEN PEOPLE ARE WATCHING. CAN EVERYONE JUST LOOK AWAY, PLEASE?
MMMM. IT'S NOT WORKING. I FORGOT HOW TO USE MY POWERS.
PIKACHU FAILED!
BUT HE DIDN'T!
WHACK

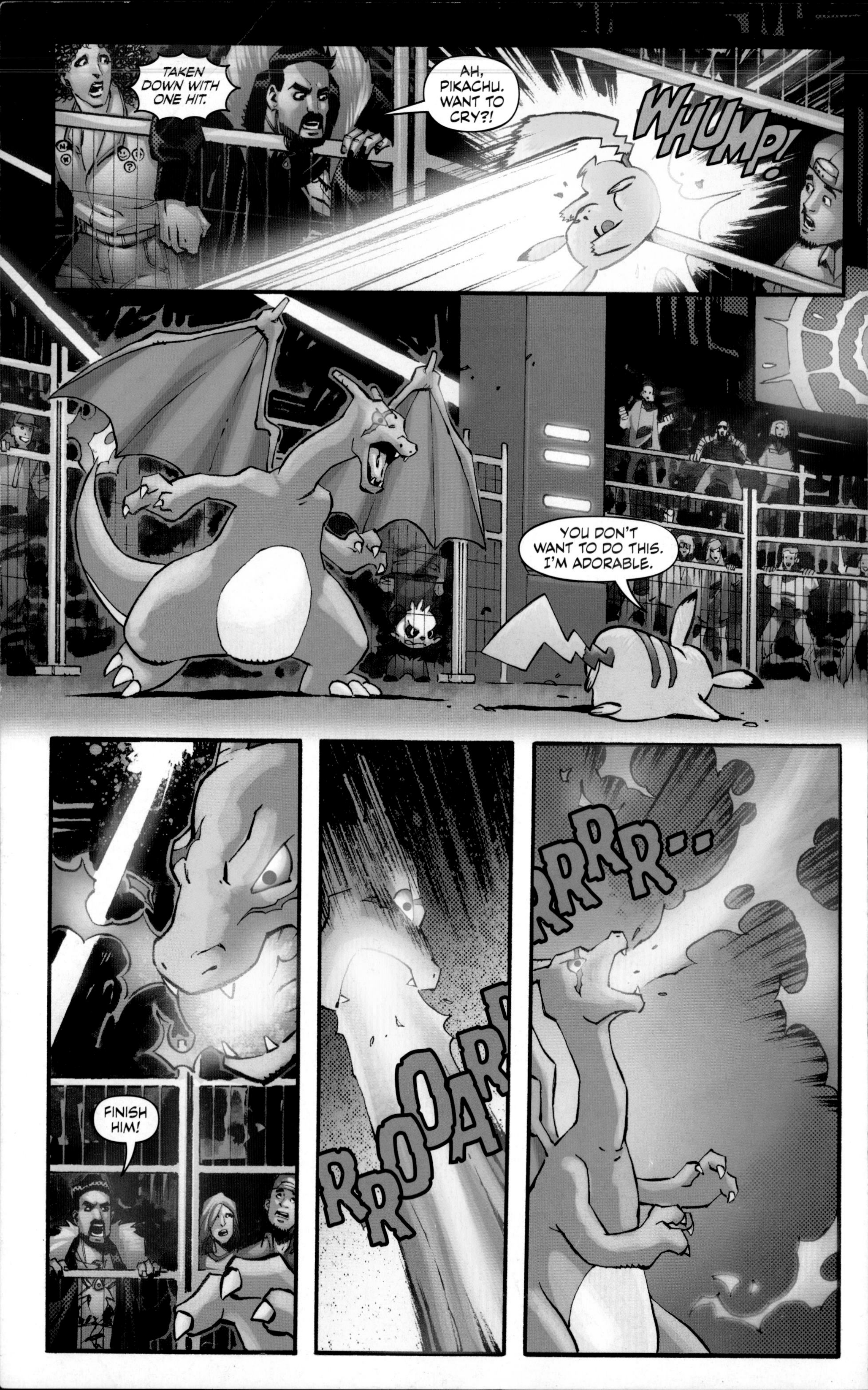
TAKEN DOWN WITH ONE HIT.
AH, PIKACHU. WANT TO CRY?!
WHUMP!
YOU DON'T WANT TO DO THIS. I'M ADORABLE.
FINISH HIM!
RROOAR
RRRR-..

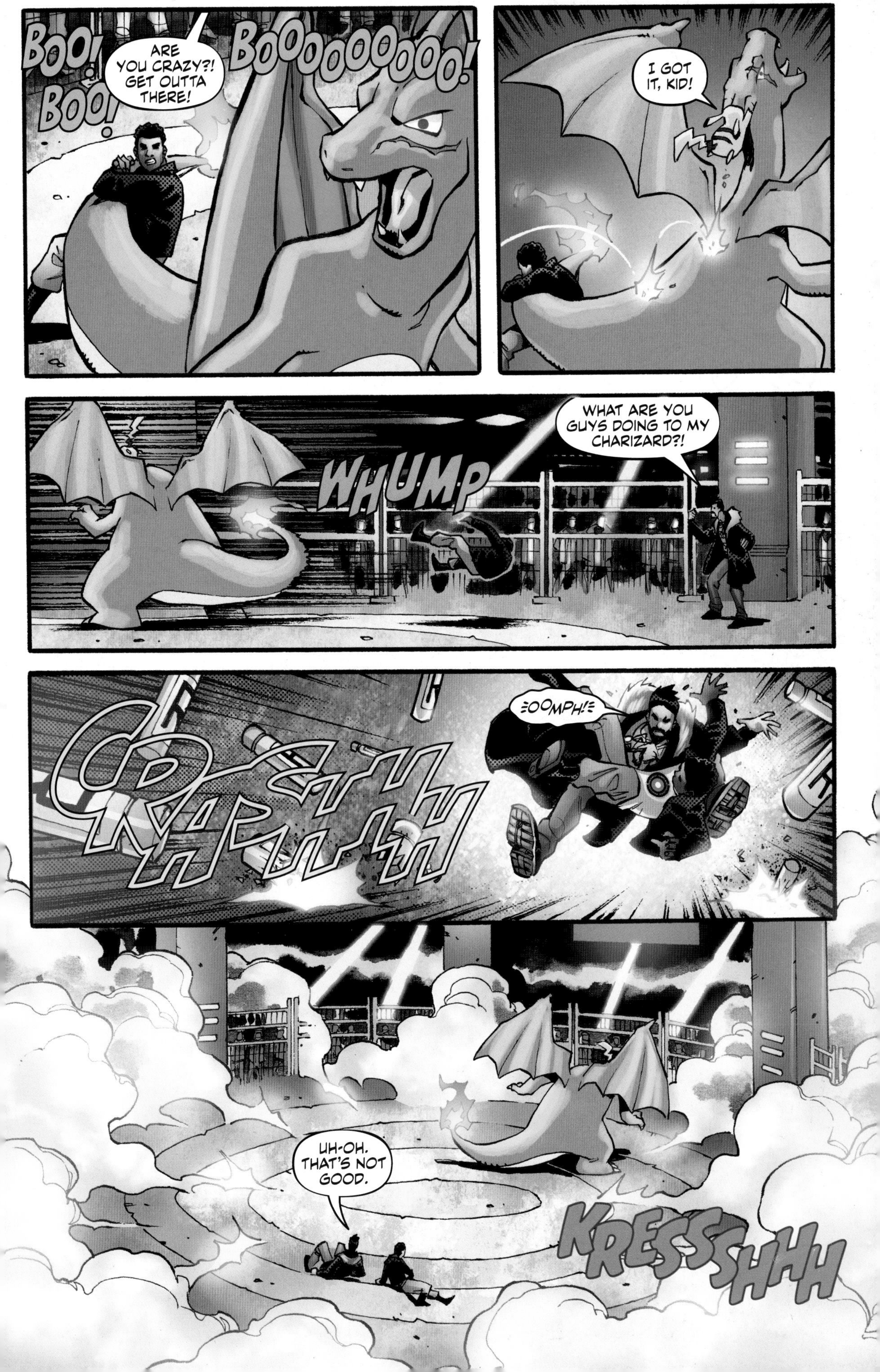
BOO! BOO!
ARE YOU CRAZY?! GET OUTTA THERE!
BOOOOOOOOO!
I GOT IT, KID!
WHUMP
WHAT ARE YOU GUYS DOING TO MY CHARIZARD?!
OOMPH!
UH-OH. THAT'S NOT GOOD.
KRESSSHHH

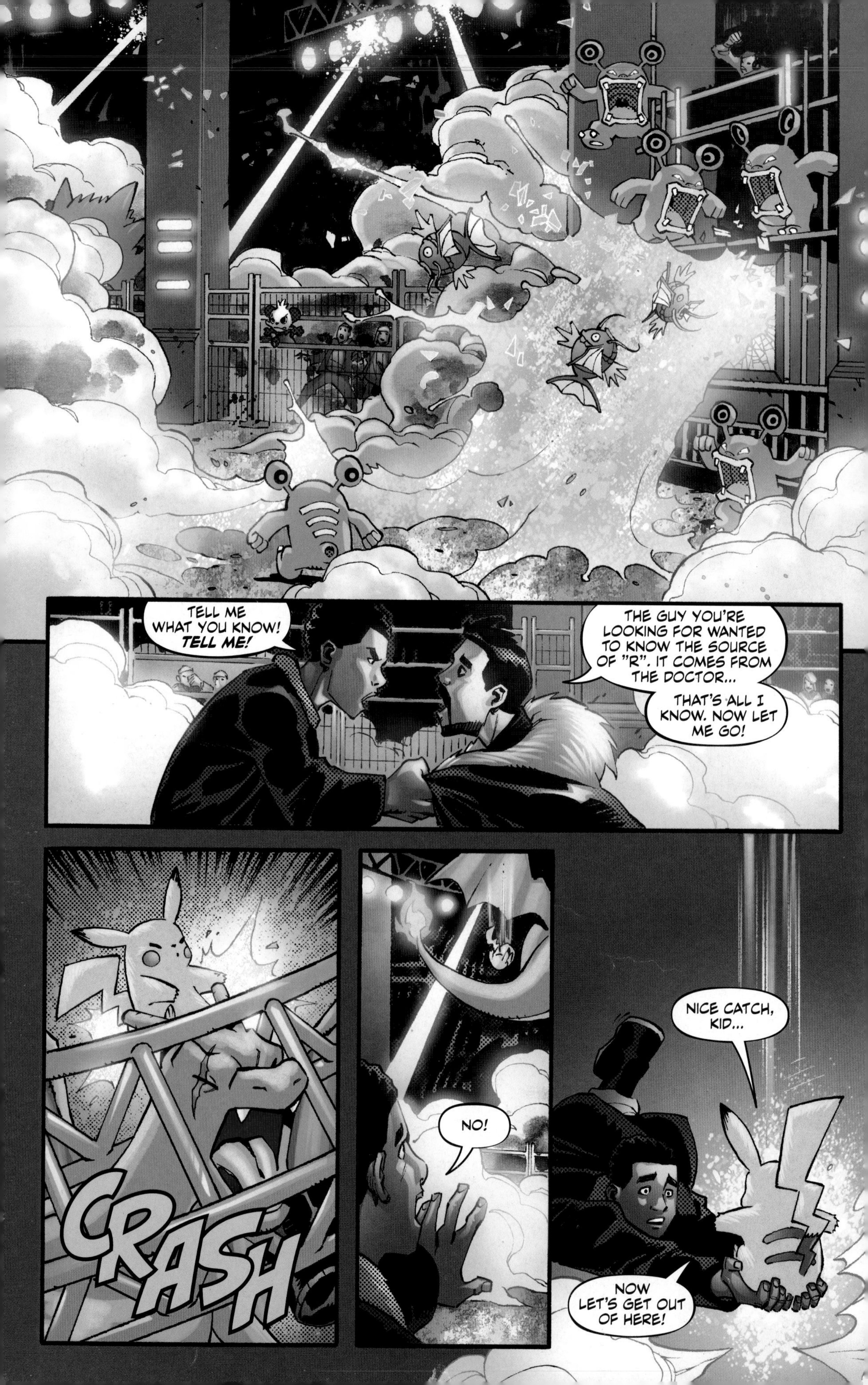
TELL ME WHAT YOU KNOW! ***TELL ME!***
THE GUY YOU'RE LOOKING FOR WANTED TO KNOW THE SOURCE OF "R". IT COMES FROM THE DOCTOR...
THAT'S ALL I KNOW. NOW LET ME GO!
CRASH
NO!
NICE CATCH, KID...
NOW LET'S GET OUT OF HERE!

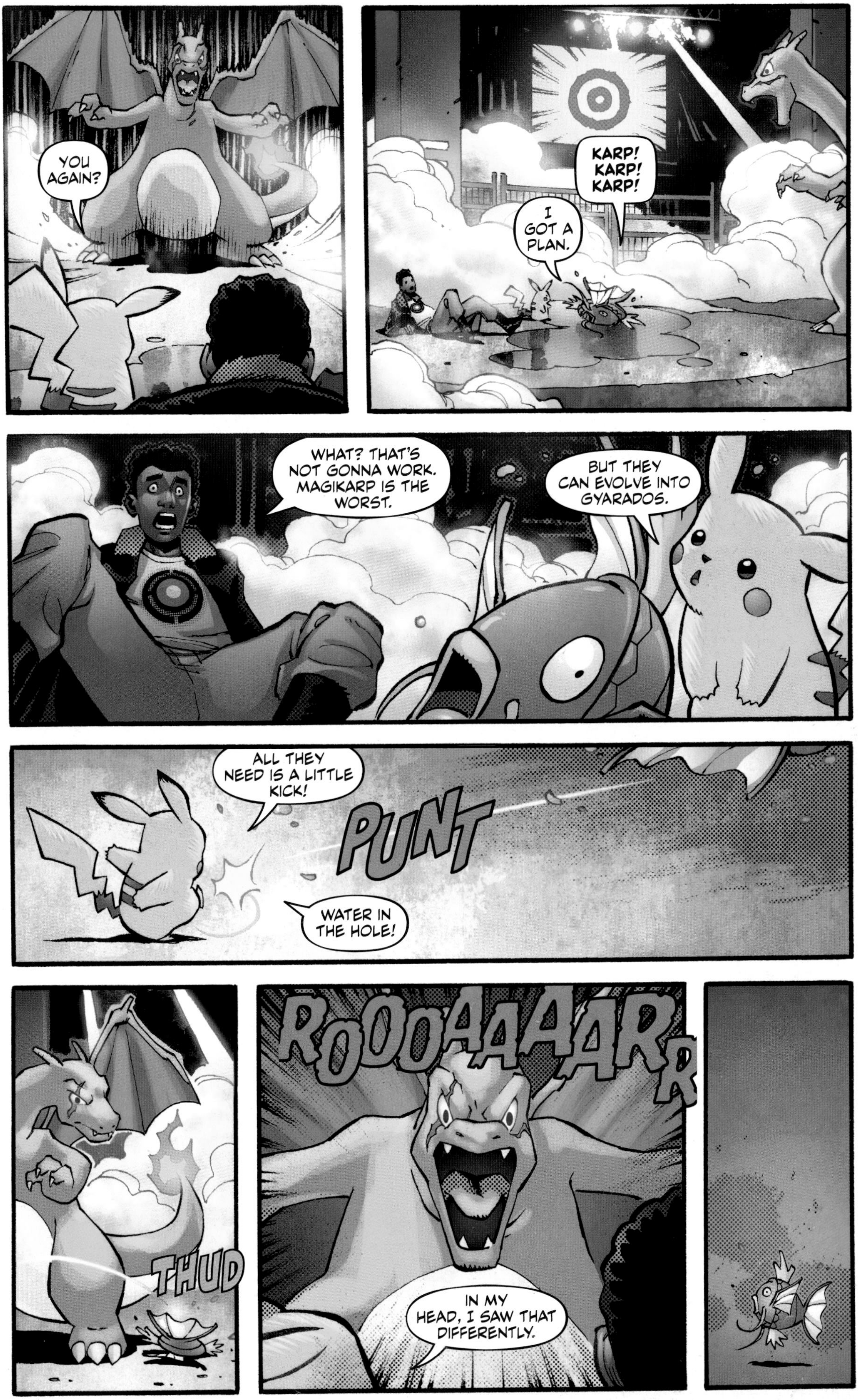
YOU AGAIN?
KARP! KARP! KARP!
I GOT A PLAN.
WHAT? THAT'S NOT GONNA WORK. MAGIKARP IS THE WORST.
BUT THEY CAN EVOLVE INTO GYARADOS.
ALL THEY NEED IS A LITTLE KICK!
PUNT
WATER IN THE HOLE!
THUD
ROOOAAAARR
IN MY HEAD, I SAW THAT DIFFERENTLY.

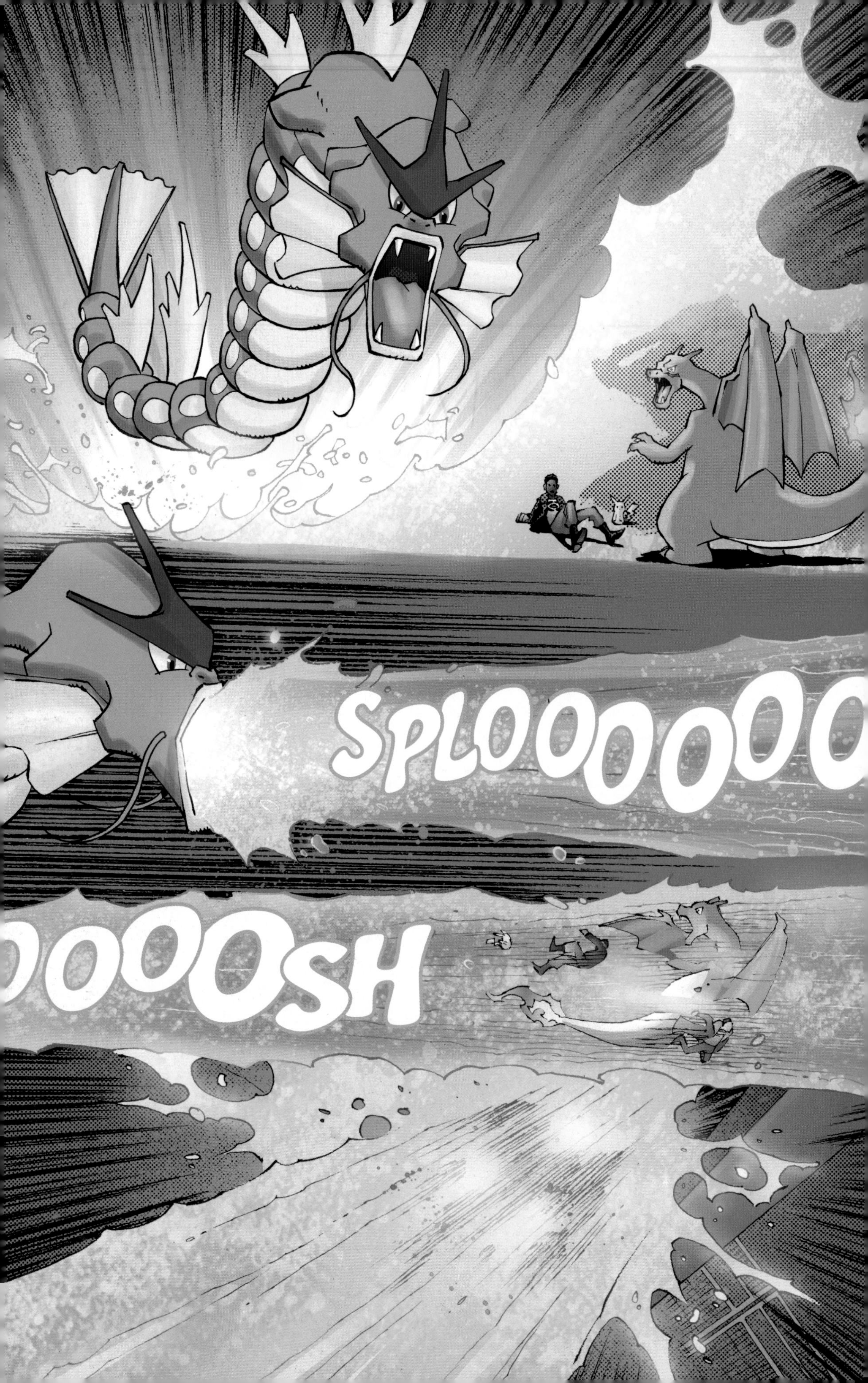
SPLOOOOOOOOOOOOSH

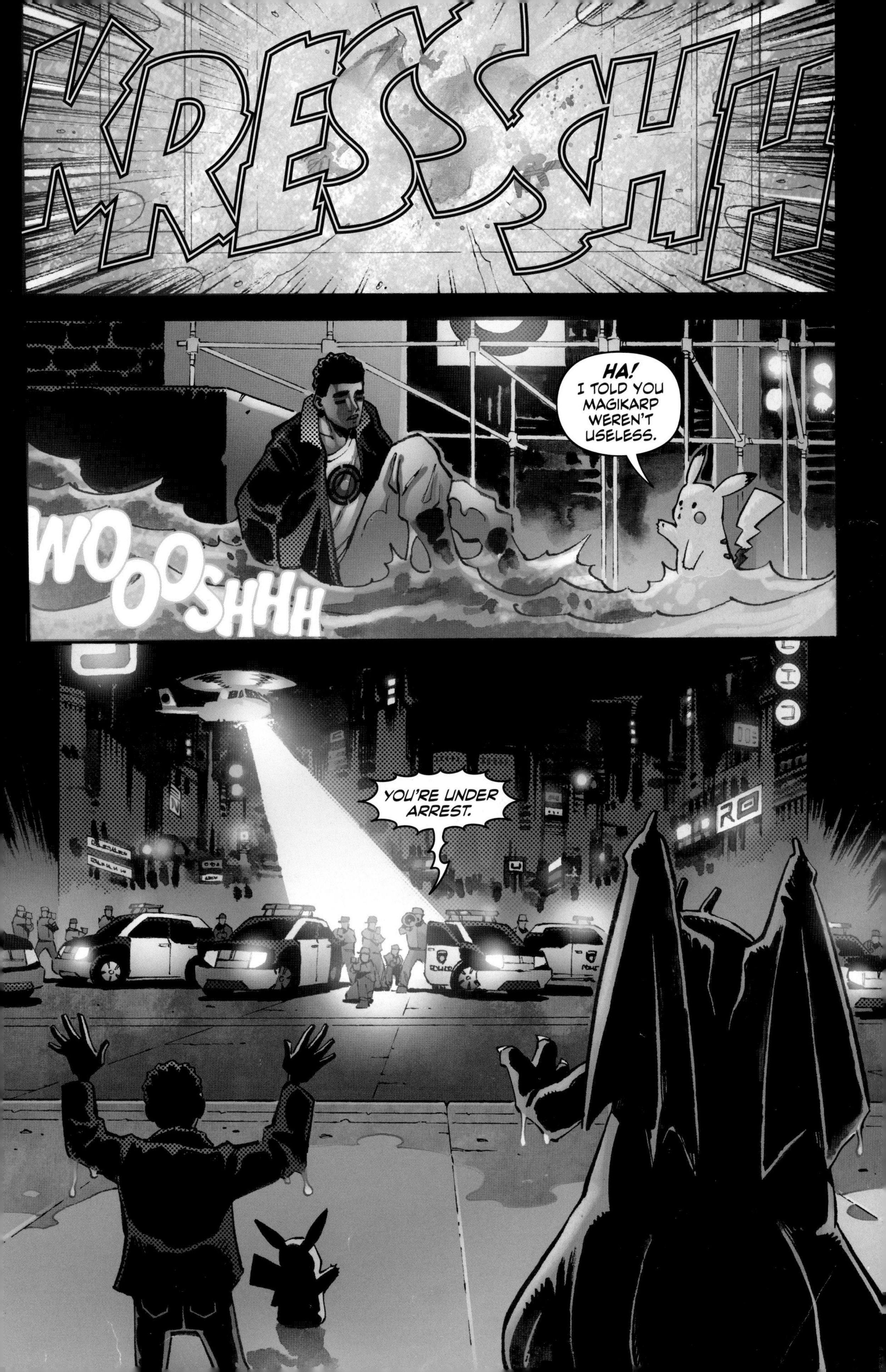
KRESSCHH
HA!
I TOLD YOU MAGIKARP WEREN'T USELESS.
WOOOSHHH
YOU'RE UNDER ARREST.
RO

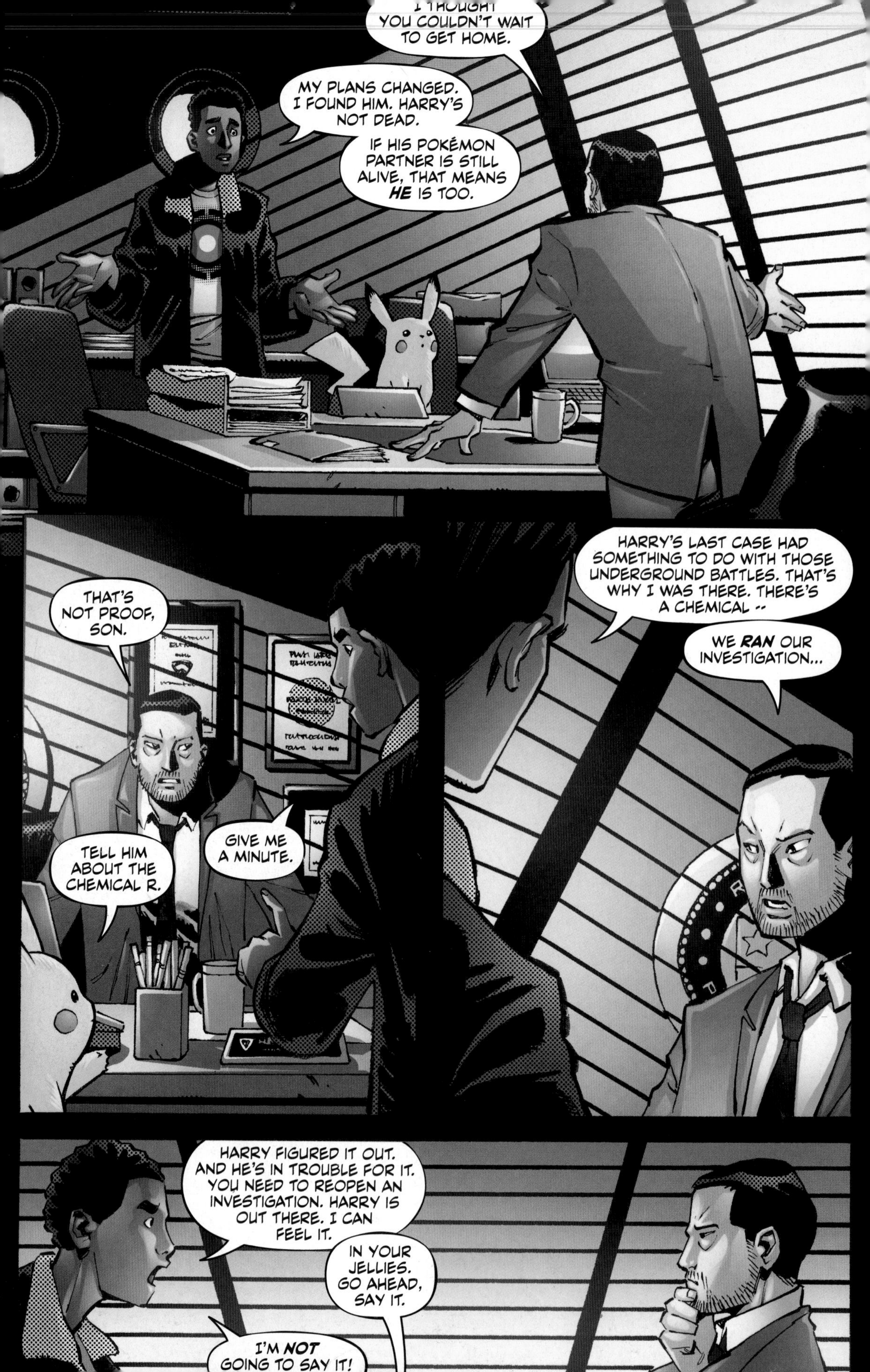
I THOUGHT YOU COULDN'T WAIT TO GET HOME.
MY PLANS CHANGED. I FOUND HIM. HARRY'S NOT DEAD.
IF HIS POKÉMON PARTNER IS STILL ALIVE, THAT MEANS HE IS TOO.
HARRY'S LAST CASE HAD SOMETHING TO DO WITH THOSE UNDERGROUND BATTLES. THAT'S WHY I WAS THERE. THERE'S A CHEMICAL --
THAT'S NOT PROOF, SON.
WE RAN OUR INVESTIGATION...
TELL HIM ABOUT THE CHEMICAL R.
GIVE ME A MINUTE.
HARRY FIGURED IT OUT. AND HE'S IN TROUBLE FOR IT. YOU NEED TO REOPEN AN INVESTIGATION. HARRY IS OUT THERE. I CAN FEEL IT.
IN YOUR JELLIES. GO AHEAD, SAY IT.
I'M NOT GOING TO SAY IT!

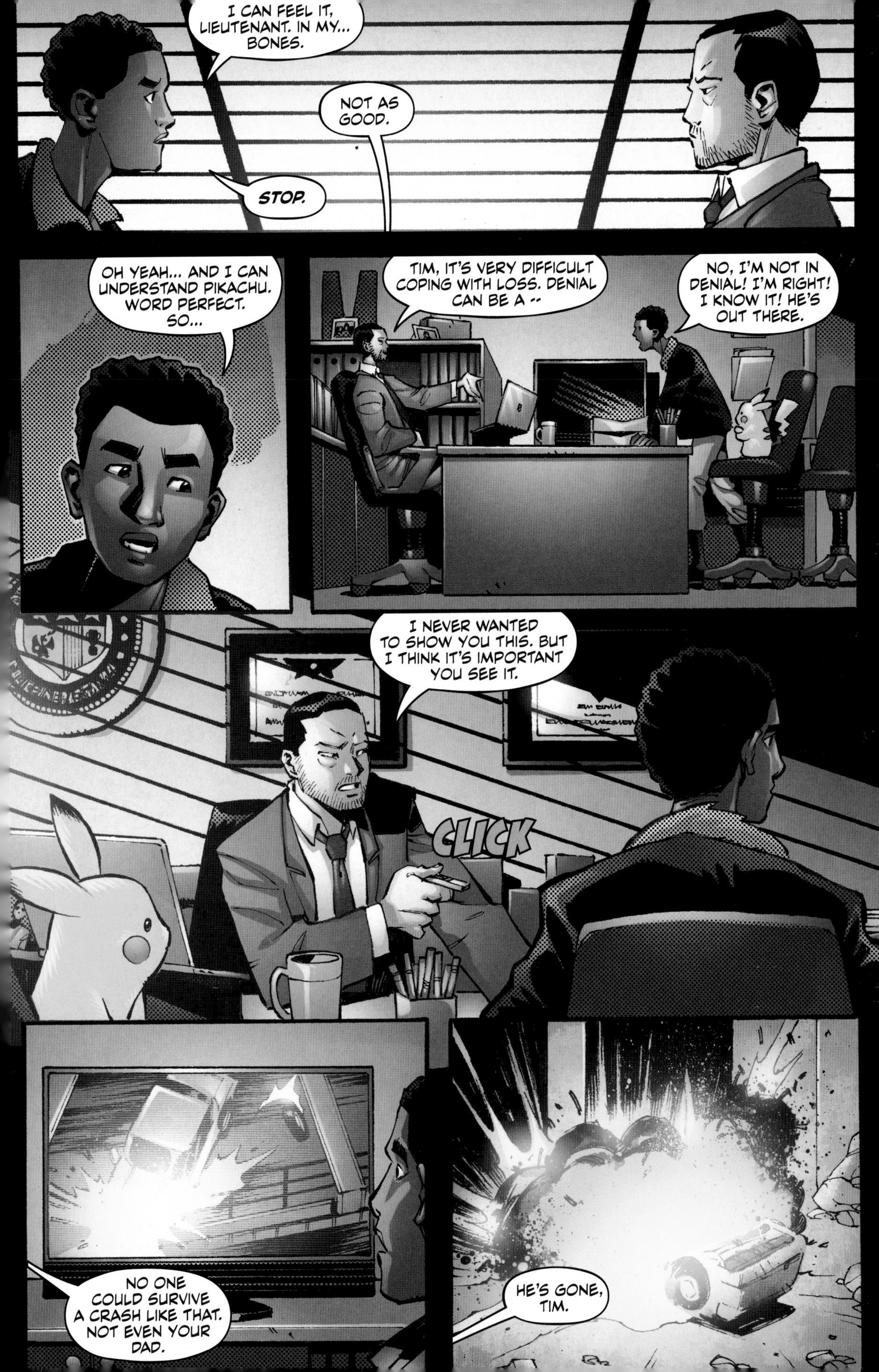

I CAN FEEL IT, LIEUTENANT. IN MY... BONES.
STOP.
NOT AS GOOD.
OH YEAH... AND I CAN UNDERSTAND PIKACHU. WORD PERFECT. SO...
TIM, IT'S VERY DIFFICULT COPING WITH LOSS. DENIAL CAN BE A --
NO, I'M NOT IN DENIAL! I'M RIGHT! I KNOW IT! HE'S OUT THERE.
I NEVER WANTED TO SHOW YOU THIS. BUT I THINK IT'S IMPORTANT YOU SEE IT.
CLICK
NO ONE COULD SURVIVE A CRASH LIKE THAT. NOT EVEN YOUR DAD.
HE'S GONE, TIM.

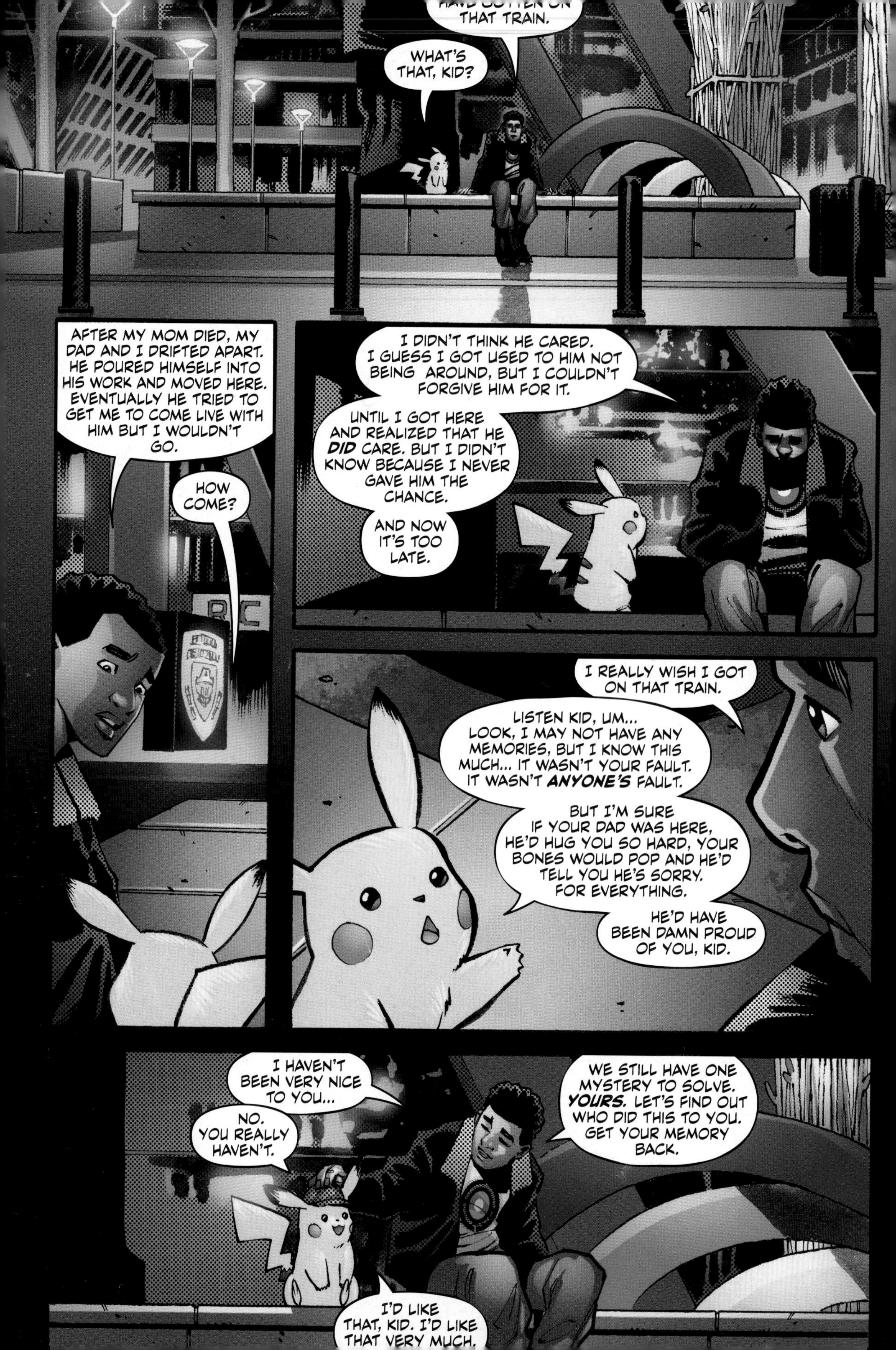

THAT TRAIN.
WHAT'S THAT, KID?
AFTER MY MOM DIED, MY DAD AND I DRIFTED APART. HE POURED HIMSELF INTO HIS WORK AND MOVED HERE. EVENTUALLY HE TRIED TO GET ME TO COME LIVE WITH HIM BUT I WOULDN'T GO.
HOW COME?
I DIDN'T THINK HE CARED. I GUESS I GOT USED TO HIM NOT BEING AROUND, BUT I COULDN'T FORGIVE HIM FOR IT.
UNTIL I GOT HERE AND REALIZED THAT HE *DID* CARE. BUT I DIDN'T KNOW BECAUSE I NEVER GAVE HIM THE CHANCE.
AND NOW IT'S TOO LATE.
I REALLY WISH I GOT ON THAT TRAIN.
LISTEN KID, UM... LOOK, I MAY NOT HAVE ANY MEMORIES, BUT I KNOW THIS MUCH... IT WASN'T YOUR FAULT. IT WASN'T *ANYONE'S* FAULT.
BUT I'M SURE IF YOUR DAD WAS HERE, HE'D HUG YOU SO HARD, YOUR BONES WOULD POP AND HE'D TELL YOU HE'S SORRY. FOR EVERYTHING.
HE'D HAVE BEEN DAMN PROUD OF YOU, KID.
I HAVEN'T BEEN VERY NICE TO YOU...
NO. YOU REALLY HAVEN'T.
WE STILL HAVE ONE MYSTERY TO SOLVE. *YOURS.* LET'S FIND OUT WHO DID THIS TO YOU. GET YOUR MEMORY BACK.
I'D LIKE THAT, KID. I'D LIKE THAT VERY MUCH.

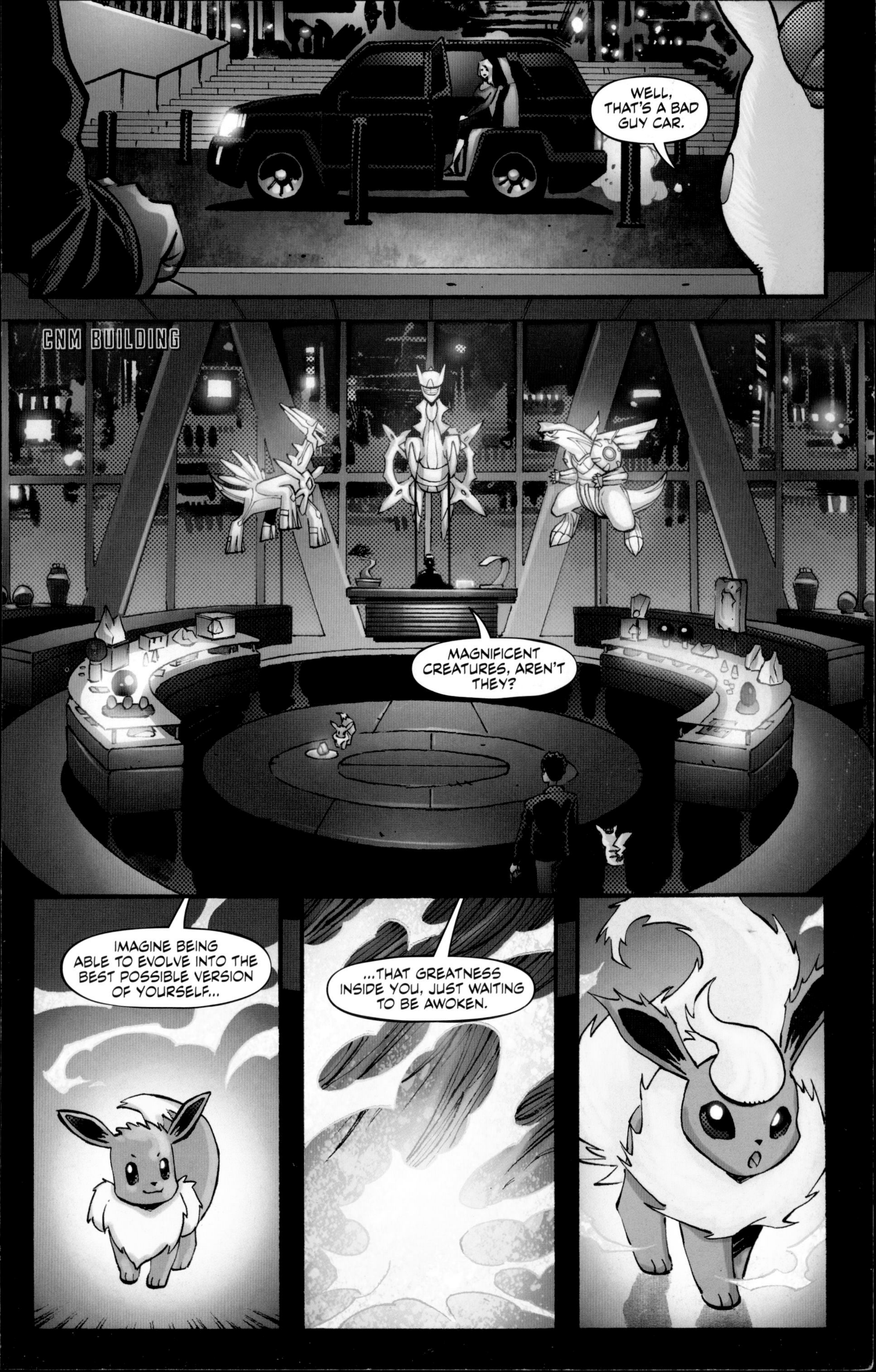
WELL, THAT'S A BAD GUY CAR.
CNM BUILDING
MAGNIFICENT CREATURES, AREN'T THEY?
IMAGINE BEING ABLE TO EVOLVE INTO THE BEST POSSIBLE VERSION OF YOURSELF...
...THAT GREATNESS INSIDE YOU, JUST WAITING TO BE AWOKEN.

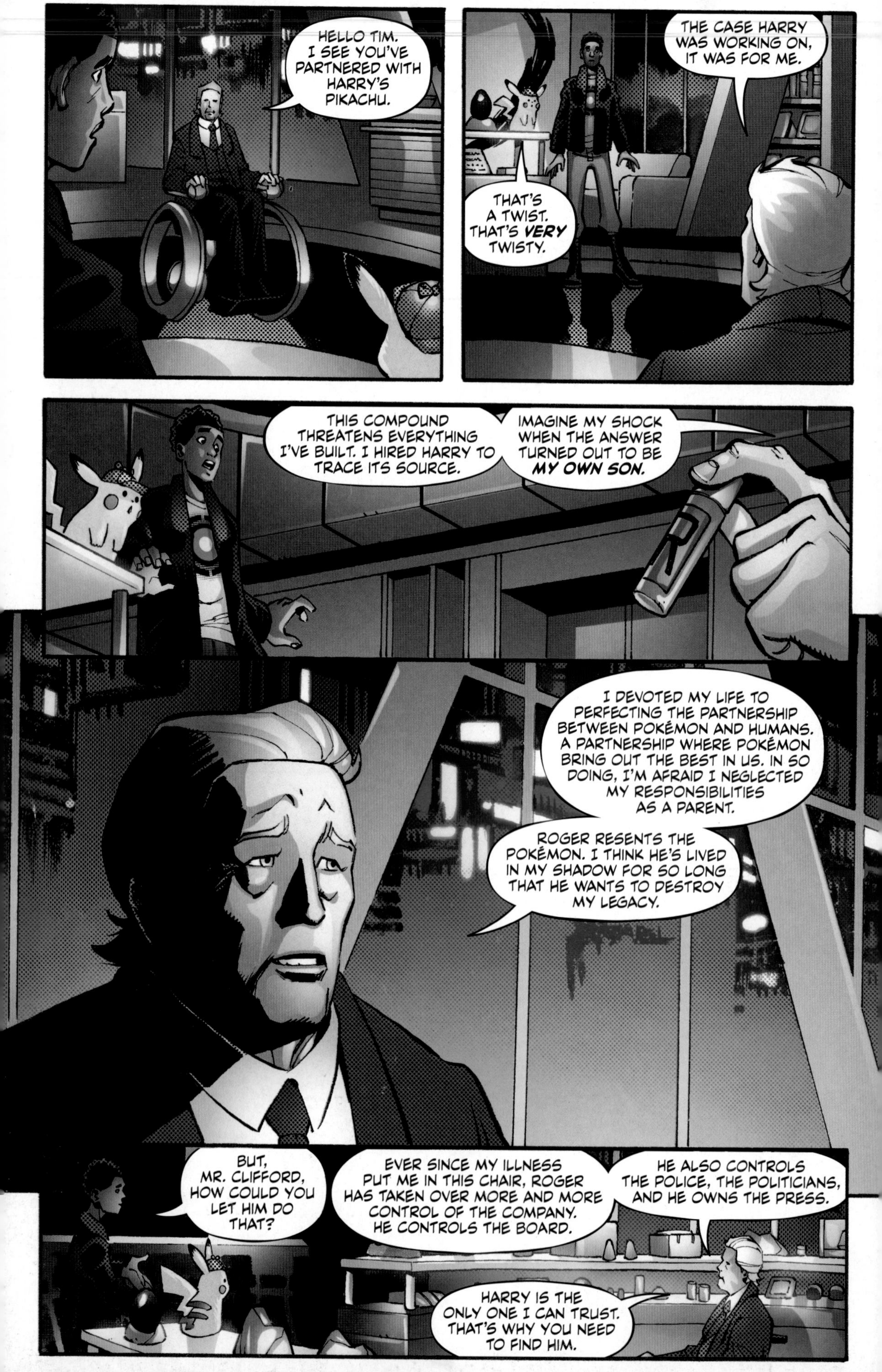
HELLO TIM. I SEE YOU'VE PARTNERED WITH HARRY'S PIKACHU.
THE CASE HARRY WAS WORKING ON, IT WAS FOR ME.
THAT'S A TWIST. THAT'S VERY TWISTY.
THIS COMPOUND THREATENS EVERYTHING I'VE BUILT. I HIRED HARRY TO TRACE ITS SOURCE.
IMAGINE MY SHOCK WHEN THE ANSWER TURNED OUT TO BE MY OWN SON.
I DEVOTED MY LIFE TO PERFECTING THE PARTNERSHIP BETWEEN POKÉMON AND HUMANS. A PARTNERSHIP WHERE POKÉMON BRING OUT THE BEST IN US. IN SO DOING, I'M AFRAID I NEGLECTED MY RESPONSIBILITIES AS A PARENT.
ROGER RESENTS THE POKÉMON. I THINK HE'S LIVED IN MY SHADOW FOR SO LONG THAT HE WANTS TO DESTROY MY LEGACY.
BUT, MR. CLIFFORD, HOW COULD YOU LET HIM DO THAT?
EVER SINCE MY ILLNESS PUT ME IN THIS CHAIR, ROGER HAS TAKEN OVER MORE AND MORE CONTROL OF THE COMPANY. HE CONTROLS THE BOARD.
HE ALSO CONTROLS THE POLICE, THE POLITICIANS, AND HE OWNS THE PRESS.
HARRY IS THE ONLY ONE I CAN TRUST. THAT'S WHY YOU NEED TO FIND HIM.

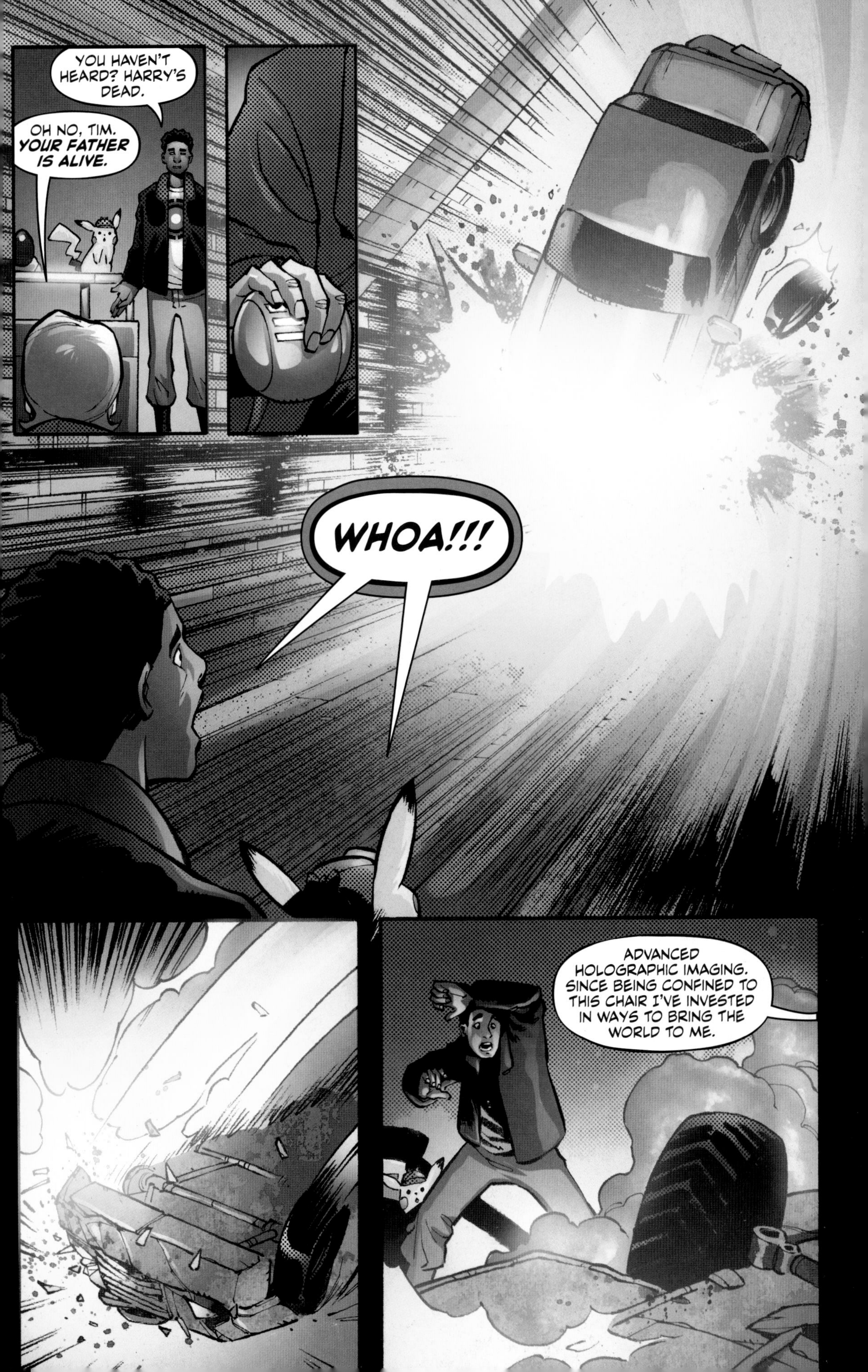
YOU HAVEN'T HEARD? HARRY'S DEAD.
OH NO, TIM. YOUR FATHER IS ALIVE.
WHOA!!!
ADVANCED HOLOGRAPHIC IMAGING. SINCE BEING CONFINED TO THIS CHAIR I'VE INVESTED IN WAYS TO BRING THE WORLD TO ME.

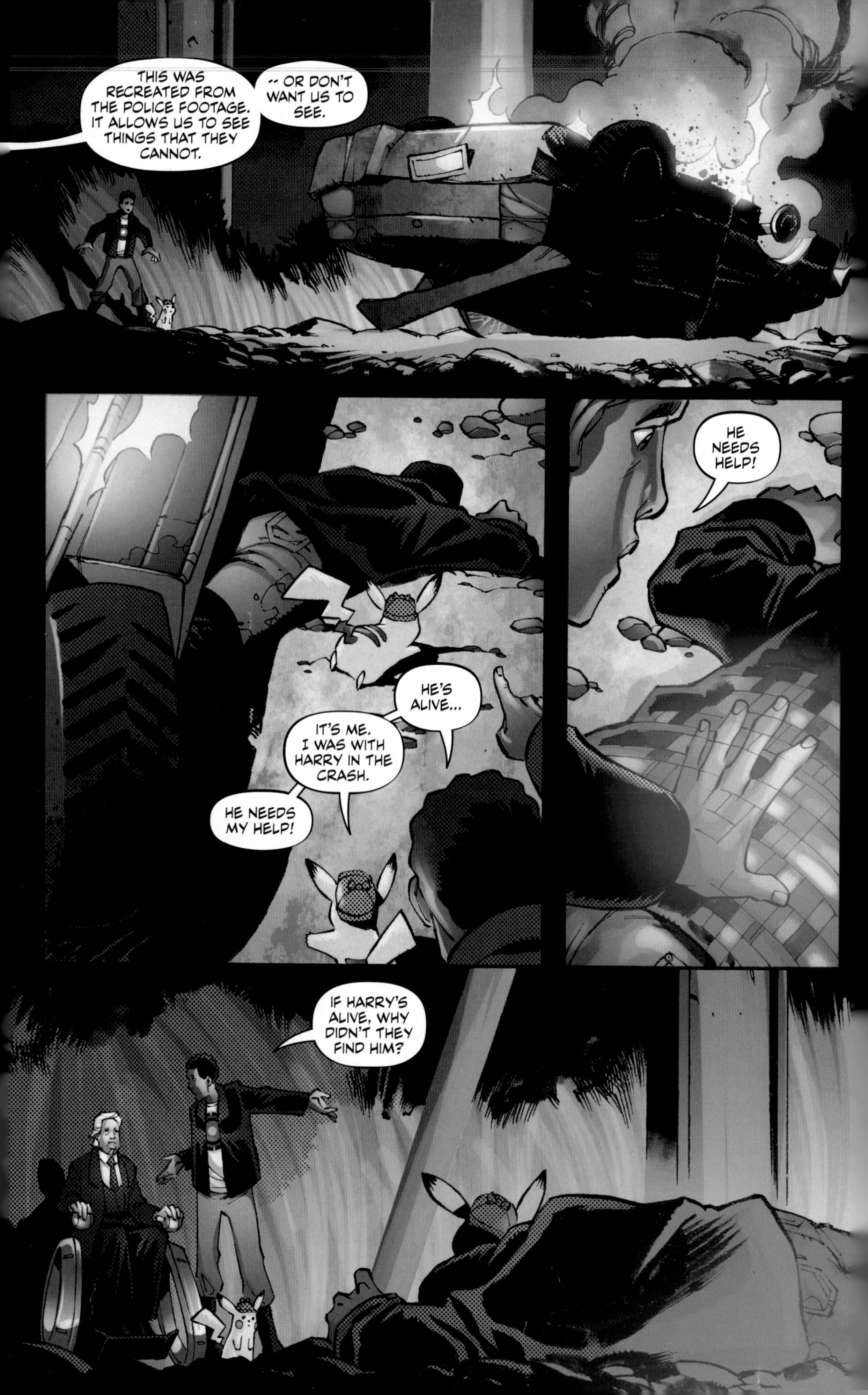
THIS WAS RECREATED FROM THE POLICE FOOTAGE. IT ALLOWS US TO SEE THINGS THAT THEY CANNOT.
-- OR DON'T WANT US TO SEE.
HE'S ALIVE...
IT'S ME. I WAS WITH HARRY IN THE CRASH.
HE NEEDS MY HELP!
HE NEEDS HELP!
IF HARRY'S ALIVE, WHY DIDN'T THEY FIND HIM?

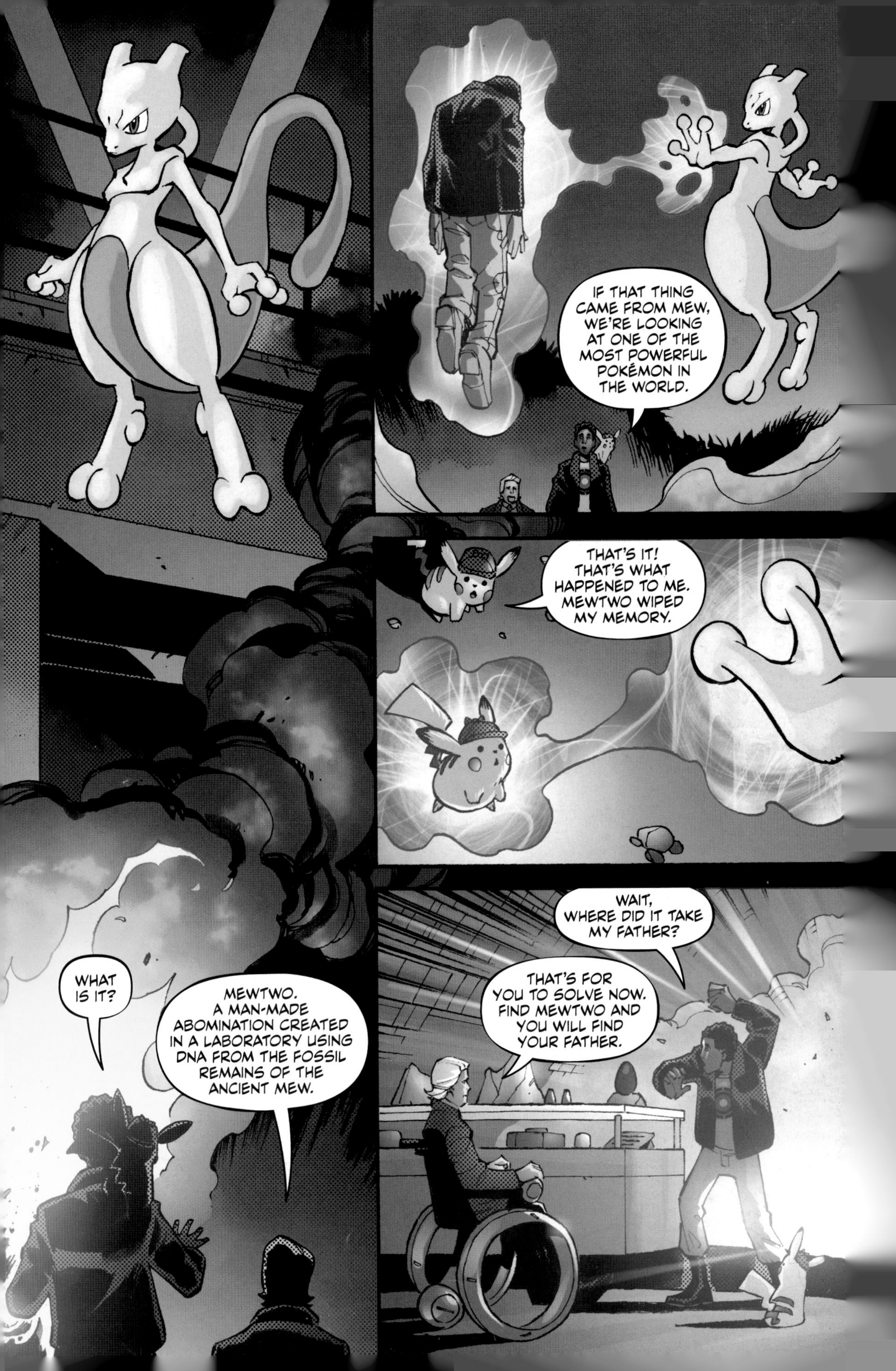
IF THAT THING CAME FROM MEW, WE'RE LOOKING AT ONE OF THE MOST POWERFUL POKÉMON IN THE WORLD.
THAT'S IT! THAT'S WHAT HAPPENED TO ME. MEWTWO WIPED MY MEMORY.
WHAT IS IT?
MEWTWO. A MAN-MADE ABOMINATION CREATED IN A LABORATORY USING DNA FROM THE FOSSIL REMAINS OF THE ANCIENT MEW.
WAIT, WHERE DID IT TAKE MY FATHER?
THAT'S FOR YOU TO SOLVE NOW. FIND MEWTWO AND YOU WILL FIND YOUR FATHER.

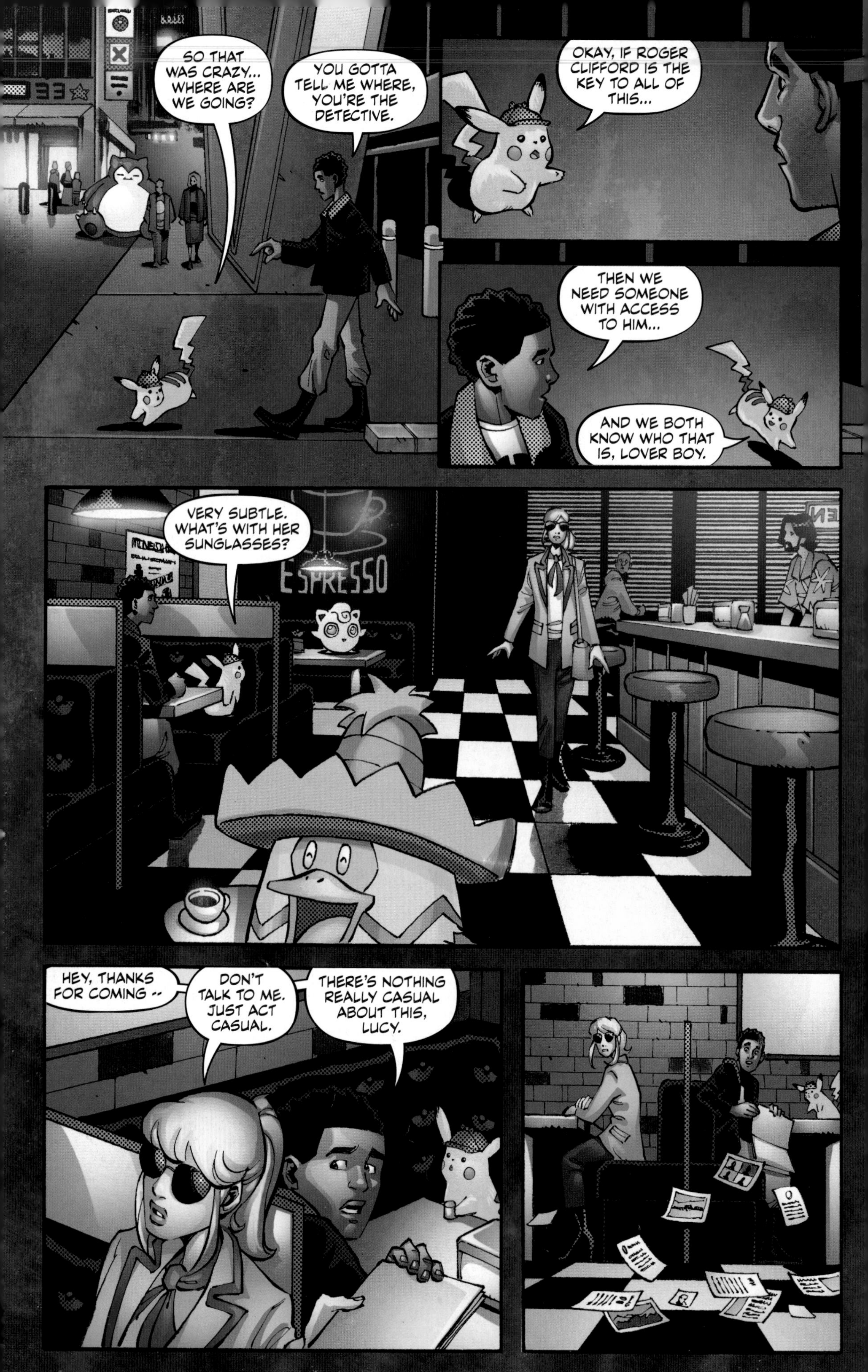
SO THAT WAS CRAZY... WHERE ARE WE GOING?
YOU GOTTA TELL ME WHERE, YOU'RE THE DETECTIVE.
OKAY, IF ROGER CLIFFORD IS THE KEY TO ALL OF THIS...
THEN WE NEED SOMEONE WITH ACCESS TO HIM...
AND WE BOTH KNOW WHO THAT IS, LOVER BOY.
VERY SUBTLE. WHAT'S WITH HER SUNGLASSES?
ESPRESSO
HEY, THANKS FOR COMING --
DON'T TALK TO ME. JUST ACT CASUAL.
THERE'S NOTHING REALLY CASUAL ABOUT THIS, LUCY.

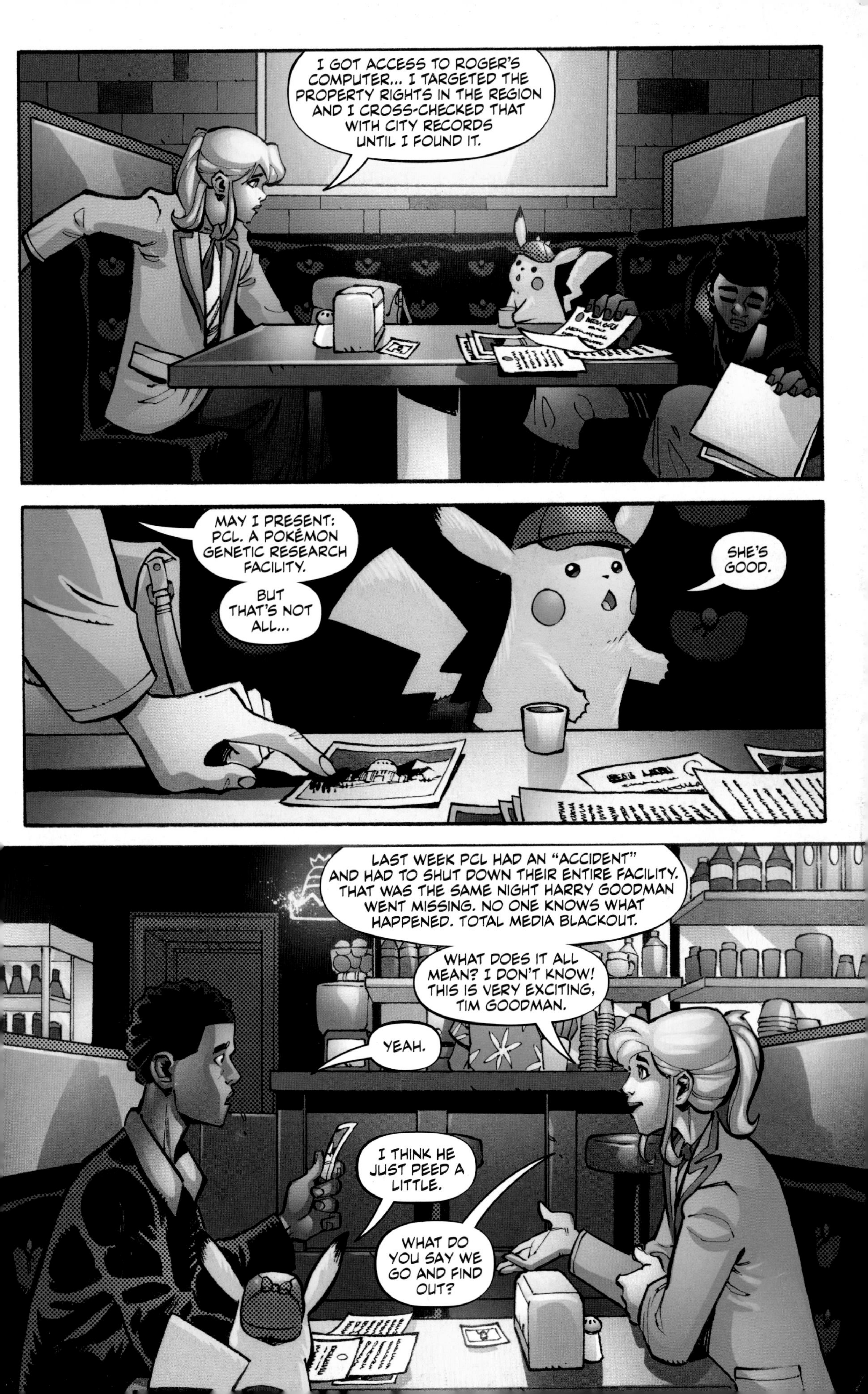
I GOT ACCESS TO ROGER'S COMPUTER... I TARGETED THE PROPERTY RIGHTS IN THE REGION AND I CROSS-CHECKED THAT WITH CITY RECORDS UNTIL I FOUND IT.
MAY I PRESENT: PCL. A POKÉMON GENETIC RESEARCH FACILITY.
BUT THAT'S NOT ALL...
SHE'S GOOD.
LAST WEEK PCL HAD AN "ACCIDENT" AND HAD TO SHUT DOWN THEIR ENTIRE FACILITY. THAT WAS THE SAME NIGHT HARRY GOODMAN WENT MISSING. NO ONE KNOWS WHAT HAPPENED. TOTAL MEDIA BLACKOUT.
WHAT DOES IT ALL MEAN? I DON'T KNOW! THIS IS VERY EXCITING, TIM GOODMAN.
YEAH.
I THINK HE JUST PEED A LITTLE.
WHAT DO YOU SAY WE GO AND FIND OUT?

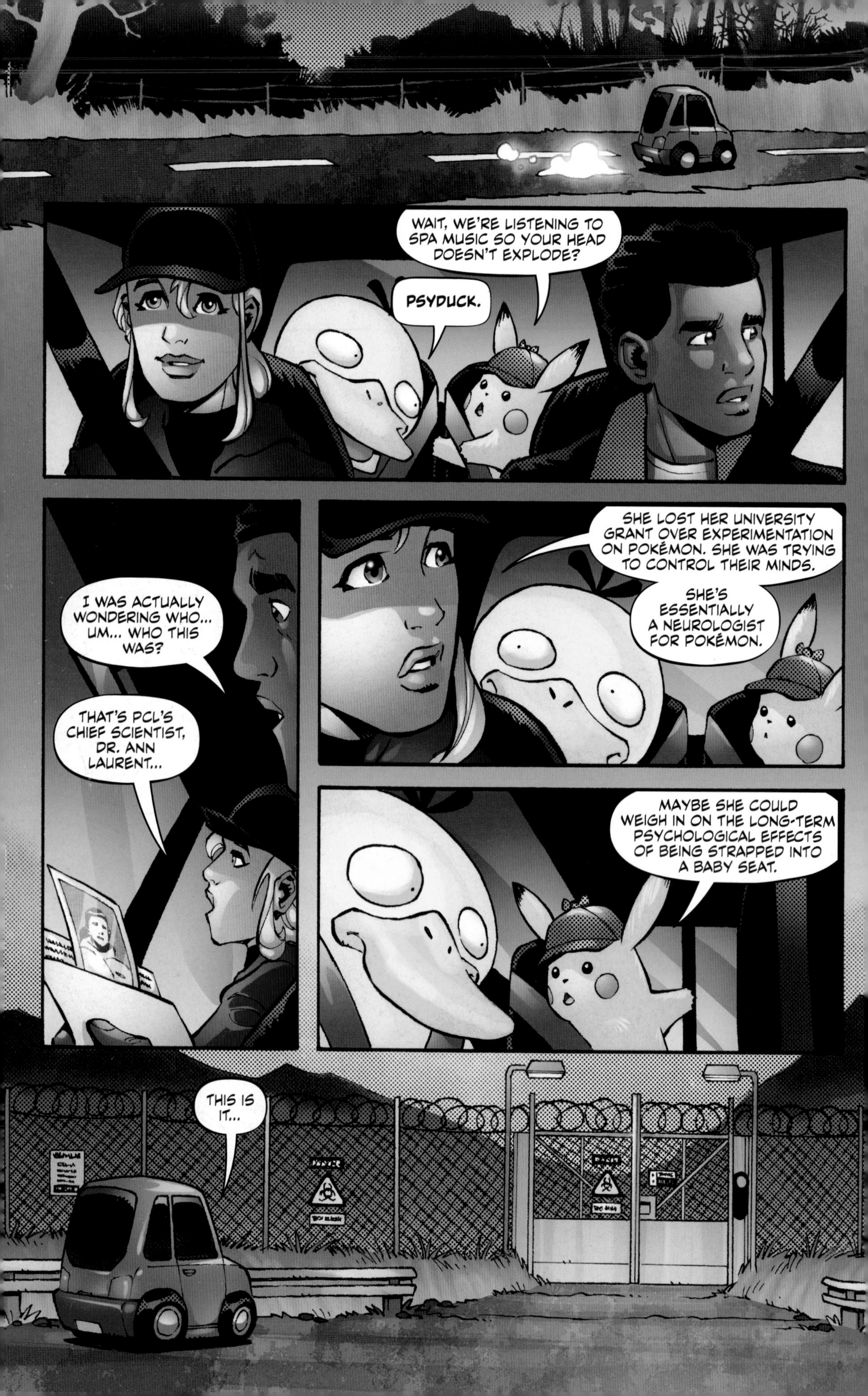
WAIT, WE'RE LISTENING TO SPA MUSIC SO YOUR HEAD DOESN'T EXPLODE?
PSYDUCK.
I WAS ACTUALLY WONDERING WHO... UM... WHO THIS WAS?
THAT'S PCL'S CHIEF SCIENTIST, DR. ANN LAURENT...
SHE LOST HER UNIVERSITY GRANT OVER EXPERIMENTATION ON POKÉMON. SHE WAS TRYING TO CONTROL THEIR MINDS.
SHE'S ESSENTIALLY A NEUROLOGIST FOR POKÉMON.
MAYBE SHE COULD WEIGH IN ON THE LONG-TERM PSYCHOLOGICAL EFFECTS OF BEING STRAPPED INTO A BABY SEAT.
THIS IS IT...

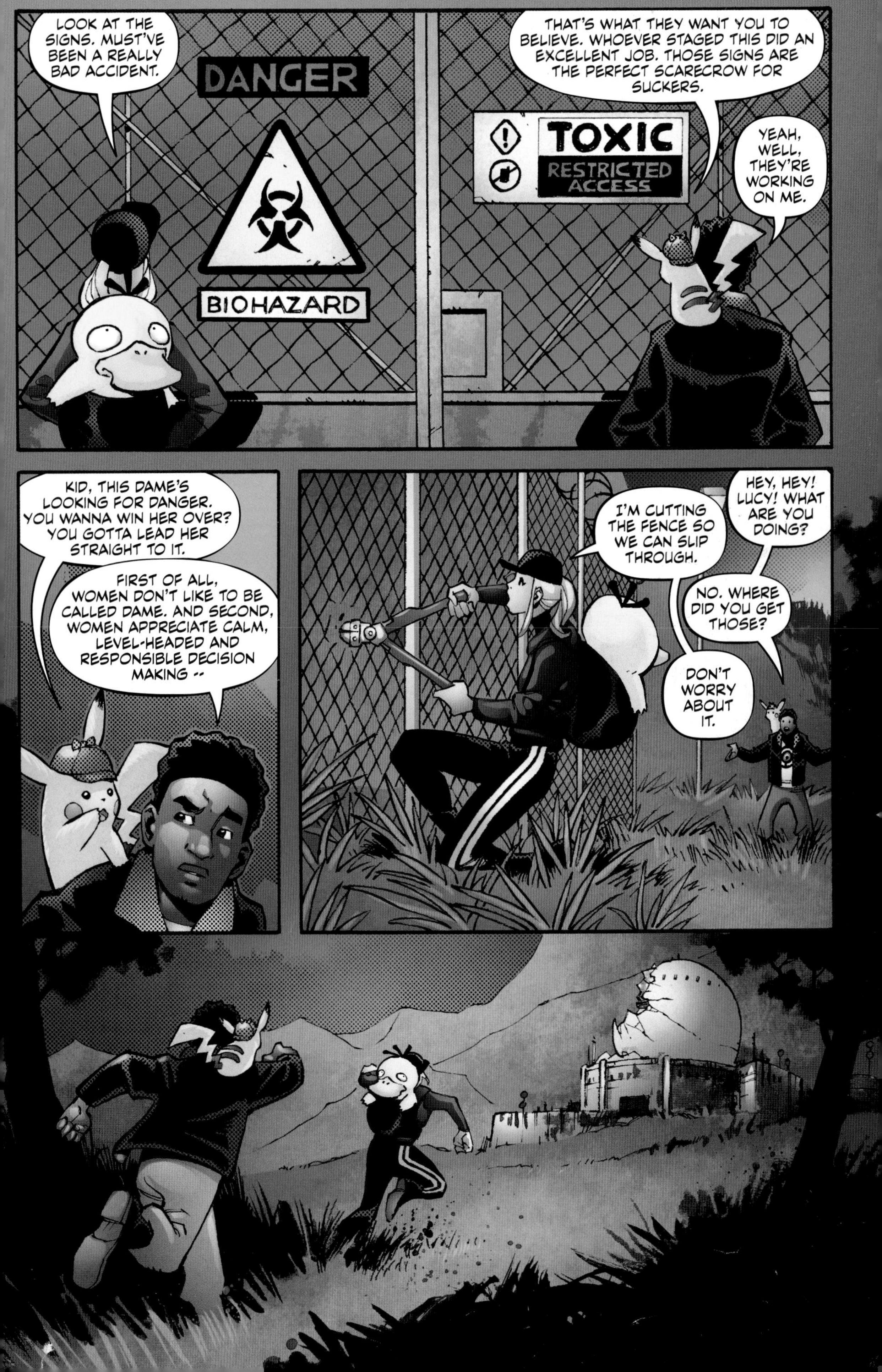

LOOK AT THE SIGNS. MUST'VE BEEN A REALLY BAD ACCIDENT.
DANGER
BIOHAZARD
TOXIC
RESTRICTED ACCESS
THAT'S WHAT THEY WANT YOU TO BELIEVE. WHOEVER STAGED THIS DID AN EXCELLENT JOB. THOSE SIGNS ARE THE PERFECT SCARECROW FOR SUCKERS.
YEAH, WELL, THEY'RE WORKING ON ME.
KID, THIS DAME'S LOOKING FOR DANGER. YOU WANNA WIN HER OVER? YOU GOTTA LEAD HER STRAIGHT TO IT.
FIRST OF ALL, WOMEN DON'T LIKE TO BE CALLED DAME. AND SECOND, WOMEN APPRECIATE CALM, LEVEL-HEADED AND RESPONSIBLE DECISION MAKING --
HEY, HEY! LUCY! WHAT ARE YOU DOING?
I'M CUTTING THE FENCE SO WE CAN SLIP THROUGH.
NO. WHERE DID YOU GET THOSE?
DON'T WORRY ABOUT IT.

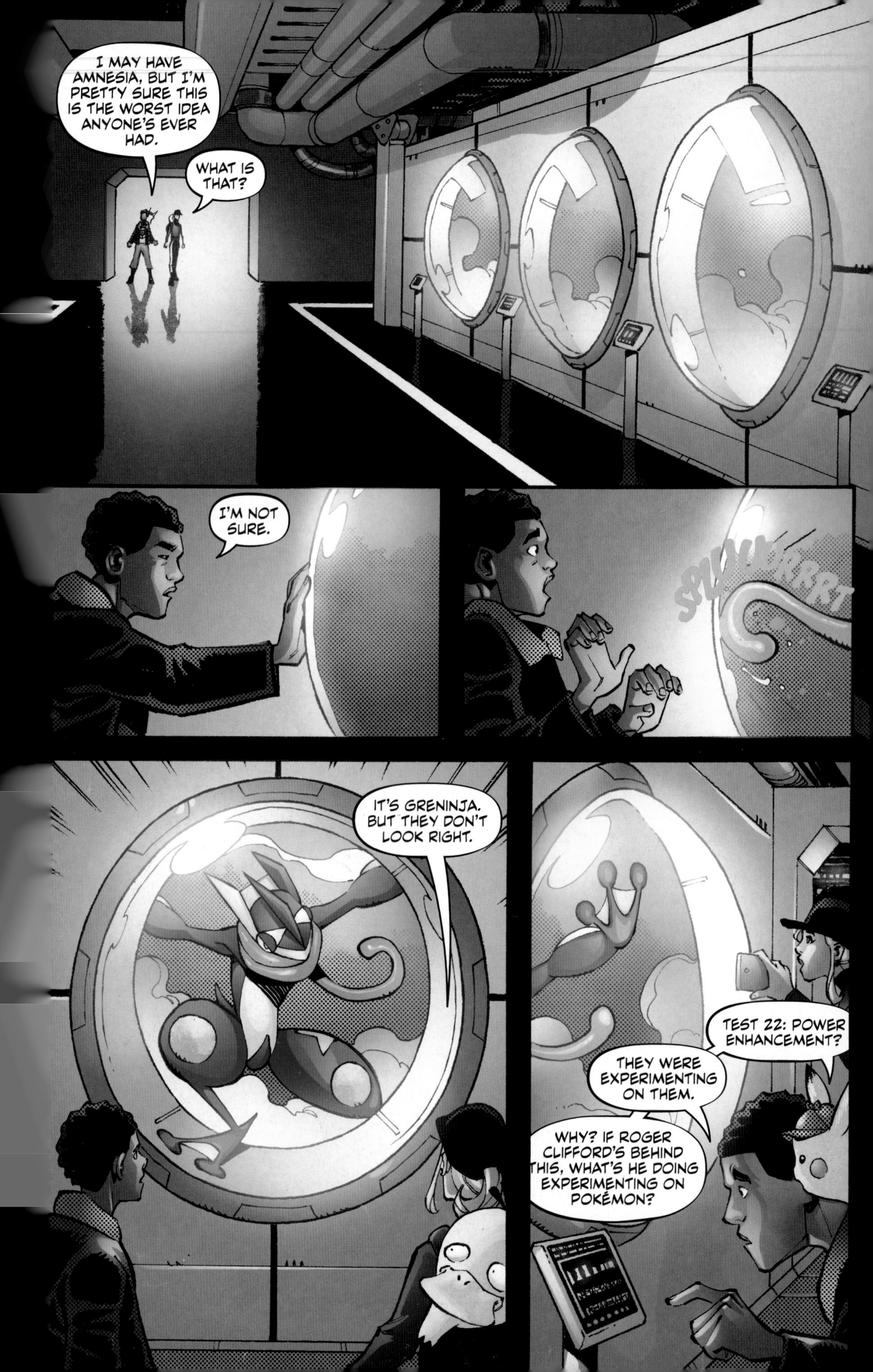
I MAY HAVE AMNESIA, BUT I'M PRETTY SURE THIS IS THE WORST IDEA ANYONE'S EVER HAD.
WHAT IS THAT?
I'M NOT SURE.
SPLUURRRT
IT'S GRENINJA. BUT THEY DON'T LOOK RIGHT.
TEST 22: POWER ENHANCEMENT?
THEY WERE EXPERIMENTING ON THEM.
WHY? IF ROGER CLIFFORD'S BEHIND THIS, WHAT'S HE DOING EXPERIMENTING ON POKÉMON?

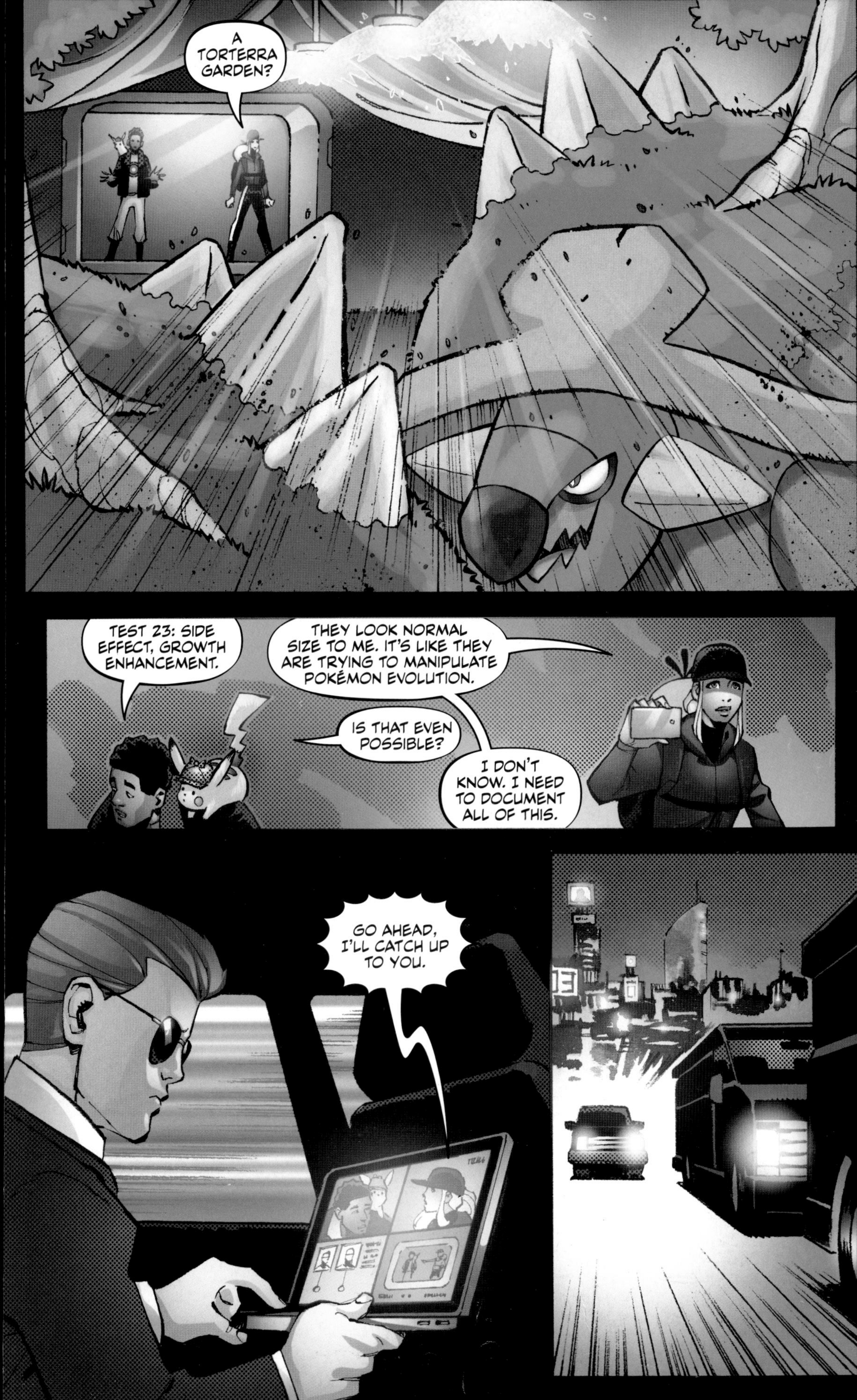
A TORTERRA GARDEN?
TEST 23: SIDE EFFECT, GROWTH ENHANCEMENT.
THEY LOOK NORMAL SIZE TO ME. IT'S LIKE THEY ARE TRYING TO MANIPULATE POKÉMON EVOLUTION.
IS THAT EVEN POSSIBLE?
I DON'T KNOW. I NEED TO DOCUMENT ALL OF THIS.
GO AHEAD, I'LL CATCH UP TO YOU.

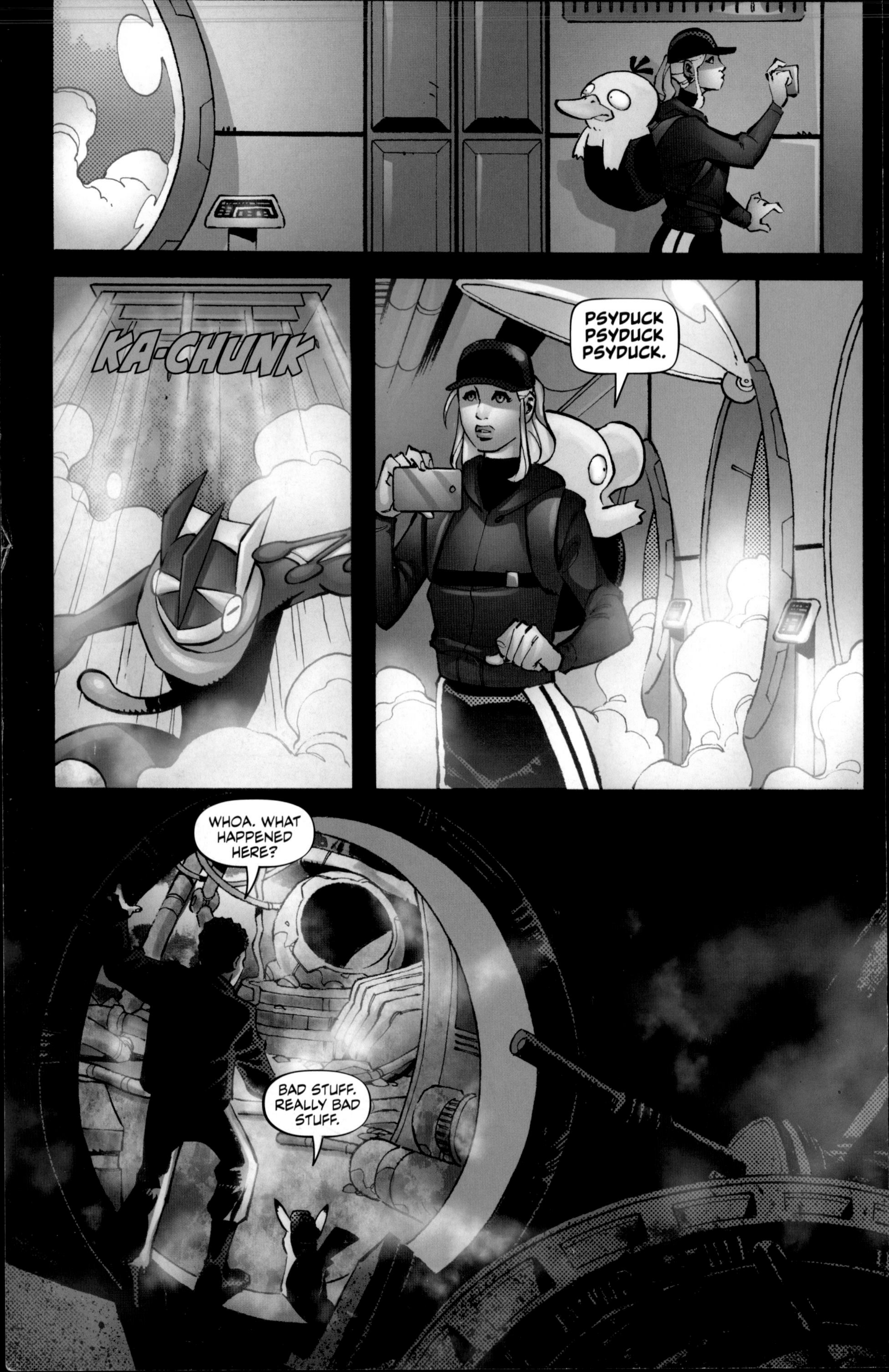
KA-CHUNK
PSYDUCK PSYDUCK PSYDUCK.
WHOA. WHAT HAPPENED HERE?
BAD STUFF. REALLY BAD STUFF.

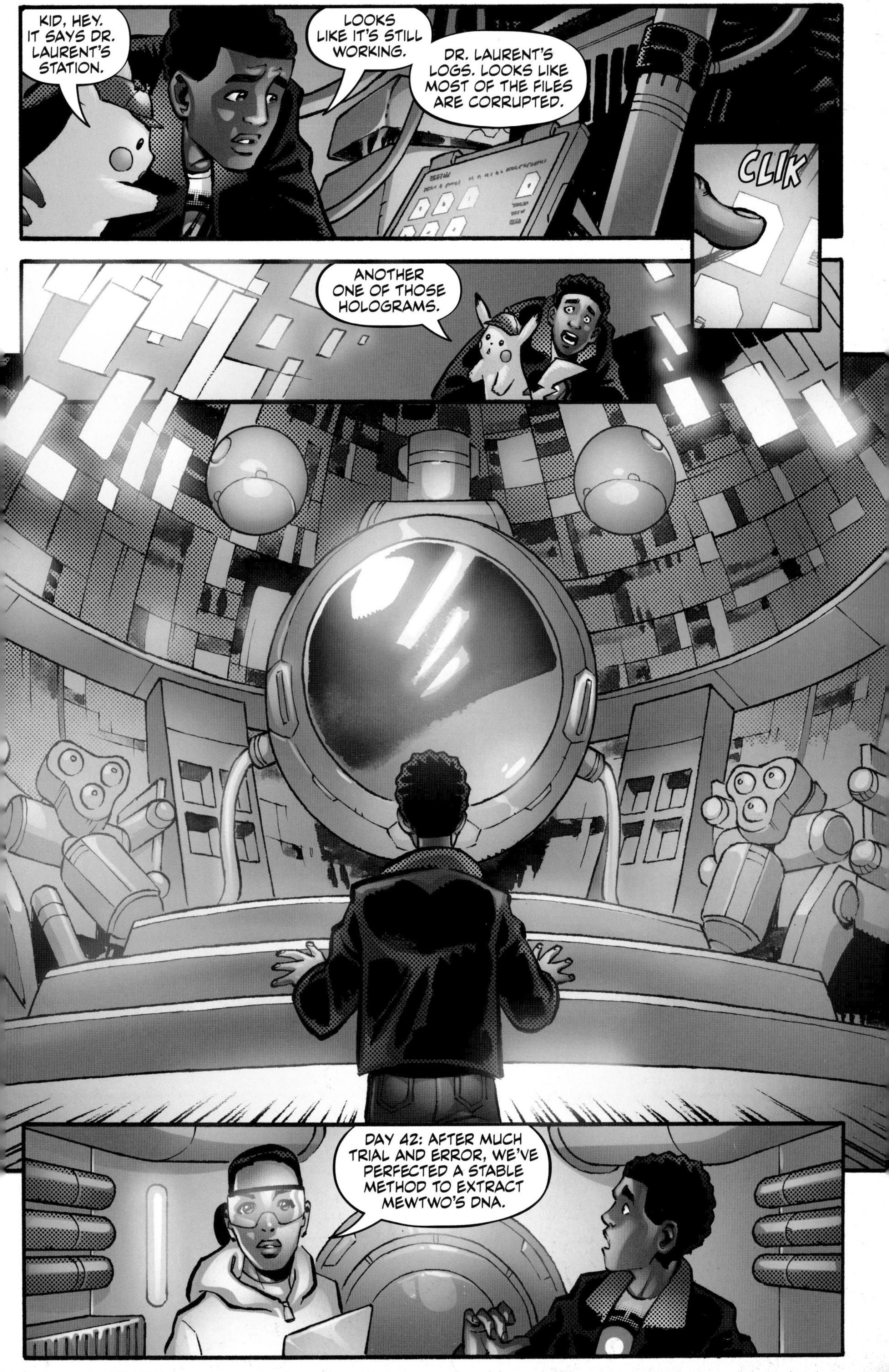
KID, HEY. IT SAYS DR. LAURENT'S STATION.
LOOKS LIKE IT'S STILL WORKING.
DR. LAURENT'S LOGS. LOOKS LIKE MOST OF THE FILES ARE CORRUPTED.
CLIK
ANOTHER ONE OF THOSE HOLOGRAMS.
DAY 42: AFTER MUCH TRIAL AND ERROR, WE'VE PERFECTED A STABLE METHOD TO EXTRACT MEWTWO'S DNA.

IT'S MEWTWO. NO WAIT, WAIT... MEWTWO CAME FROM THIS PLACE?

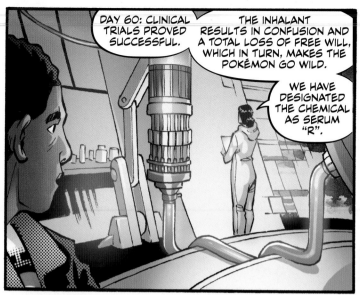

DAY 60: CLINICAL TRIALS PROVED SUCCESSFUL.

THE INHALANT RESULTS IN CONFUSION AND A TOTAL LOSS OF FREE WILL, WHICH IN TURN, MAKES THE POKÉMON GO WILD.

WE HAVE DESIGNATED THE CHEMICAL AS SERUM "R".

THEY USED MEWTWO TO MAKE "R".

AND THEY WERE TESTING IT AT THE BATTLES.

DAY 68. THE NEURAL LINK IS OPERATIONAL.

ALERT. CONDITION RED!

NO! WE'RE LOSING POWER TO THE CONTAINMENT CH--!

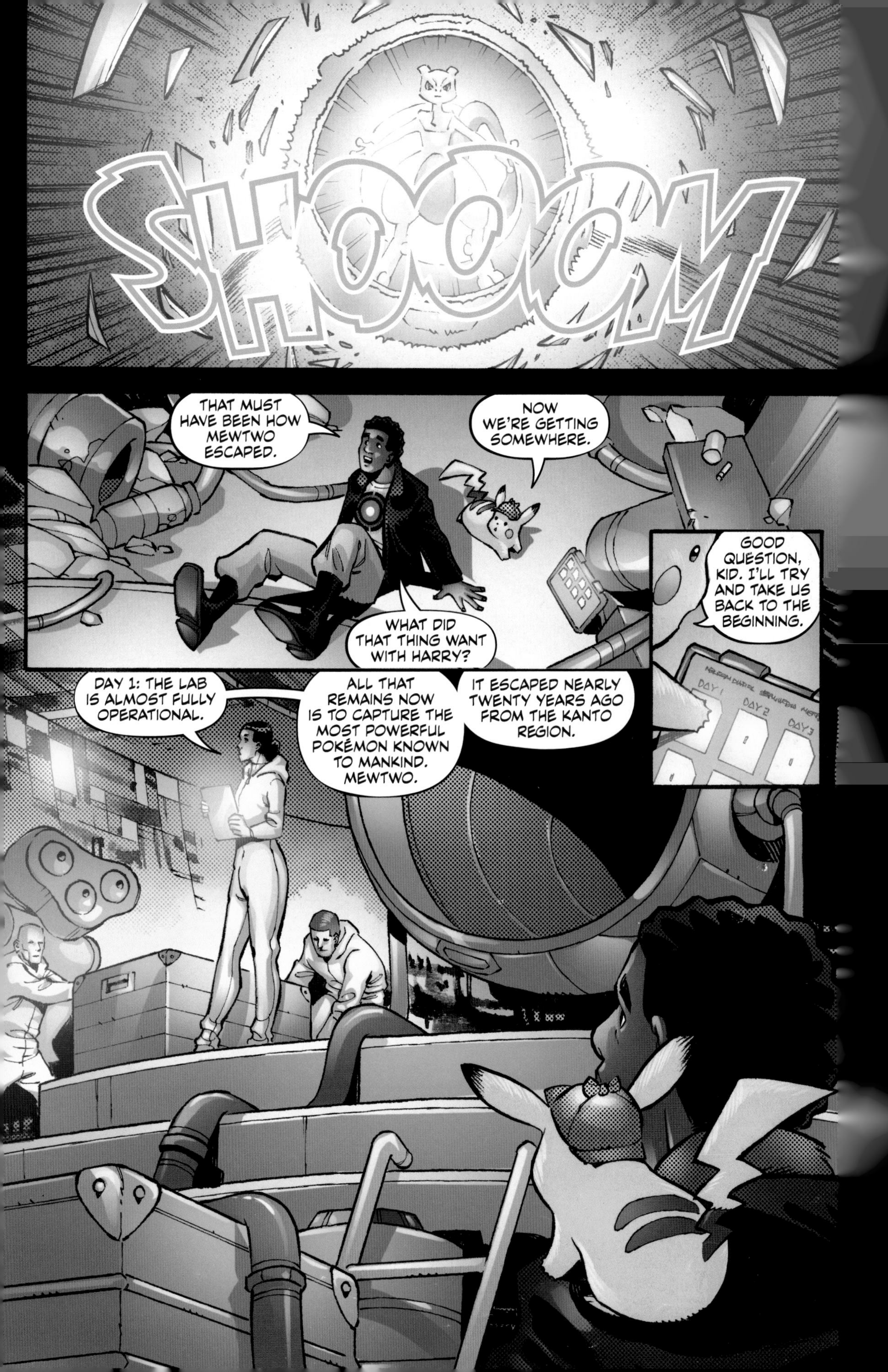
SHOOOM
THAT MUST HAVE BEEN HOW MEWTWO ESCAPED.
NOW WE'RE GETTING SOMEWHERE.
WHAT DID THAT THING WANT WITH HARRY?
GOOD QUESTION, KID. I'LL TRY AND TAKE US BACK TO THE BEGINNING.
DAY 1
DAY 2
DAY 3
DAY 1: THE LAB IS ALMOST FULLY OPERATIONAL.
ALL THAT REMAINS NOW IS TO CAPTURE THE MOST POWERFUL POKÉMON KNOWN TO MANKIND. MEWTWO.
IT ESCAPED NEARLY TWENTY YEARS AGO FROM THE KANTO REGION.

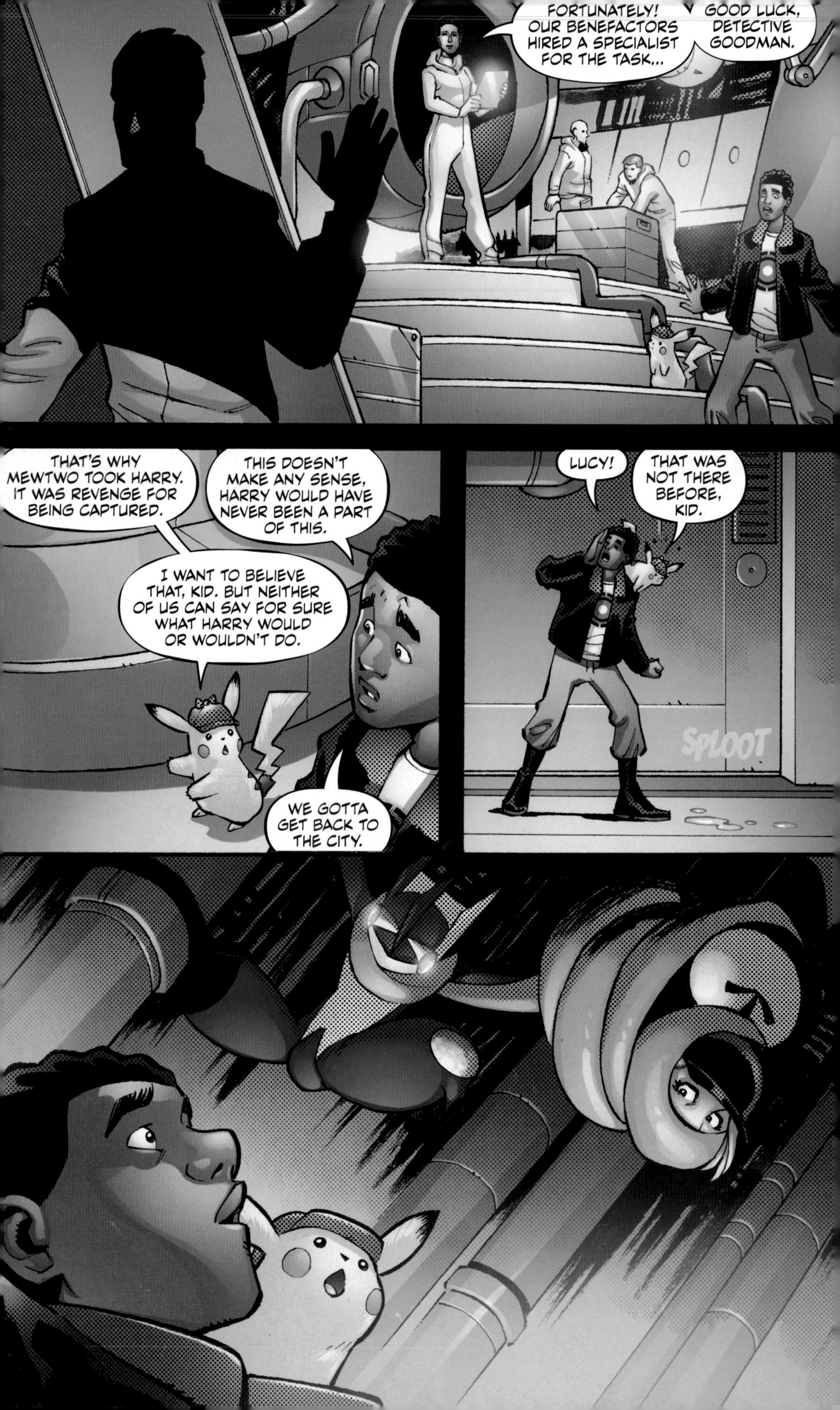
FORTUNATELY! OUR BENEFACTORS HIRED A SPECIALIST FOR THE TASK...
GOOD LUCK, DETECTIVE GOODMAN.
THAT'S WHY MEWTWO TOOK HARRY. IT WAS REVENGE FOR BEING CAPTURED.
THIS DOESN'T MAKE ANY SENSE, HARRY WOULD HAVE NEVER BEEN A PART OF THIS.
I WANT TO BELIEVE THAT, KID. BUT NEITHER OF US CAN SAY FOR SURE WHAT HARRY WOULD OR WOULDN'T DO.
WE GOTTA GET BACK TO THE CITY.
LUCY!
THAT WAS NOT THERE BEFORE, KID.
SPLOOT

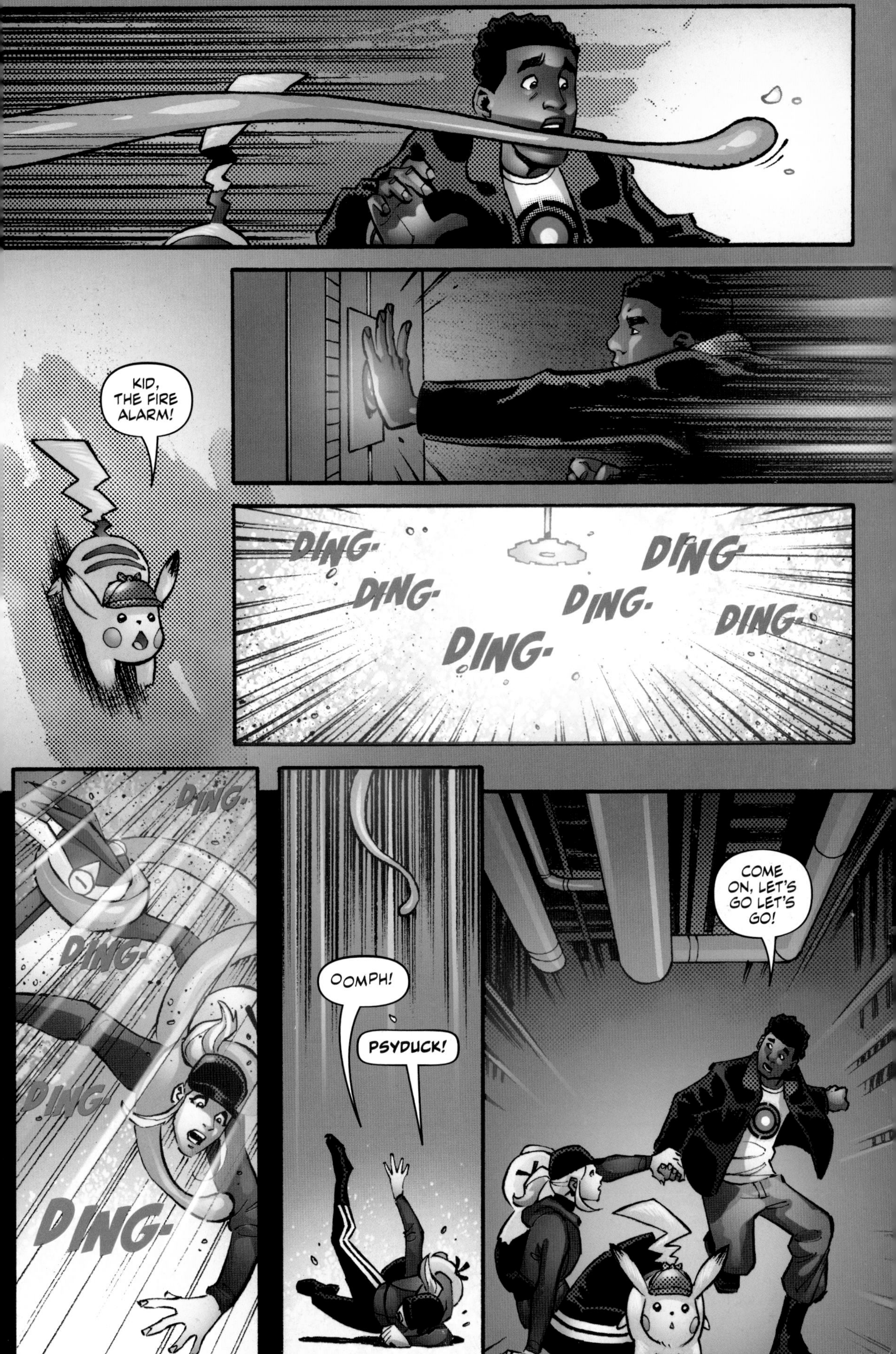
KID, THE FIRE ALARM!
DING-
DING-
DING-
DING-
DING
DING-
DING-
DING-
DING-
DING-
OOMPH!
PSYDUCK!
COME ON, LET'S GO LET'S GO!

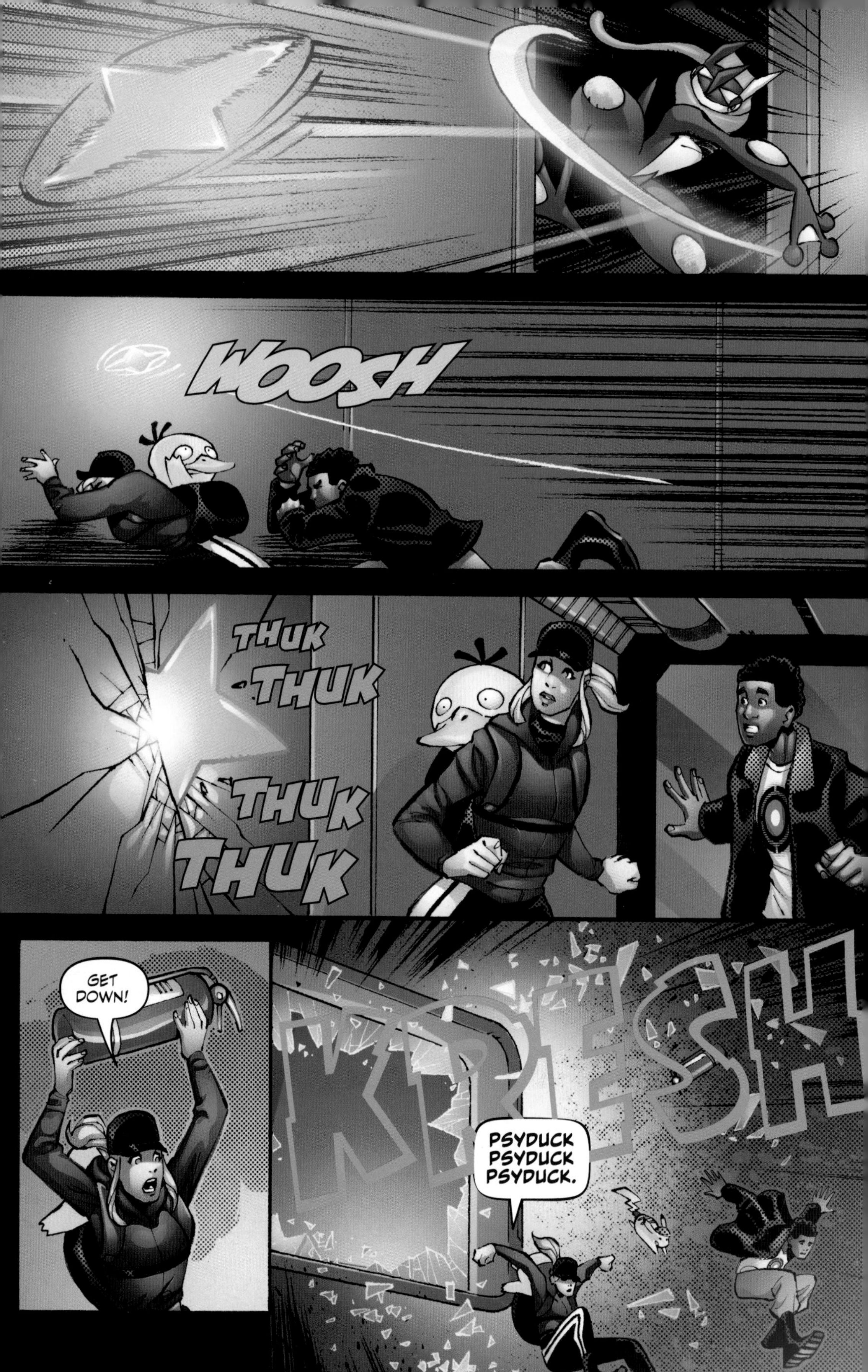
WOOSH
THUK
THUK
THUK
THUK
GET DOWN!
KRESH
PSYDUCK PSYDUCK PSYDUCK.

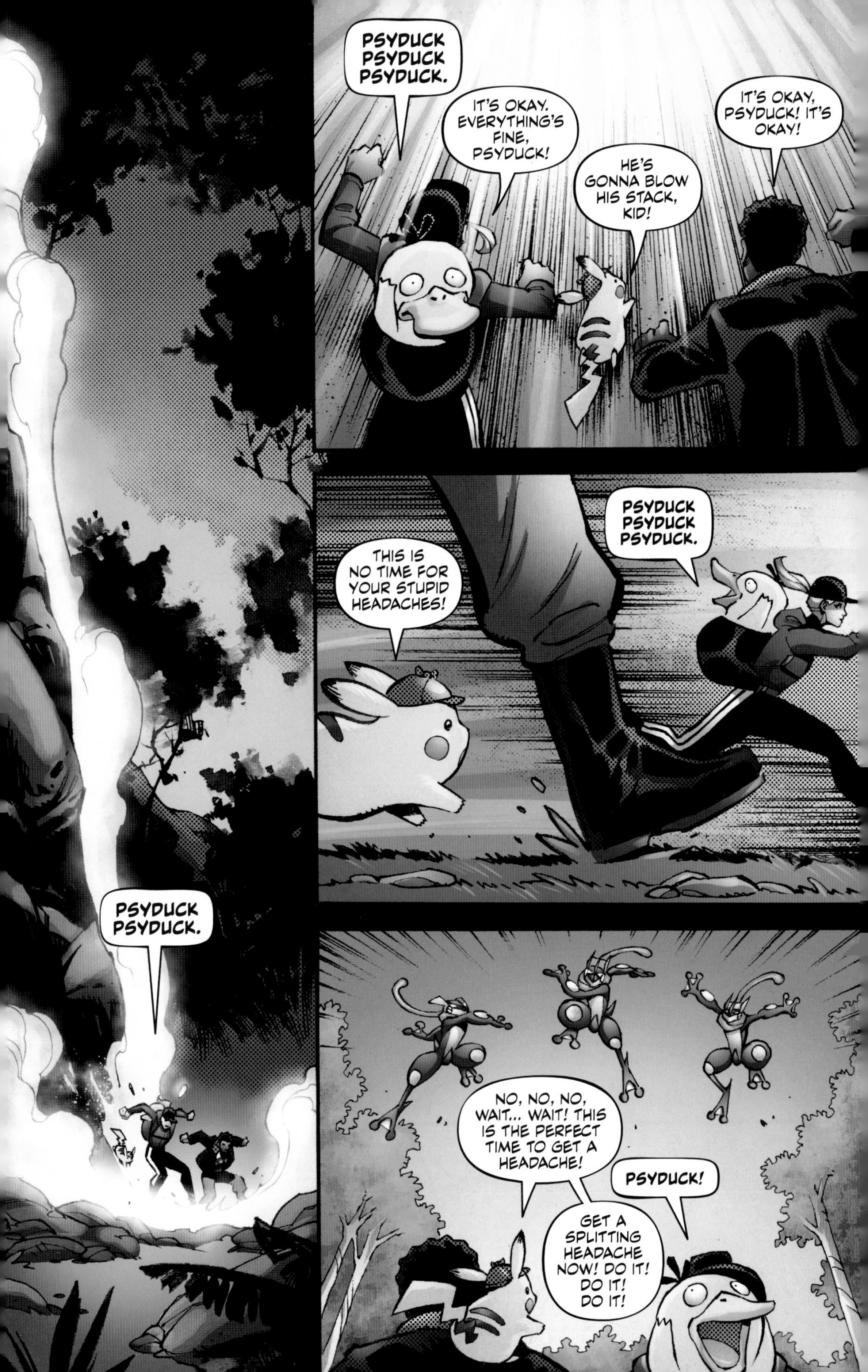
PSYDUCK PSYDUCK PSYDUCK.
IT'S OKAY. EVERYTHING'S FINE, PSYDUCK!
HE'S GONNA BLOW HIS STACK, KID!
IT'S OKAY, PSYDUCK! IT'S OKAY!
PSYDUCK PSYDUCK.
PSYDUCK PSYDUCK PSYDUCK.
THIS IS NO TIME FOR YOUR STUPID HEADACHES!
NO, NO, NO, WAIT... WAIT! THIS IS THE PERFECT TIME TO GET A HEADACHE!
GET A SPLITTING HEADACHE NOW! DO IT! DO IT! DO IT!
PSYDUCK!

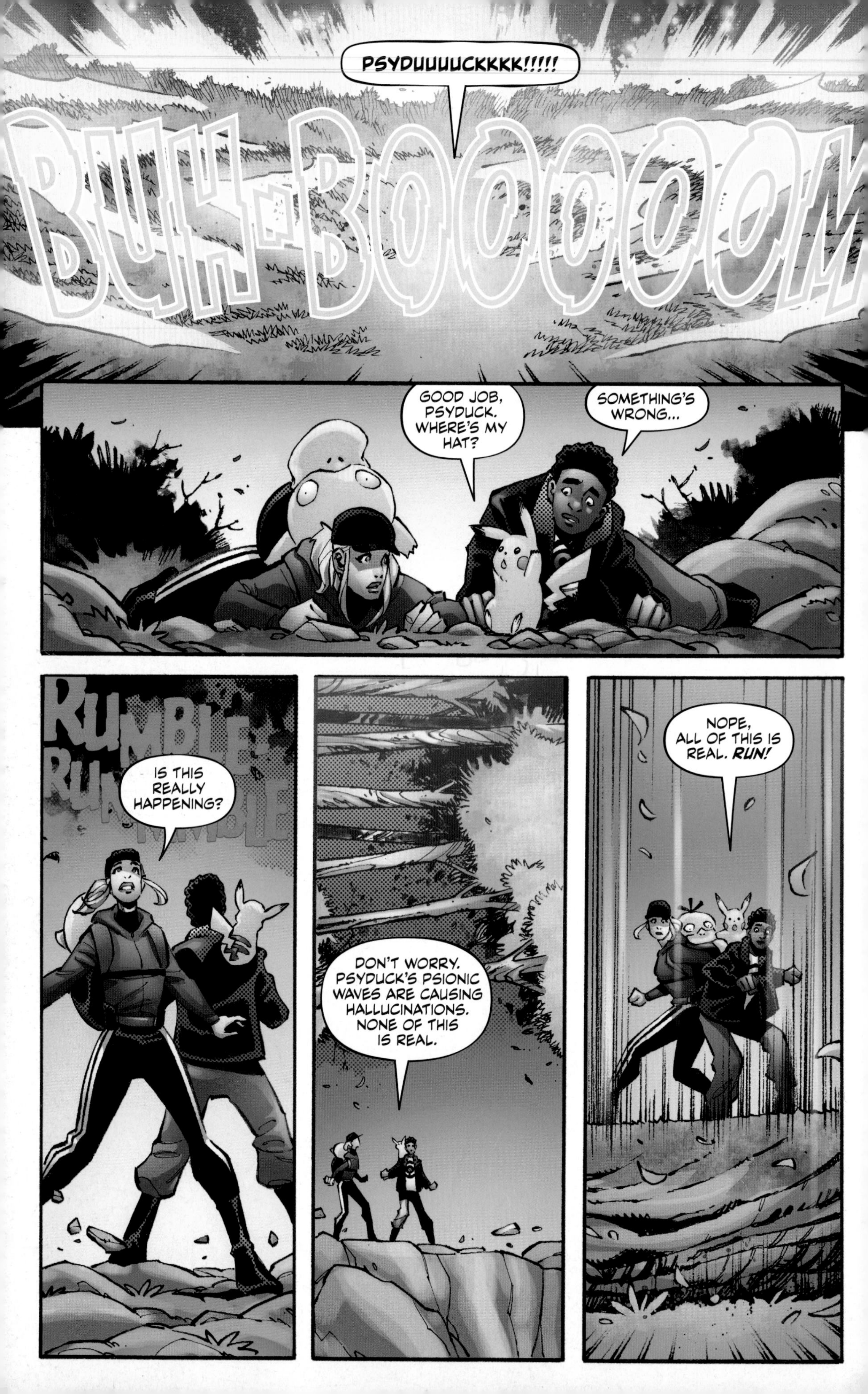
PSYDUUUUCKKKK!!!!!
BUH-BOOOOOM
GOOD JOB, PSYDUCK. WHERE'S MY HAT?
SOMETHING'S WRONG...
RUMBLE-RUMBLE
IS THIS REALLY HAPPENING?
DON'T WORRY. PSYDUCK'S PSIONIC WAVES ARE CAUSING HALLUCINATIONS. NONE OF THIS IS REAL.
NOPE, ALL OF THIS IS REAL. *RUN!*

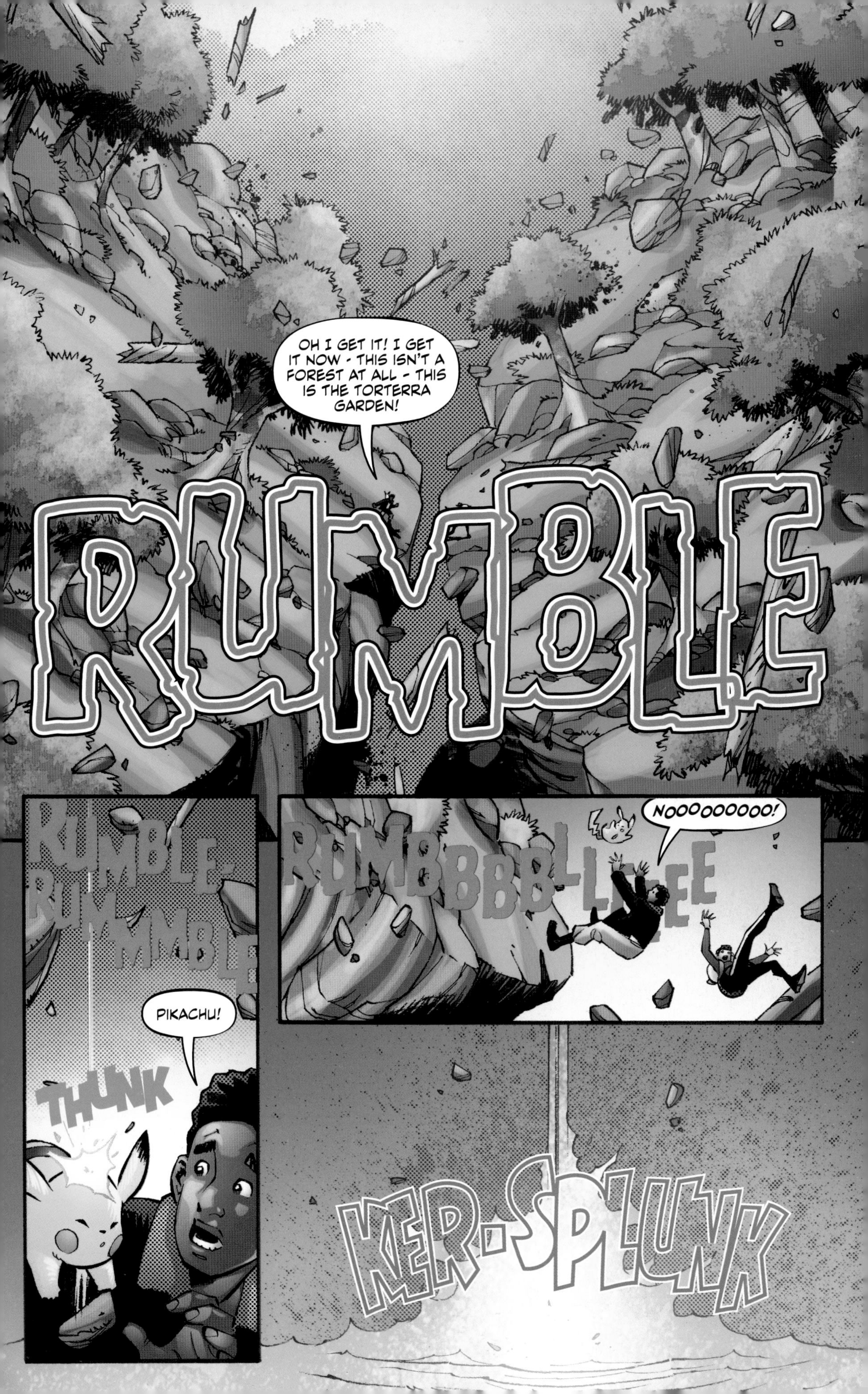
OH I GET IT! I GET IT NOW - THIS ISN'T A FOREST AT ALL - THIS IS THE TORTERRA GARDEN!
RUMBLE
RUMBLE RUMMMBLE
PIKACHU!
THUNK
RUMBBBBLLEEE
NOOOOOOOOO!
KER-SPLUNK

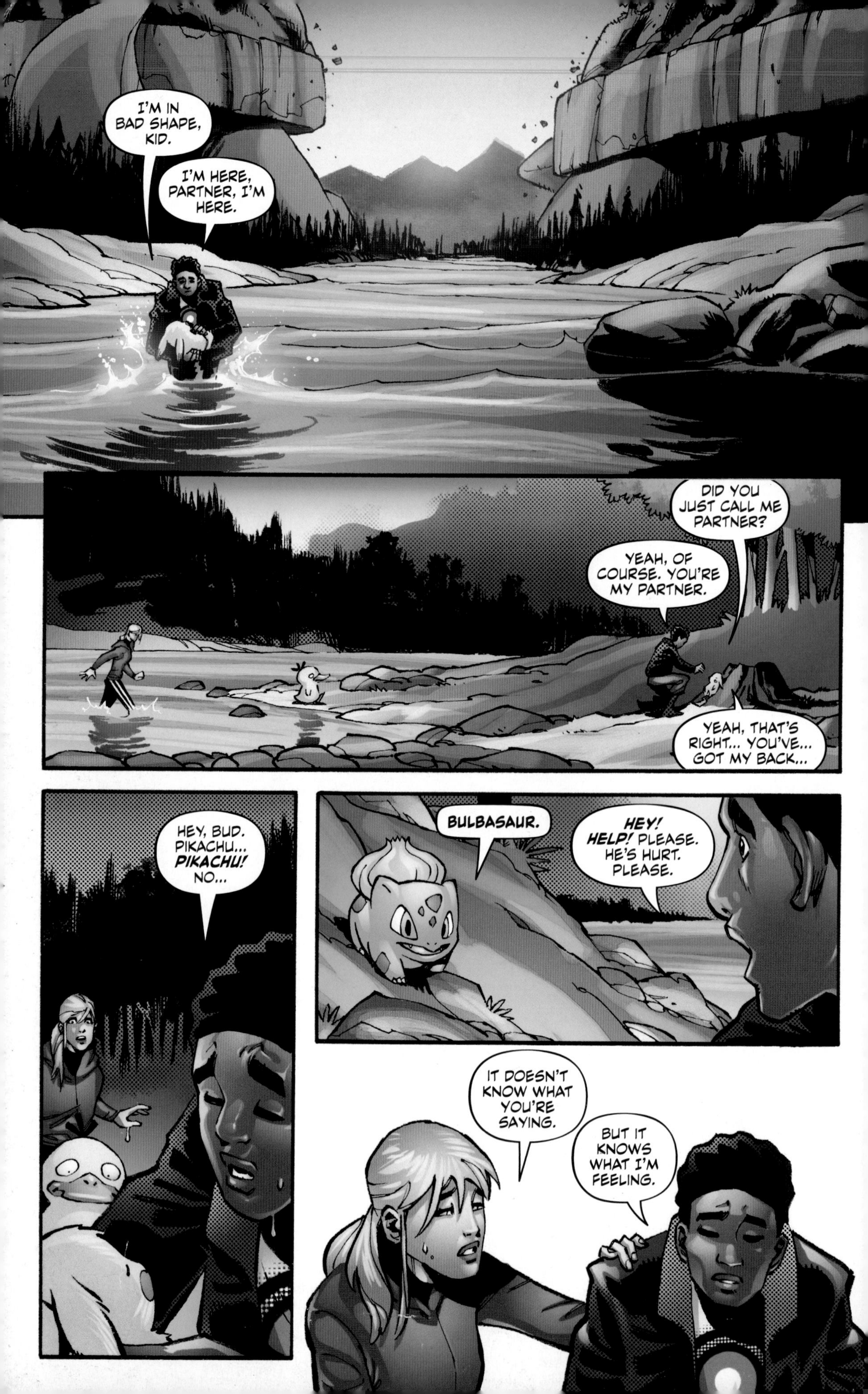
I'M IN BAD SHAPE, KID.
I'M HERE, PARTNER, I'M HERE.
DID YOU JUST CALL ME PARTNER?
YEAH, OF COURSE. YOU'RE MY PARTNER.
YEAH, THAT'S RIGHT... YOU'VE... GOT MY BACK...
HEY, BUD. PIKACHU... *PIKACHU!* NO...
BULBASAUR.
HEY! HELP! PLEASE. HE'S HURT. PLEASE.
IT DOESN'T KNOW WHAT YOU'RE SAYING.
BUT IT KNOWS WHAT I'M FEELING.

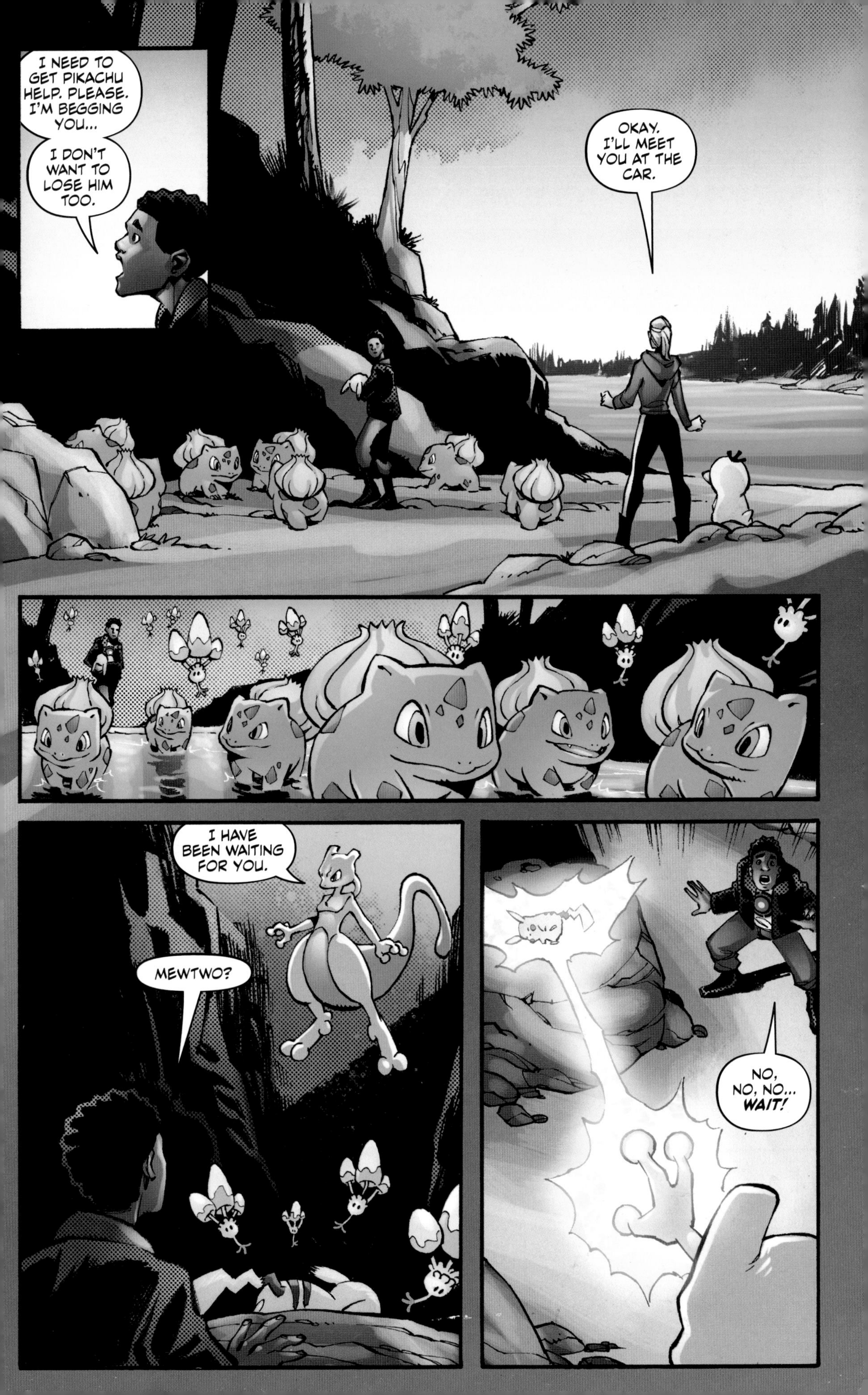

I NEED TO GET PIKACHU HELP. PLEASE. I'M BEGGING YOU...
I DON'T WANT TO LOSE HIM TOO.
OKAY. I'LL MEET YOU AT THE CAR.
I HAVE BEEN WAITING FOR YOU.
MEWTWO?
NO, NO, NO... *WAIT!*

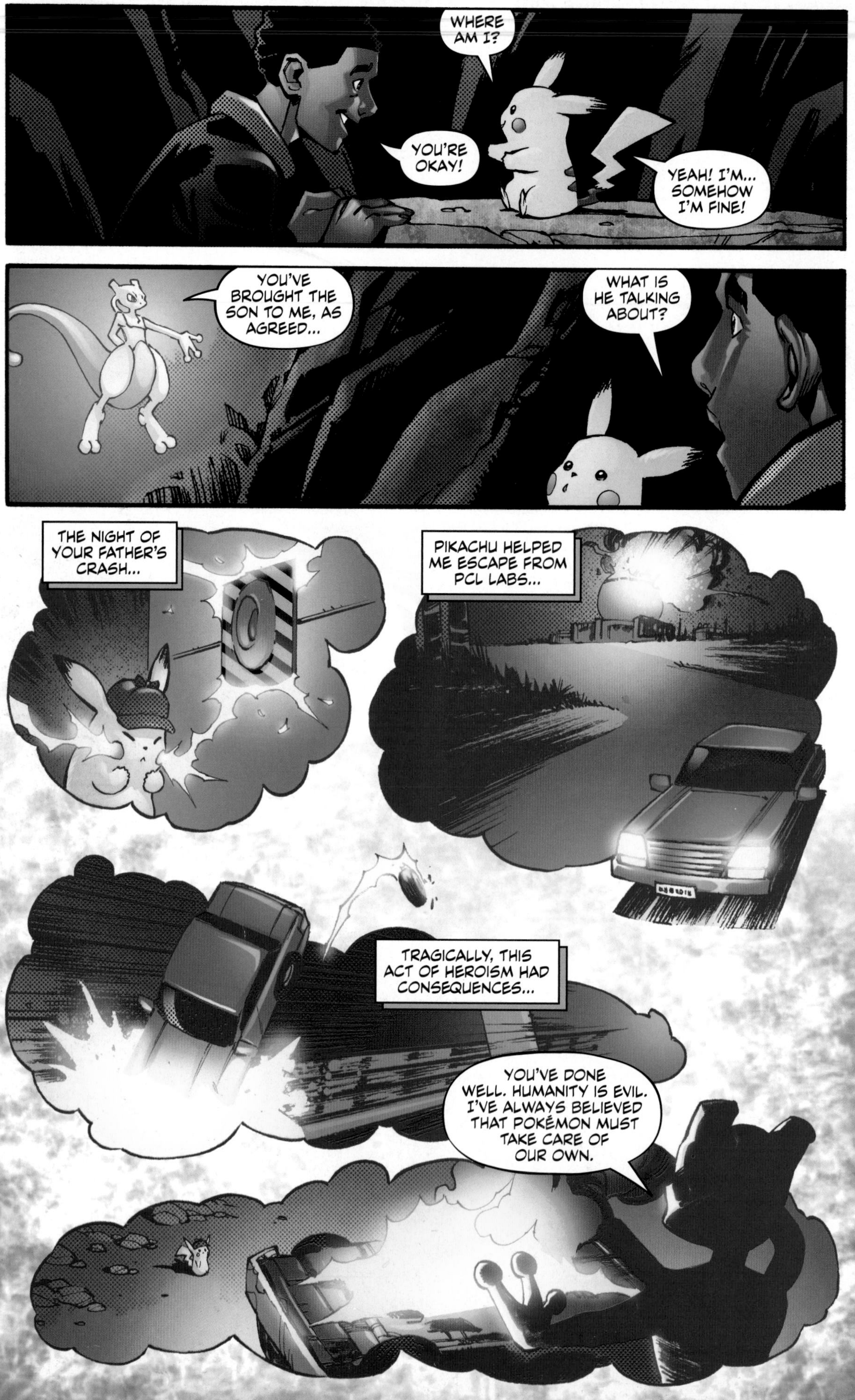
WHERE AM I?
YOU'RE OKAY!
YEAH! I'M... SOMEHOW I'M FINE!
YOU'VE BROUGHT THE SON TO ME, AS AGREED...
WHAT IS HE TALKING ABOUT?
THE NIGHT OF YOUR FATHER'S CRASH...
PIKACHU HELPED ME ESCAPE FROM PCL LABS...
TRAGICALLY, THIS ACT OF HEROISM HAD CONSEQUENCES...
YOU'VE DONE WELL. HUMANITY IS EVIL. I'VE ALWAYS BELIEVED THAT POKÉMON MUST TAKE CARE OF OUR OWN.

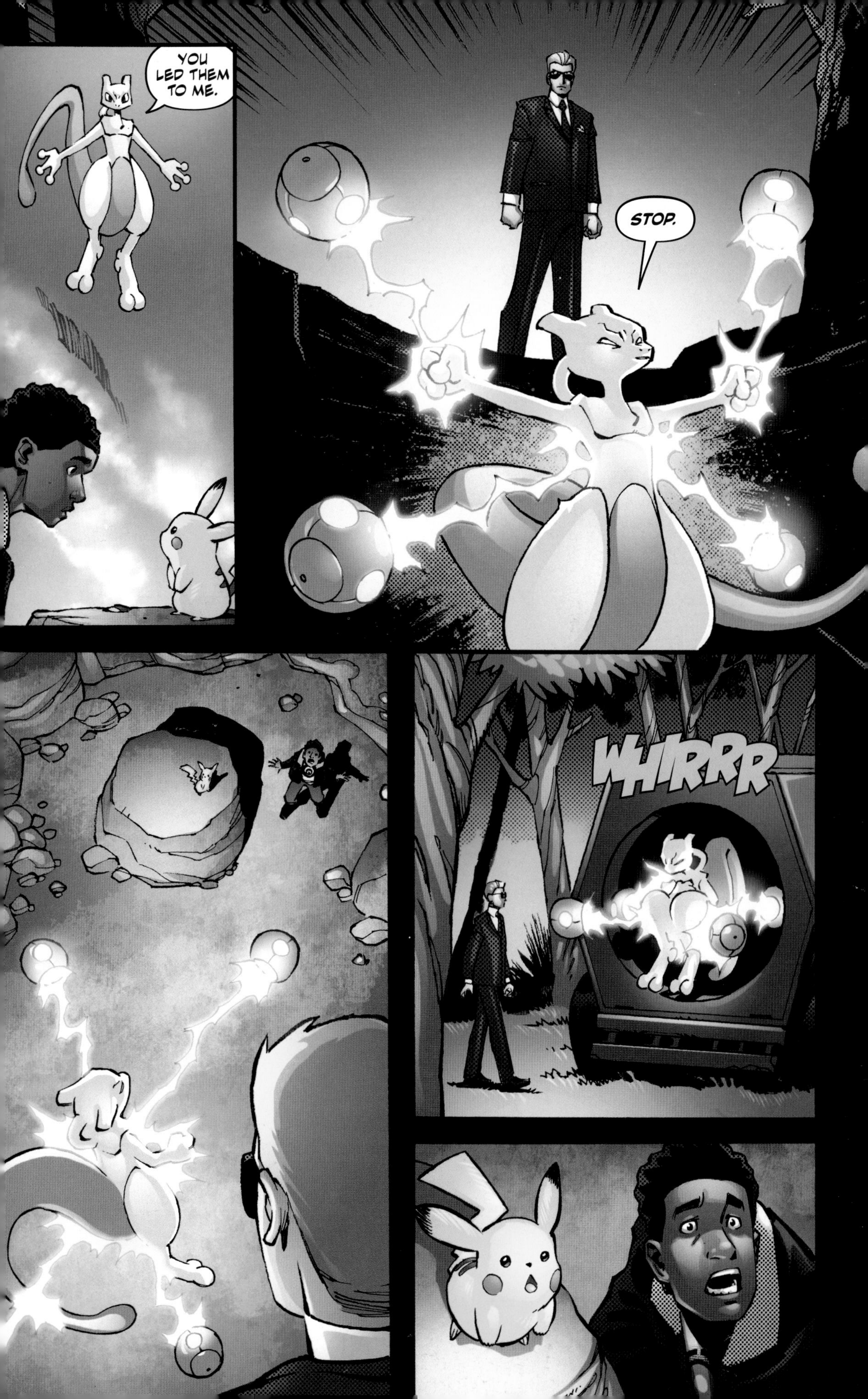

YOU LED THEM TO ME.
STOP.
WHIRRR

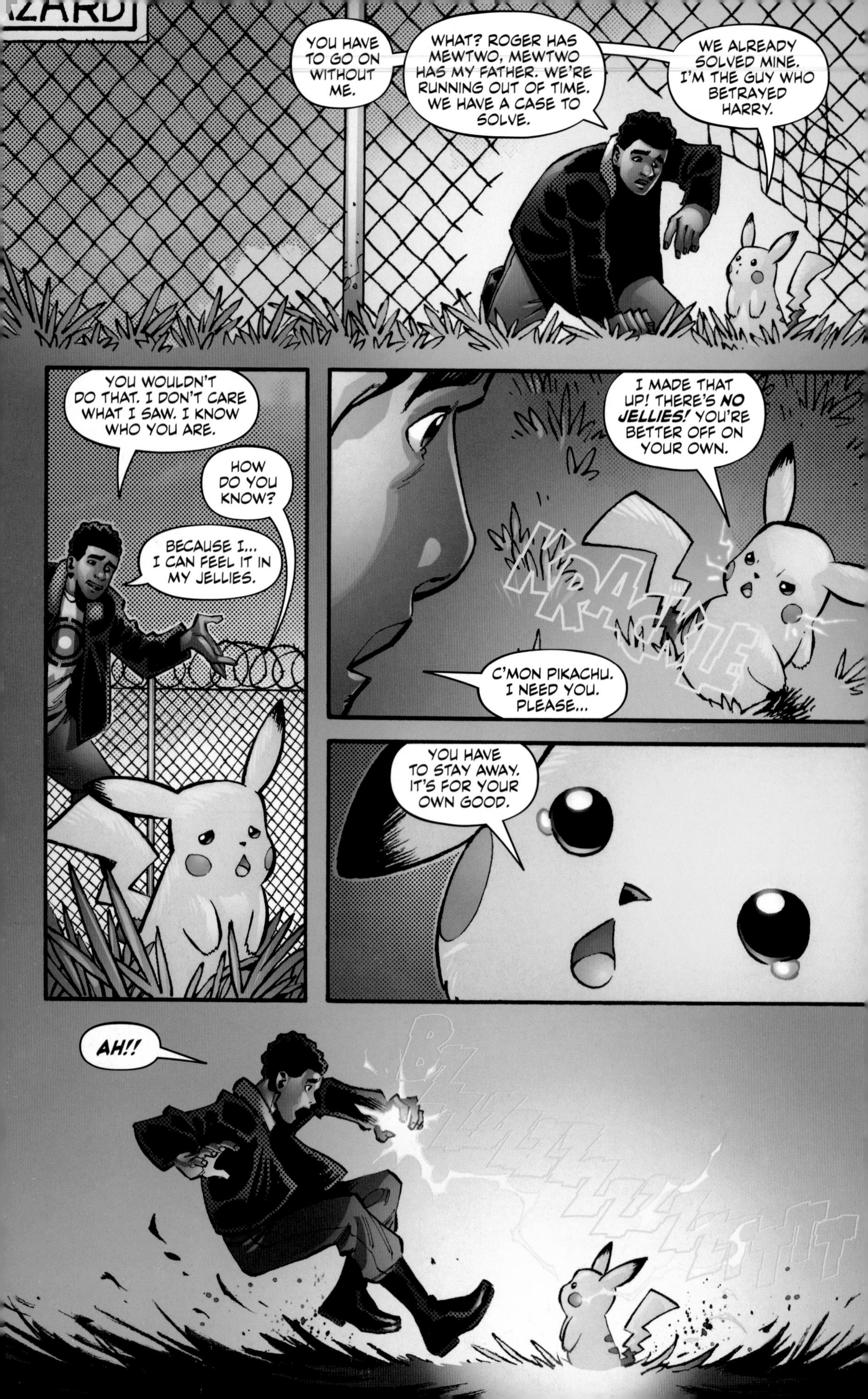

ZARD
YOU HAVE TO GO ON WITHOUT ME.
WHAT? ROGER HAS MEWTWO, MEWTWO HAS MY FATHER. WE'RE RUNNING OUT OF TIME. WE HAVE A CASE TO SOLVE.
WE ALREADY SOLVED MINE. I'M THE GUY WHO BETRAYED HARRY.
YOU WOULDN'T DO THAT. I DON'T CARE WHAT I SAW. I KNOW WHO YOU ARE.
HOW DO YOU KNOW?
BECAUSE I... I CAN FEEL IT IN MY JELLIES.
I MADE THAT UP! THERE'S **NO JELLIES!** YOU'RE BETTER OFF ON YOUR OWN.
KRACKLE
C'MON PIKACHU. I NEED YOU. PLEASE...
YOU HAVE TO STAY AWAY. IT'S FOR YOUR OWN GOOD.
AH!!

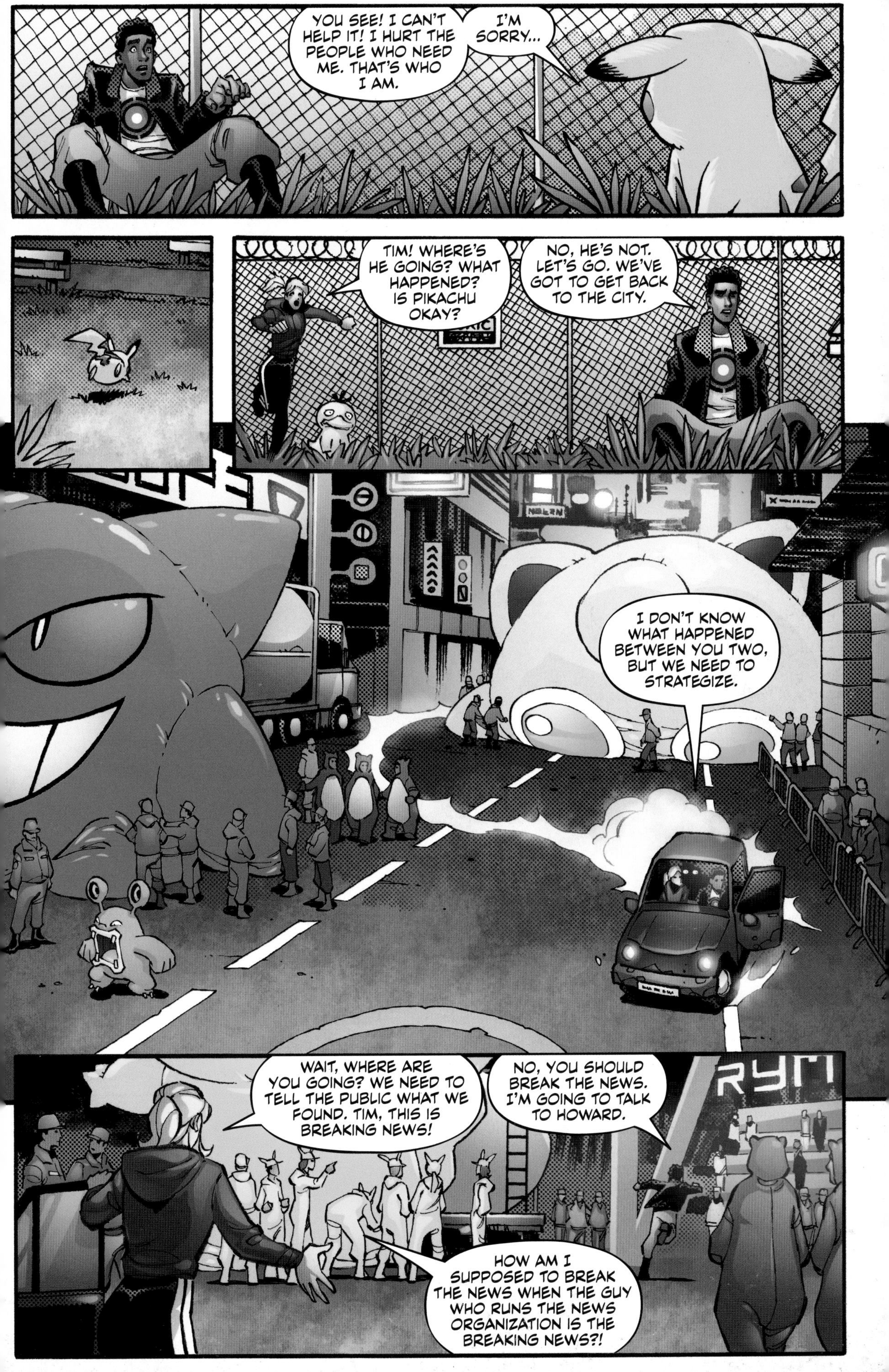
YOU SEE! I CAN'T HELP IT! I HURT THE PEOPLE WHO NEED ME. THAT'S WHO I AM.
I'M SORRY...
TIM! WHERE'S HE GOING? WHAT HAPPENED? IS PIKACHU OKAY?
NO, HE'S NOT. LET'S GO. WE'VE GOT TO GET BACK TO THE CITY.
I DON'T KNOW WHAT HAPPENED BETWEEN YOU TWO, BUT WE NEED TO STRATEGIZE.
WAIT, WHERE ARE YOU GOING? WE NEED TO TELL THE PUBLIC WHAT WE FOUND. TIM, THIS IS BREAKING NEWS!
NO, YOU SHOULD BREAK THE NEWS. I'M GOING TO TALK TO HOWARD.
HOW AM I SUPPOSED TO BREAK THE NEWS WHEN THE GUY WHO RUNS THE NEWS ORGANIZATION IS THE BREAKING NEWS?!

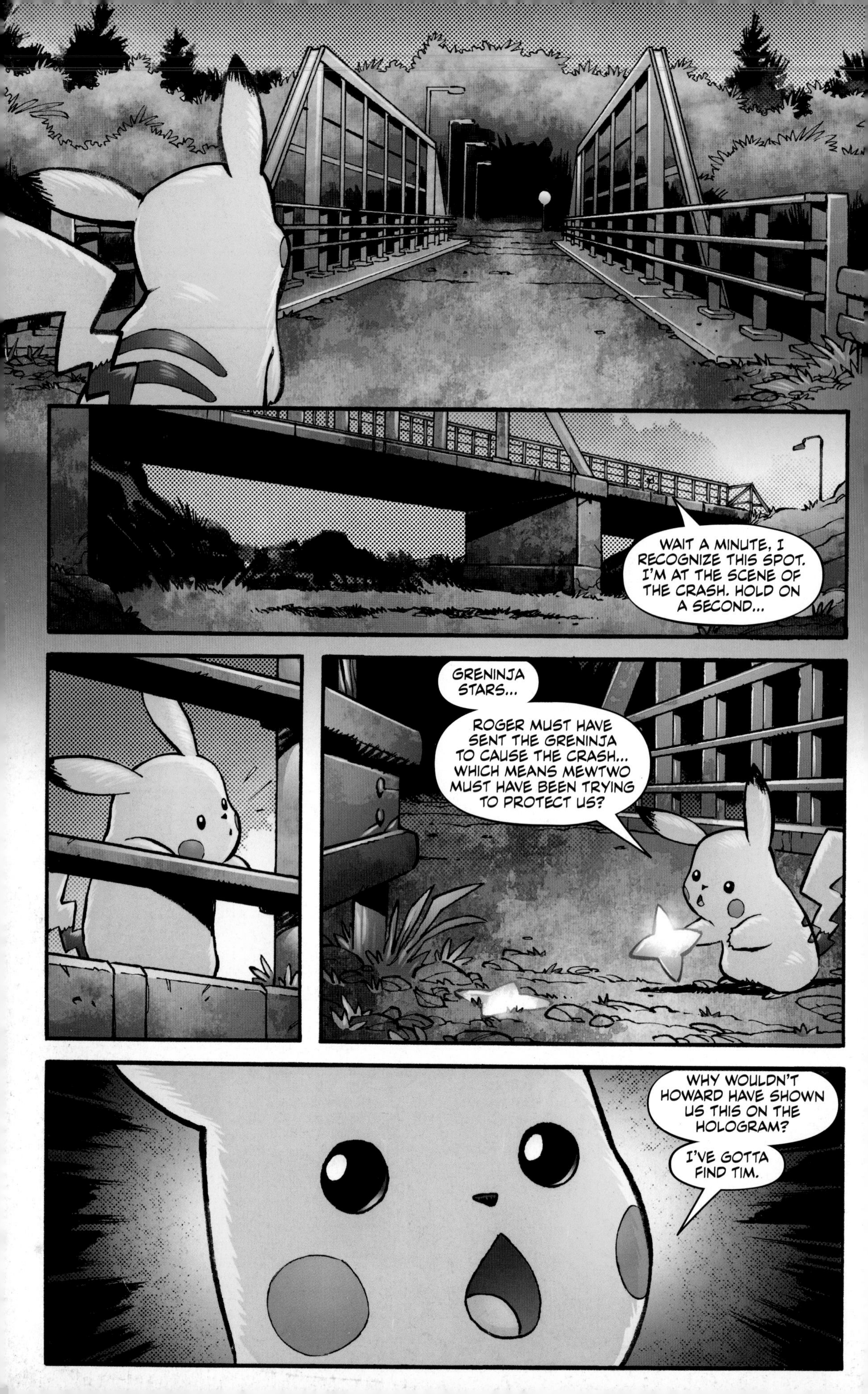
WAIT A MINUTE, I RECOGNIZE THIS SPOT. I'M AT THE SCENE OF THE CRASH. HOLD ON A SECOND...
GRENINJA STARS...
ROGER MUST HAVE SENT THE GRENINJA TO CAUSE THE CRASH... WHICH MEANS MEWTWO MUST HAVE BEEN TRYING TO PROTECT US?
WHY WOULDN'T HOWARD HAVE SHOWN US THIS ON THE HOLOGRAM?
I'VE GOTTA FIND TIM.

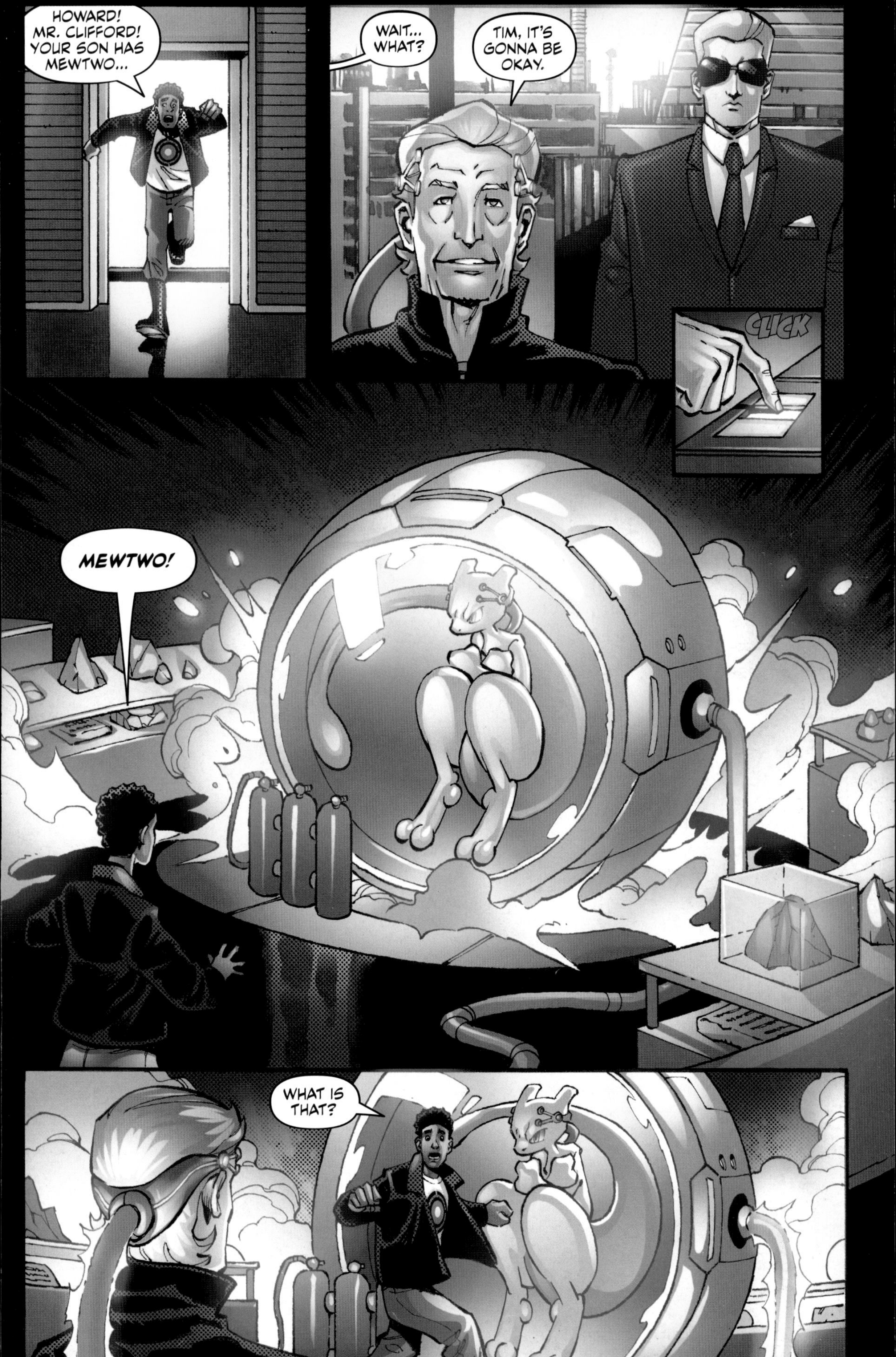
HOWARD! MR. CLIFFORD! YOUR SON HAS MEWTWO...
WAIT... WHAT?
TIM, IT'S GONNA BE OKAY.
CLICK
MEWTWO!
WHAT IS THAT?

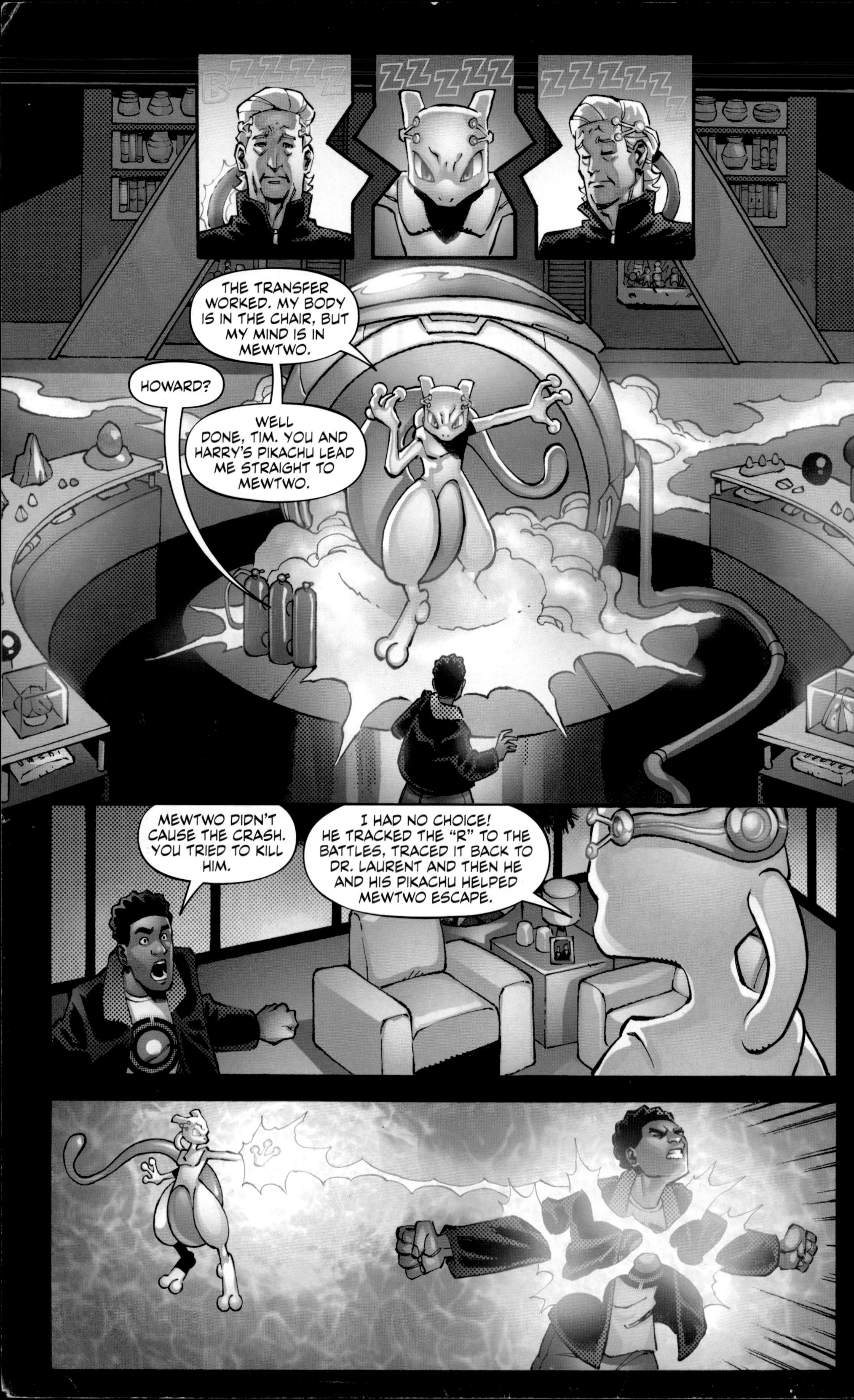
BZZZZZ
ZZZZZ
ZZZZZZ
THE TRANSFER WORKED. MY BODY IS IN THE CHAIR, BUT MY MIND IS IN MEWTWO.
HOWARD?
WELL DONE, TIM. YOU AND HARRY'S PIKACHU LEAD ME STRAIGHT TO MEWTWO.
MEWTWO DIDN'T CAUSE THE CRASH. YOU TRIED TO KILL HIM.
I HAD NO CHOICE! HE TRACKED THE "R" TO THE BATTLES, TRACED IT BACK TO DR. LAURENT AND THEN HE AND HIS PIKACHU HELPED MEWTWO ESCAPE.

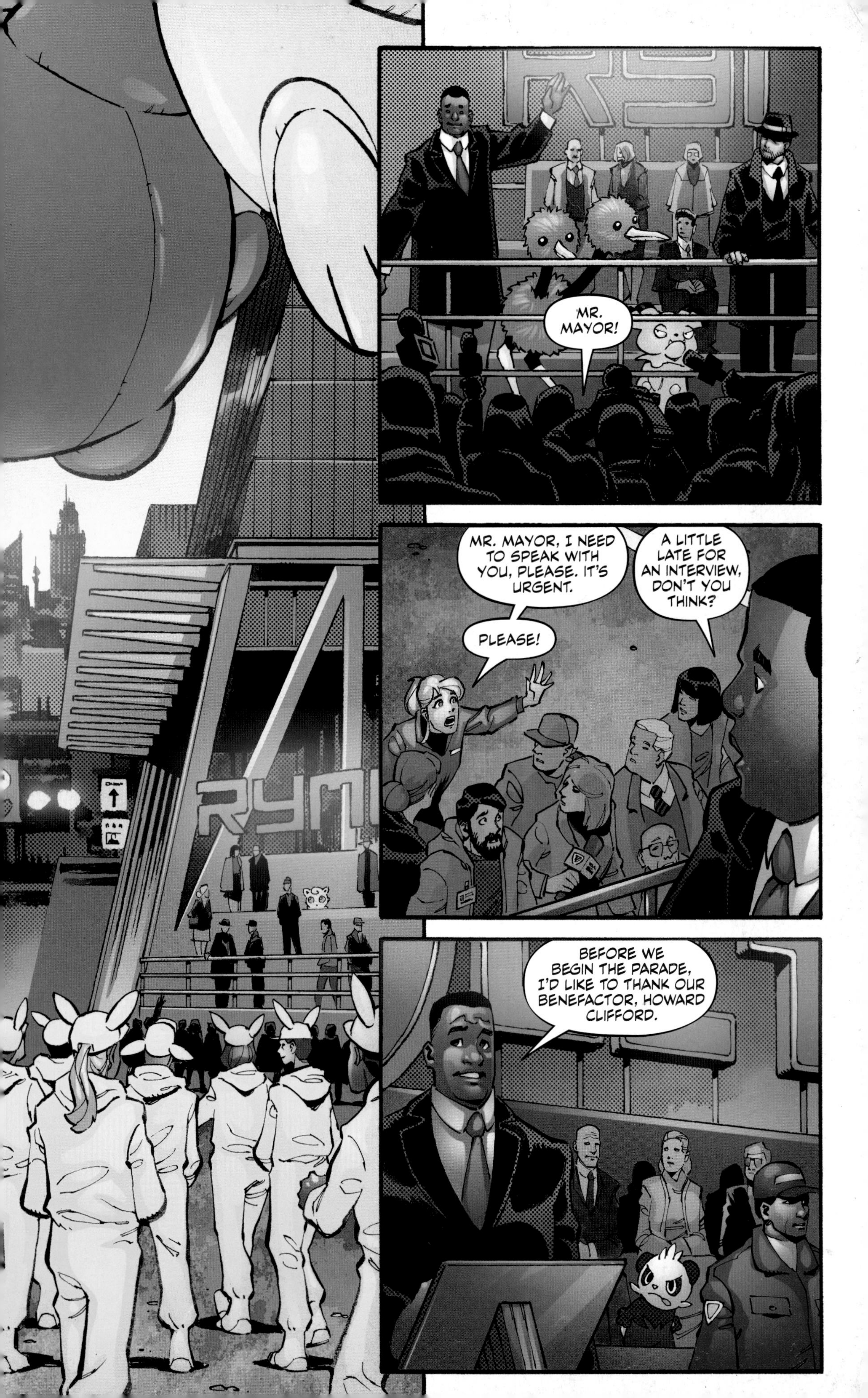
MR. MAYOR!
MR. MAYOR, I NEED TO SPEAK WITH YOU, PLEASE. IT'S URGENT.
PLEASE!
A LITTLE LATE FOR AN INTERVIEW, DON'T YOU THINK?
BEFORE WE BEGIN THE PARADE, I'D LIKE TO THANK OUR BENEFACTOR, HOWARD CLIFFORD.

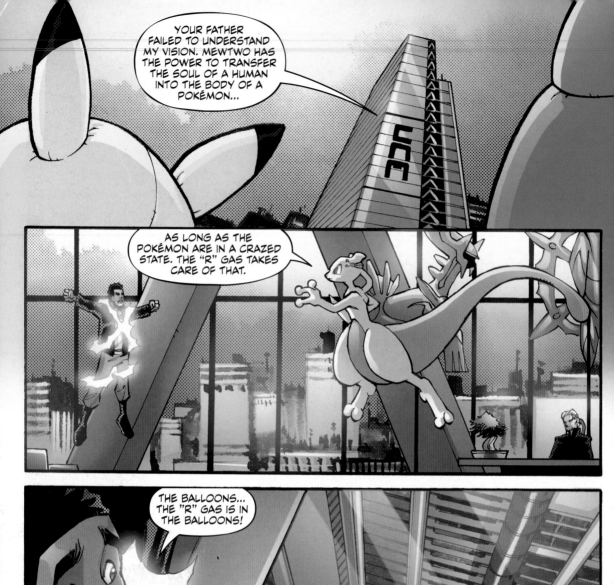

YOUR FATHER FAILED TO UNDERSTAND MY VISION. MEWTWO HAS THE POWER TO TRANSFER THE SOUL OF A HUMAN INTO THE BODY OF A POKÉMON...

AS LONG AS THE POKÉMON ARE IN A CRAZED STATE. THE "R" GAS TAKES CARE OF THAT.

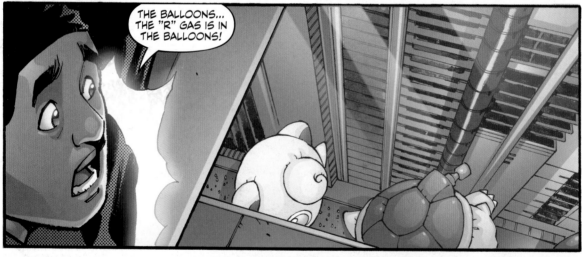

THE BALLOONS... THE "R" GAS IS IN THE BALLOONS!

WHAM

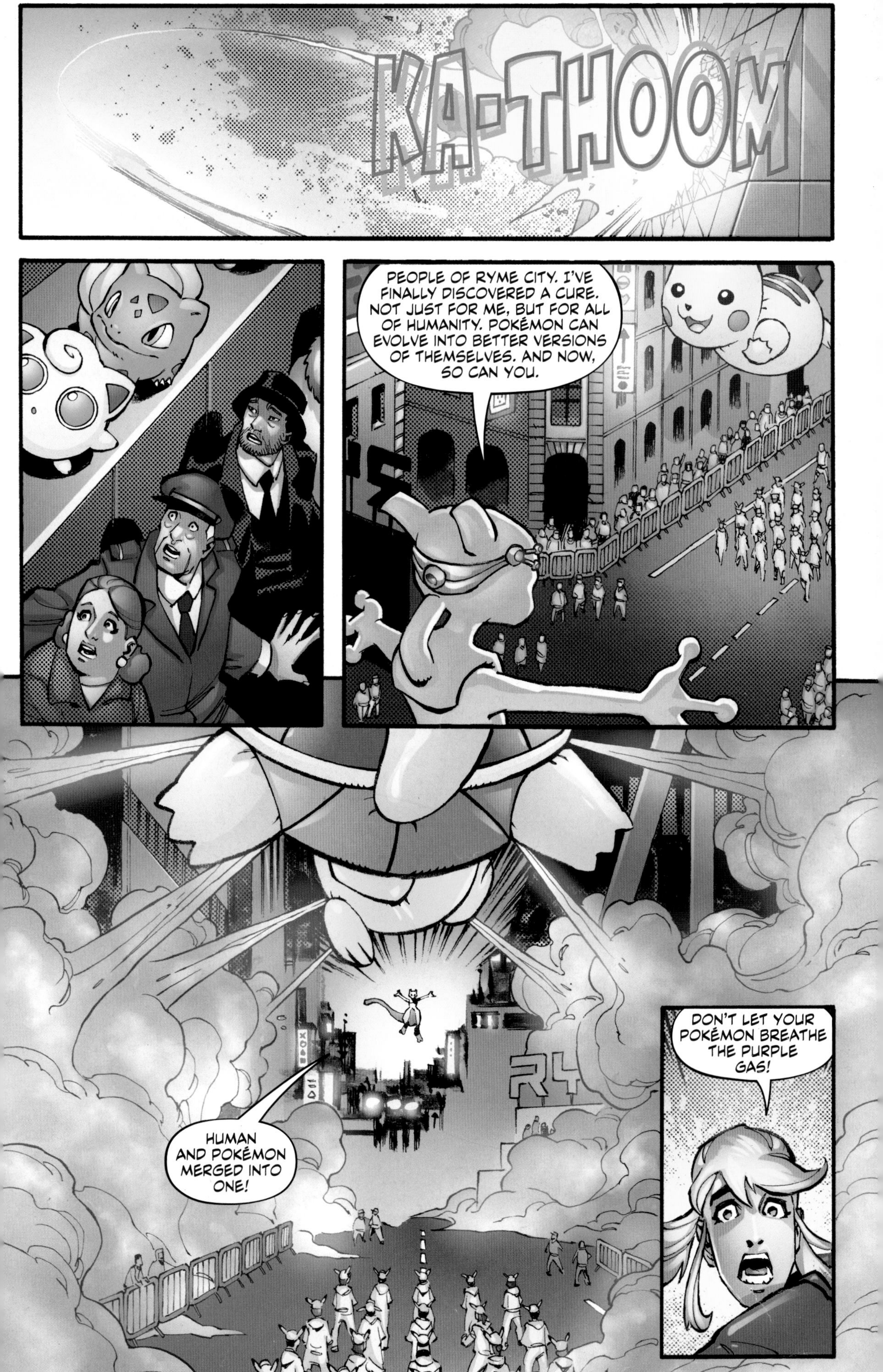
KA-THOOM
PEOPLE OF RYME CITY. I'VE FINALLY DISCOVERED A CURE. NOT JUST FOR ME, BUT FOR ALL OF HUMANITY. POKÉMON CAN EVOLVE INTO BETTER VERSIONS OF THEMSELVES. AND NOW, SO CAN YOU.
HUMAN AND POKÉMON MERGED INTO ONE!
DON'T LET YOUR POKÉMON BREATHE THE PURPLE GAS!

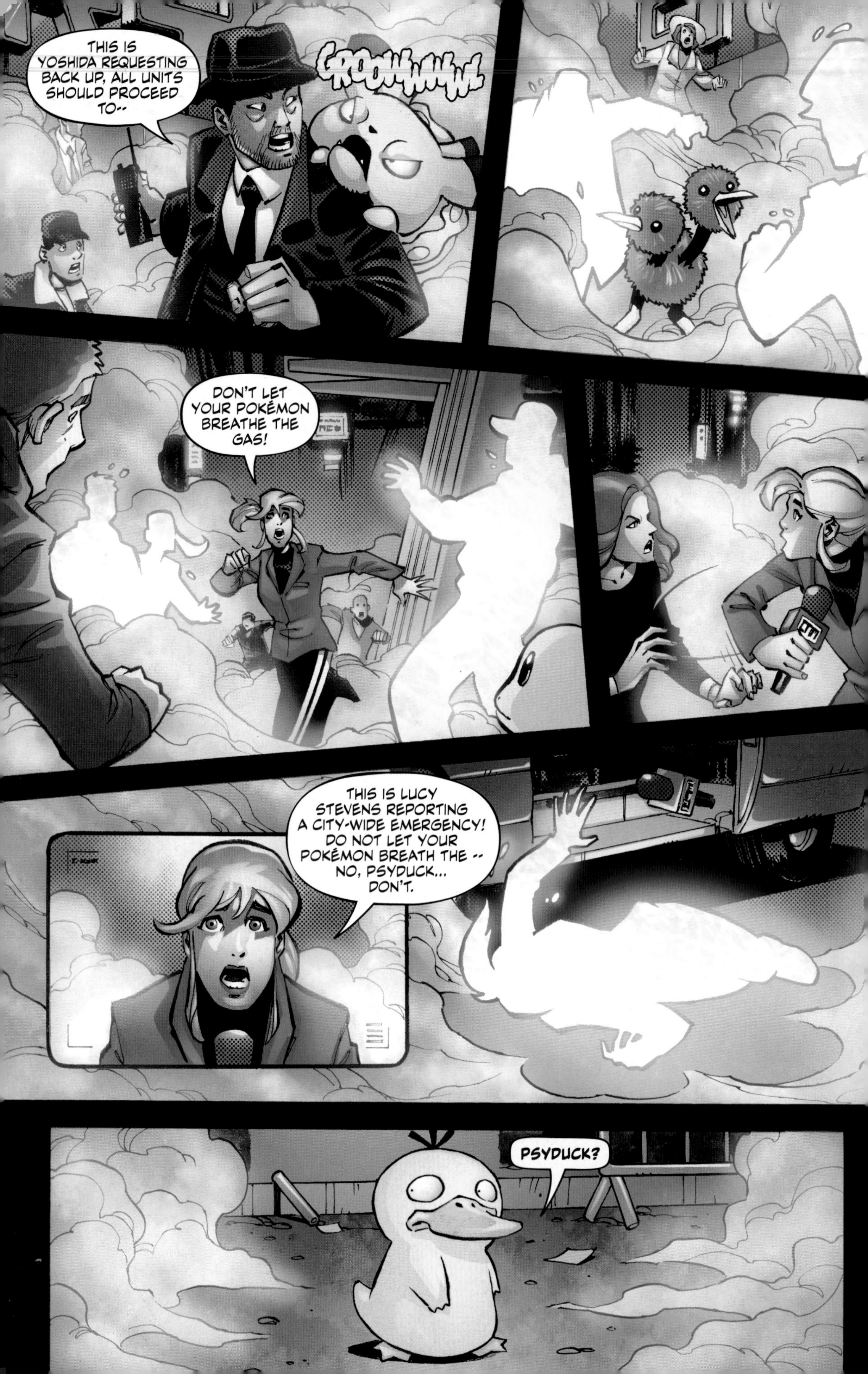
THIS IS YOSHIDA REQUESTING BACK UP, ALL UNITS SHOULD PROCEED TO--
GROOWWWW
DON'T LET YOUR POKÉMON BREATHE THE GAS!
THIS IS LUCY STEVENS REPORTING A CITY-WIDE EMERGENCY! DO NOT LET YOUR POKÉMON BREATH THE -- NO, PSYDUCK... DON'T.
PSYDUCK?

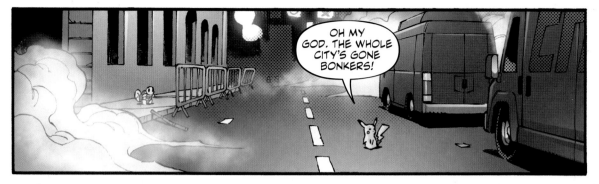

OH MY GOD. THE WHOLE CITY'S GONE BONKERS!

PSYDUCK? WHAT HAPPENED TO YOU? WHERE'S TIM?

PSYDUCK! PSYDUCK! PSYDUCK!

PSYDUCK! PSYDUCK! PSYDUCK!

HOWARD IS MEWTWO? THE NEURAL LINK... YEAH, THIS WAS HIS PLAN ALL ALONG!

I GOTTA STOP THIS.

OKAY, TIM SAID VOLT TACKLE IS MY BEST MOVE. MY POWERS ARE SOMEWHERE IN HERE. COME ON, A LITTLE SPARK TO GET THIS PARTY STARTED...

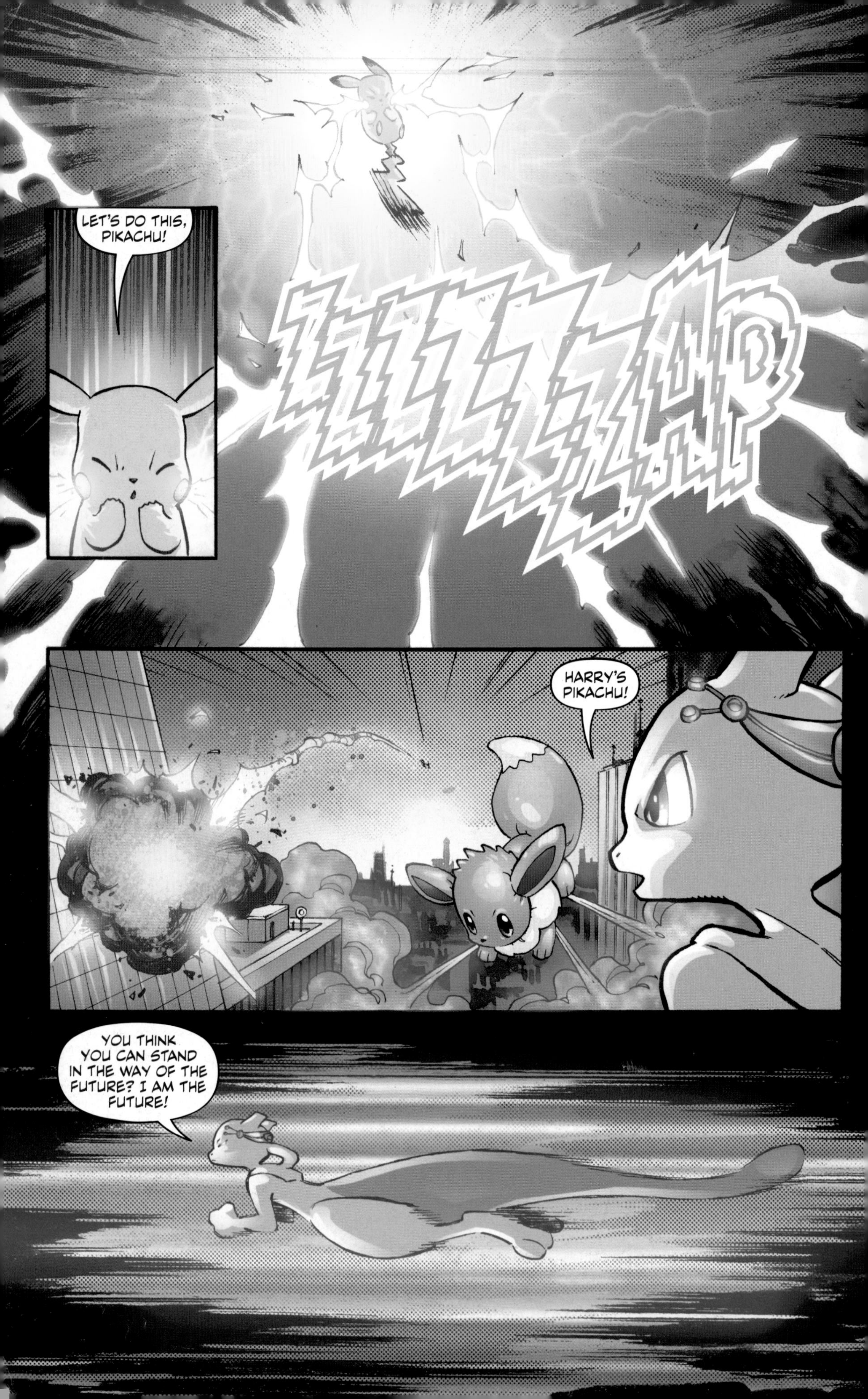
LET'S DO THIS, PIKACHU!
HARRY'S PIKACHU!
YOU THINK YOU CAN STAND IN THE WAY OF THE FUTURE? I AM THE FUTURE!

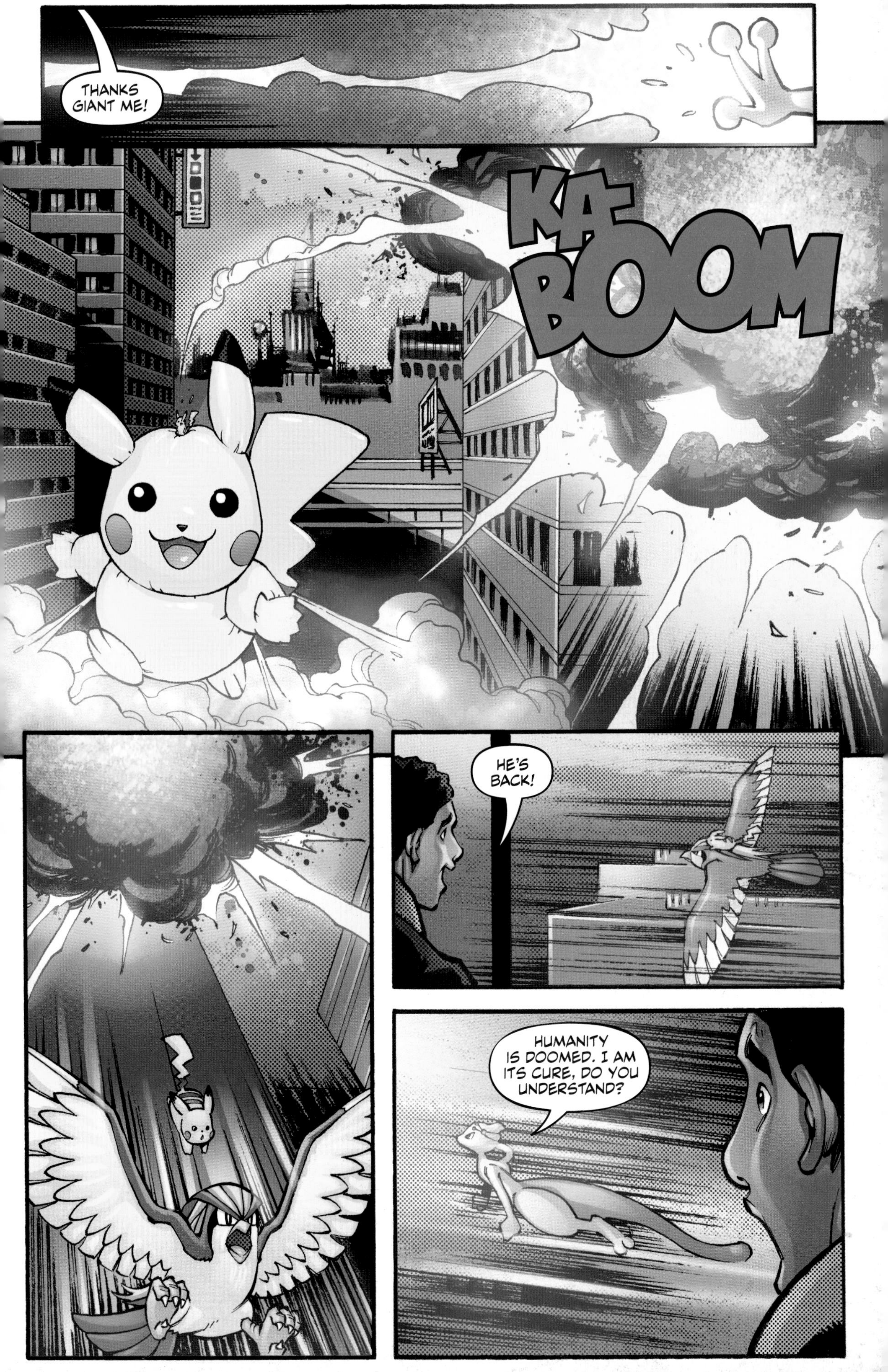
THANKS GIANT ME!
KA-BOOM
HE'S BACK!
HUMANITY IS DOOMED. I AM ITS CURE, DO YOU UNDERSTAND?

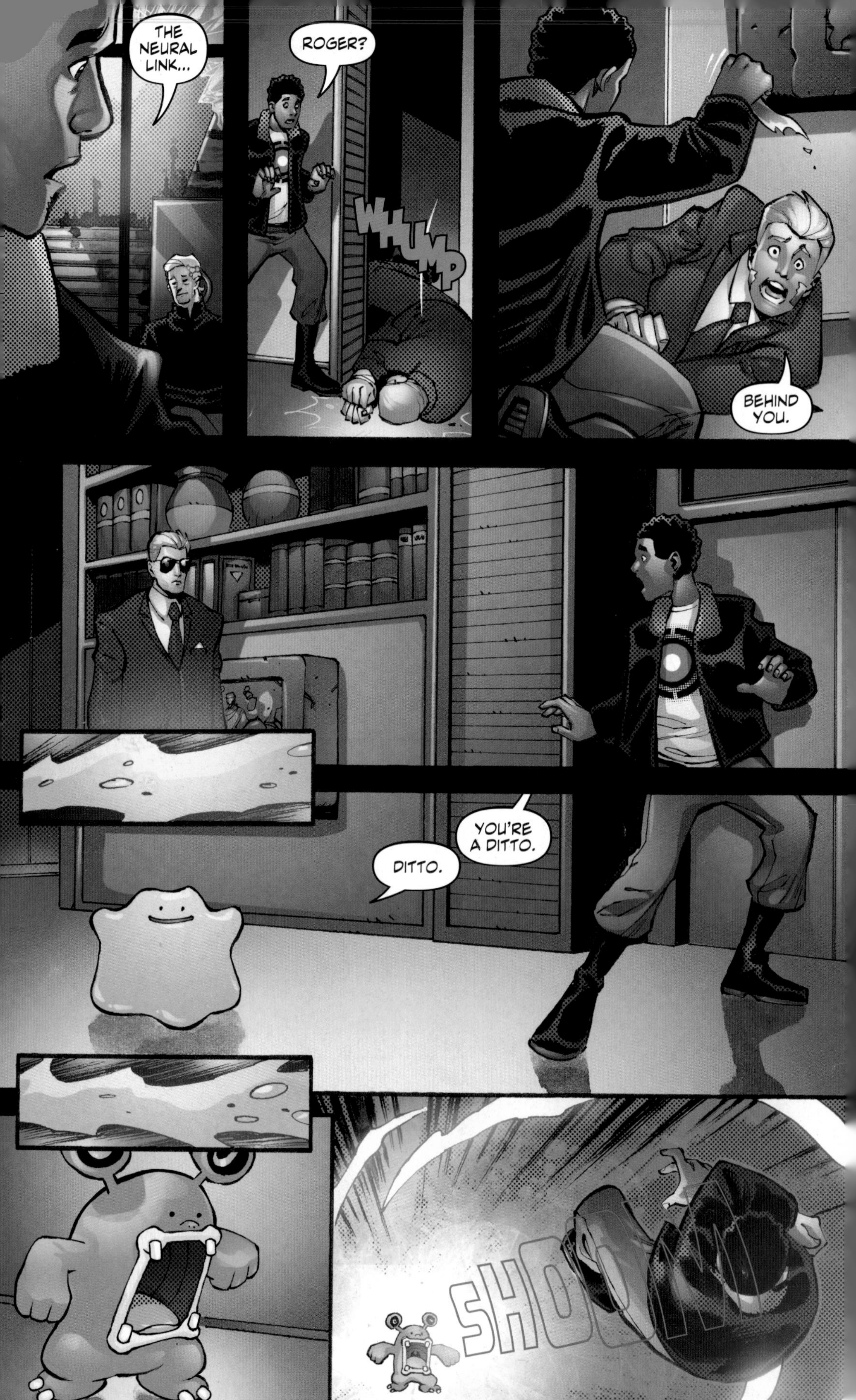
THE NEURAL LINK...
ROGER?
WHUMP
BEHIND YOU.
YOU'RE A DITTO.
DITTO.
SHOOM

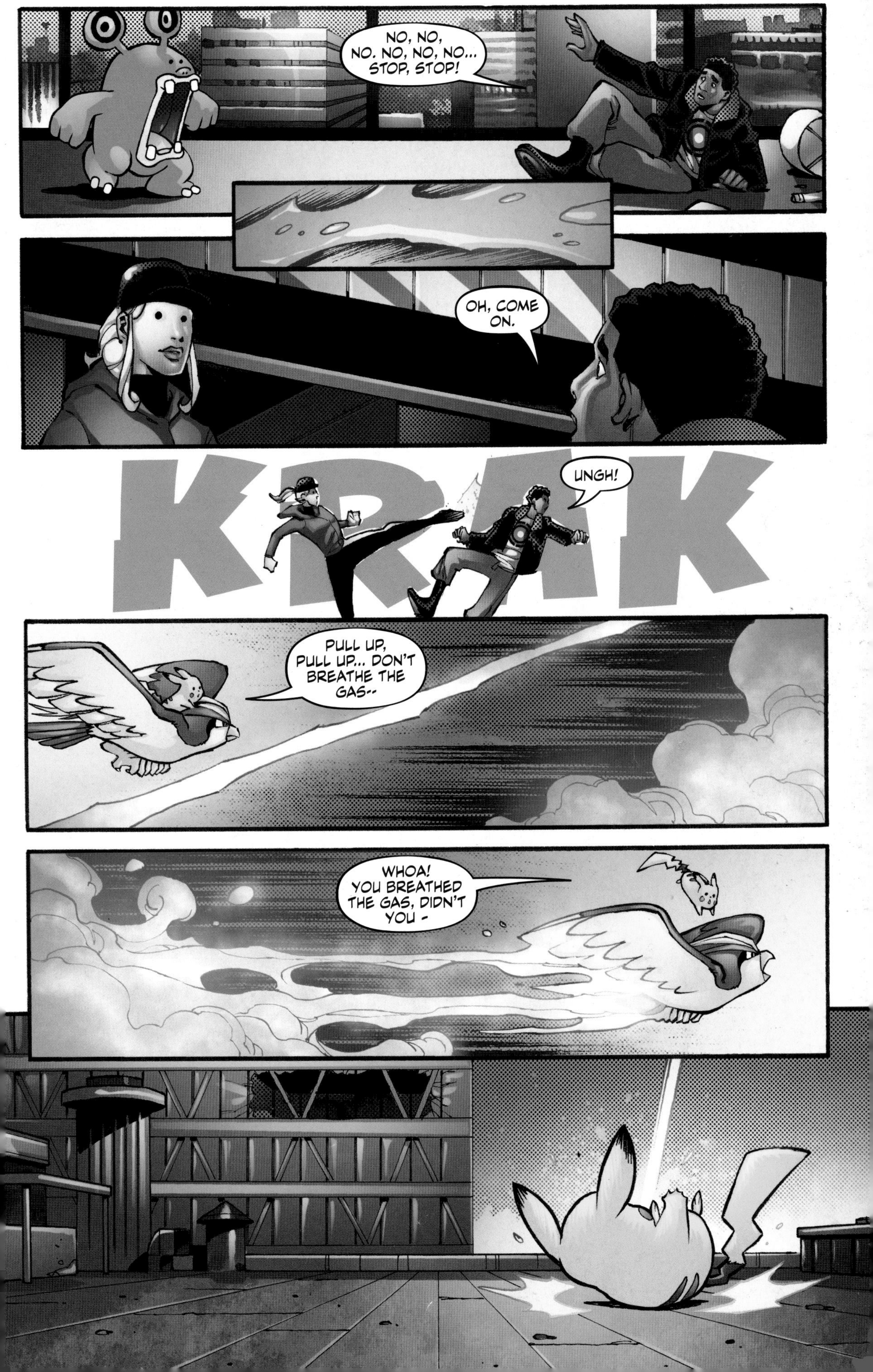
NO, NO,
NO. NO, NO, NO...
STOP, STOP!
OH, COME
ON.
KRAK
UNGH!
PULL UP,
PULL UP... DON'T
BREATHE THE
GAS--
WHOA!
YOU BREATHED
THE GAS, DIDN'T
YOU -

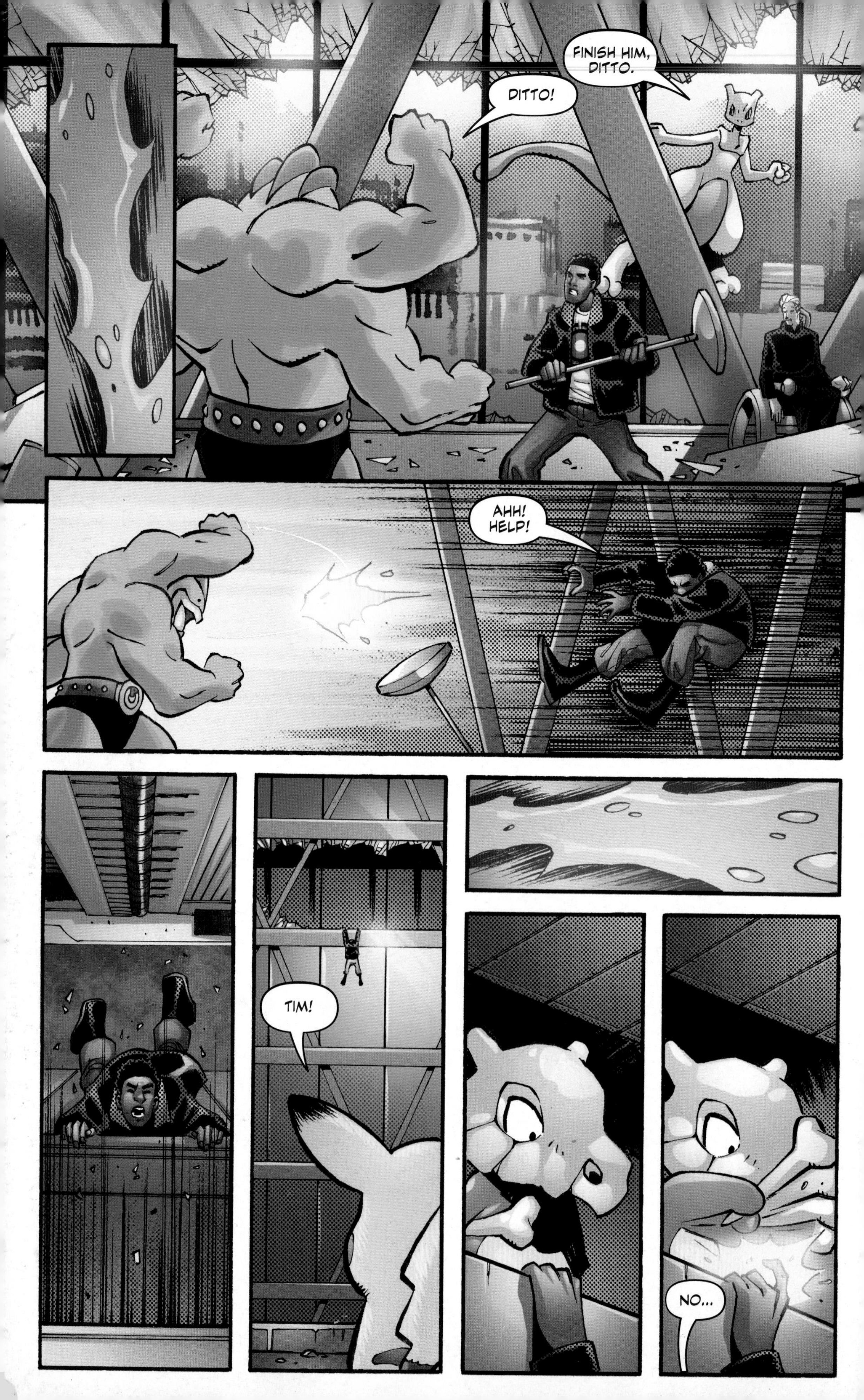
FINISH HIM, DITTO.
DITTO!
AHH! HELP!
TIM!
NO...

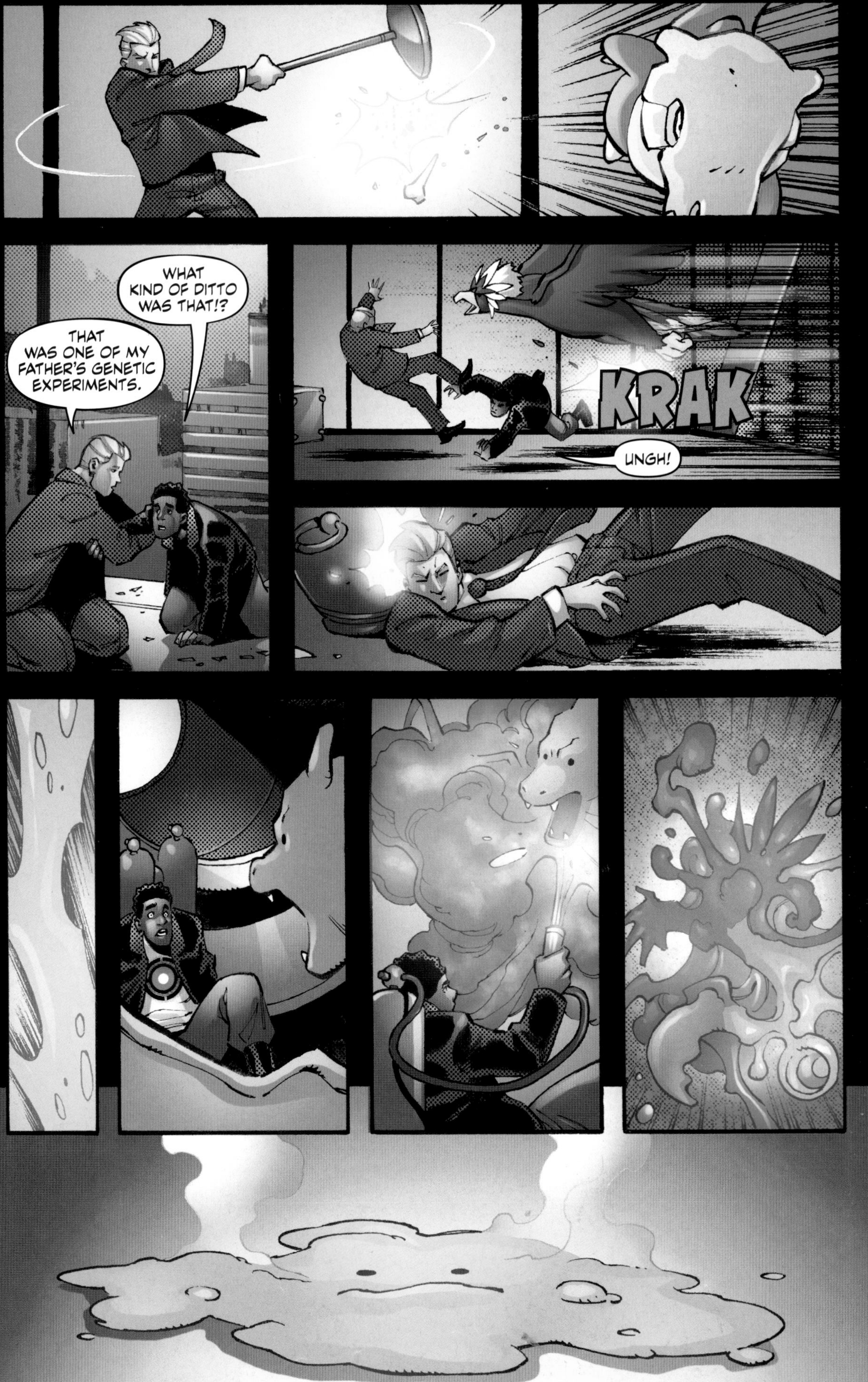
WHAT KIND OF DITTO WAS THAT!?
THAT WAS ONE OF MY FATHER'S GENETIC EXPERIMENTS.
KRAK
UNGH!

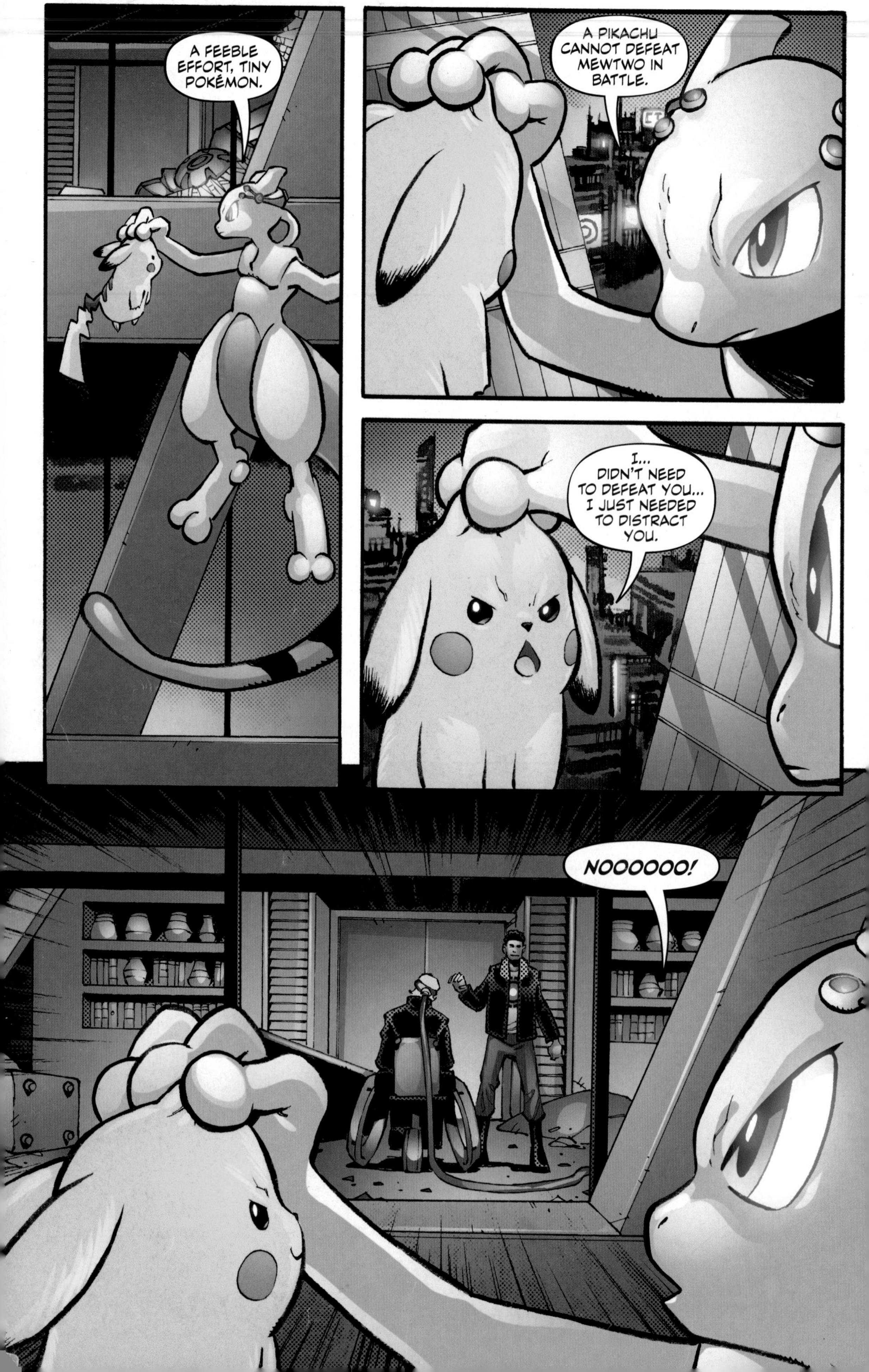
A FEEBLE EFFORT, TINY POKÉMON.
A PIKACHU CANNOT DEFEAT MEWTWO IN BATTLE.
I... DIDN'T NEED TO DEFEAT YOU... I JUST NEEDED TO DISTRACT YOU.
NOOOOOO!

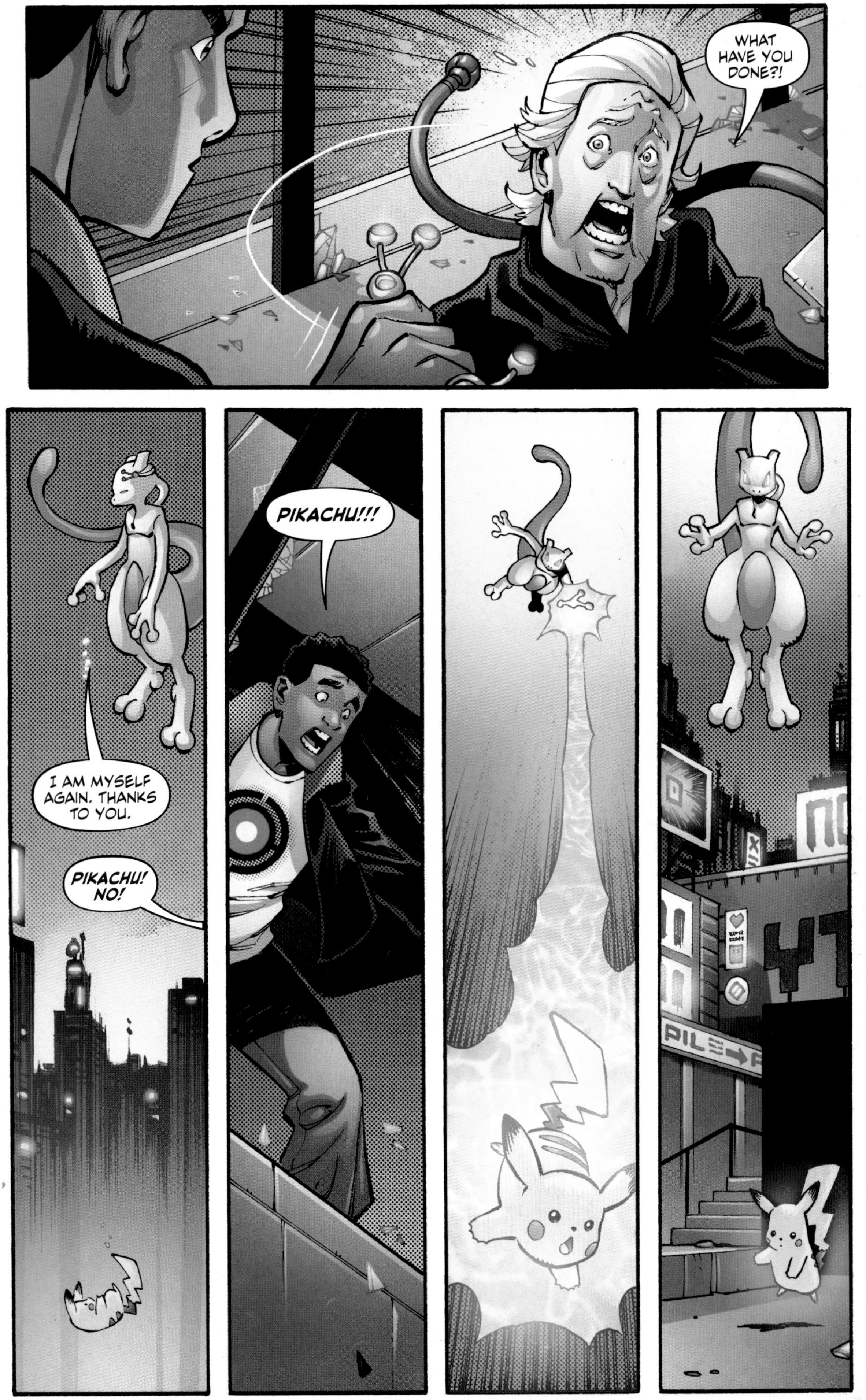
WHAT HAVE YOU DONE?!
I AM MYSELF AGAIN. THANKS TO YOU.
PIKACHU! NO!
PIKACHU!!!

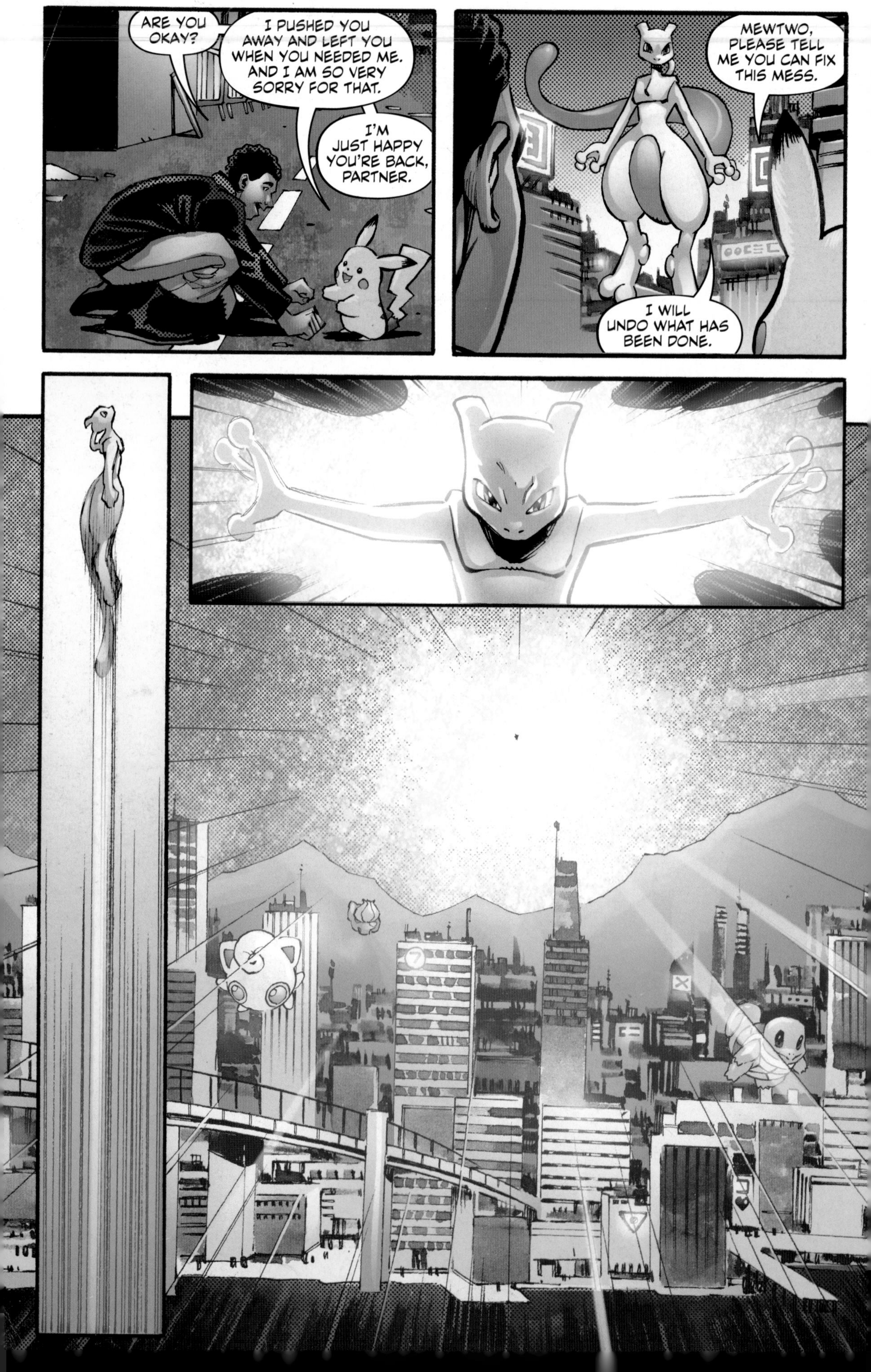
ARE YOU OKAY?
I PUSHED YOU AWAY AND LEFT YOU WHEN YOU NEEDED ME. AND I AM SO VERY SORRY FOR THAT.
I'M JUST HAPPY YOU'RE BACK, PARTNER.
MEWTWO, PLEASE TELL ME YOU CAN FIX THIS MESS.
I WILL UNDO WHAT HAS BEEN DONE.

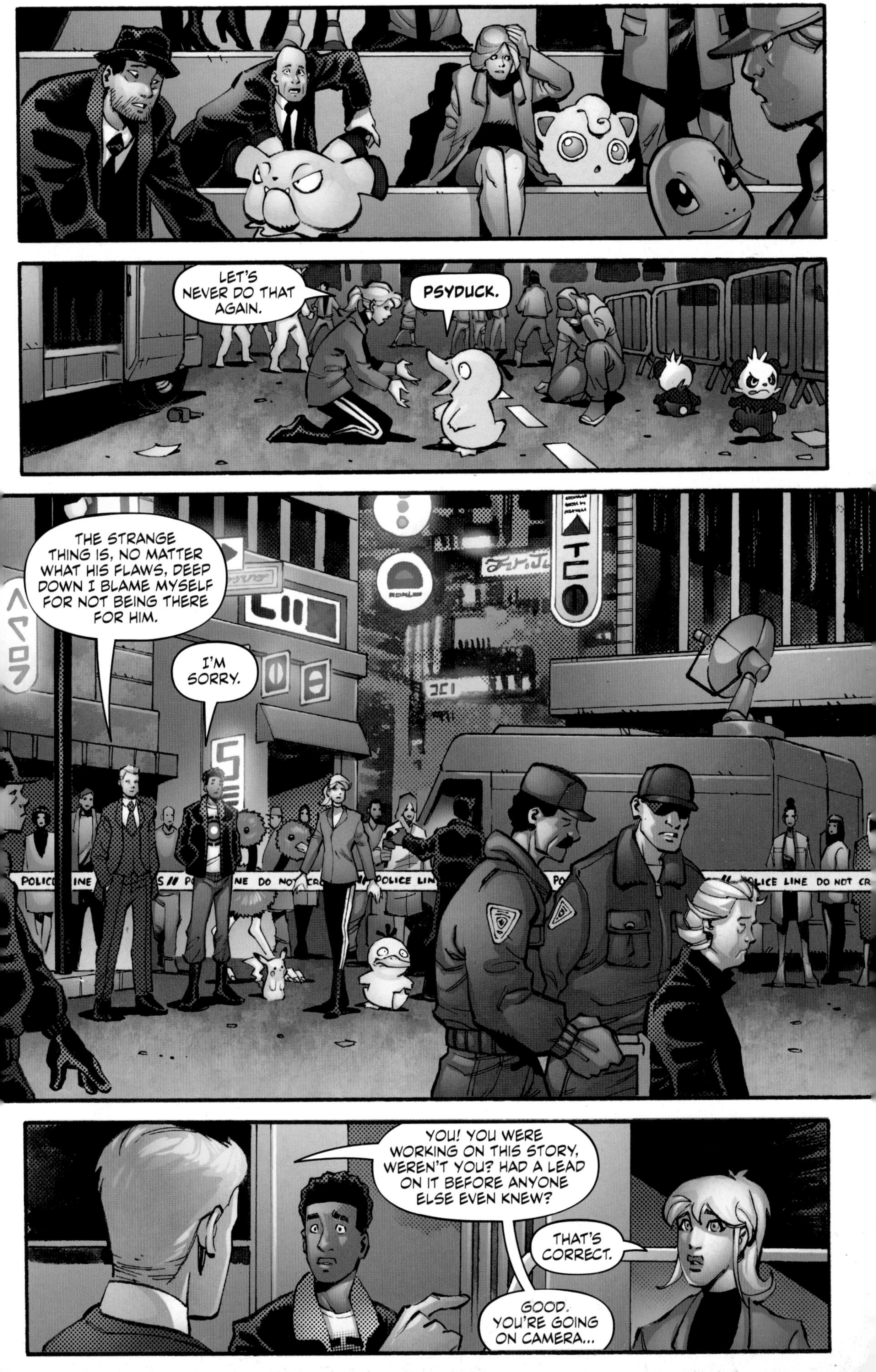
LET'S NEVER DO THAT AGAIN.
PSYDUCK.
THE STRANGE THING IS, NO MATTER WHAT HIS FLAWS, DEEP DOWN I BLAME MYSELF FOR NOT BEING THERE FOR HIM.
I'M SORRY.
POLICE LINE
YOU! YOU WERE WORKING ON THIS STORY, WEREN'T YOU? HAD A LEAD ON IT BEFORE ANYONE ELSE EVEN KNEW?
THAT'S CORRECT.
GOOD. YOU'RE GOING ON CAMERA...

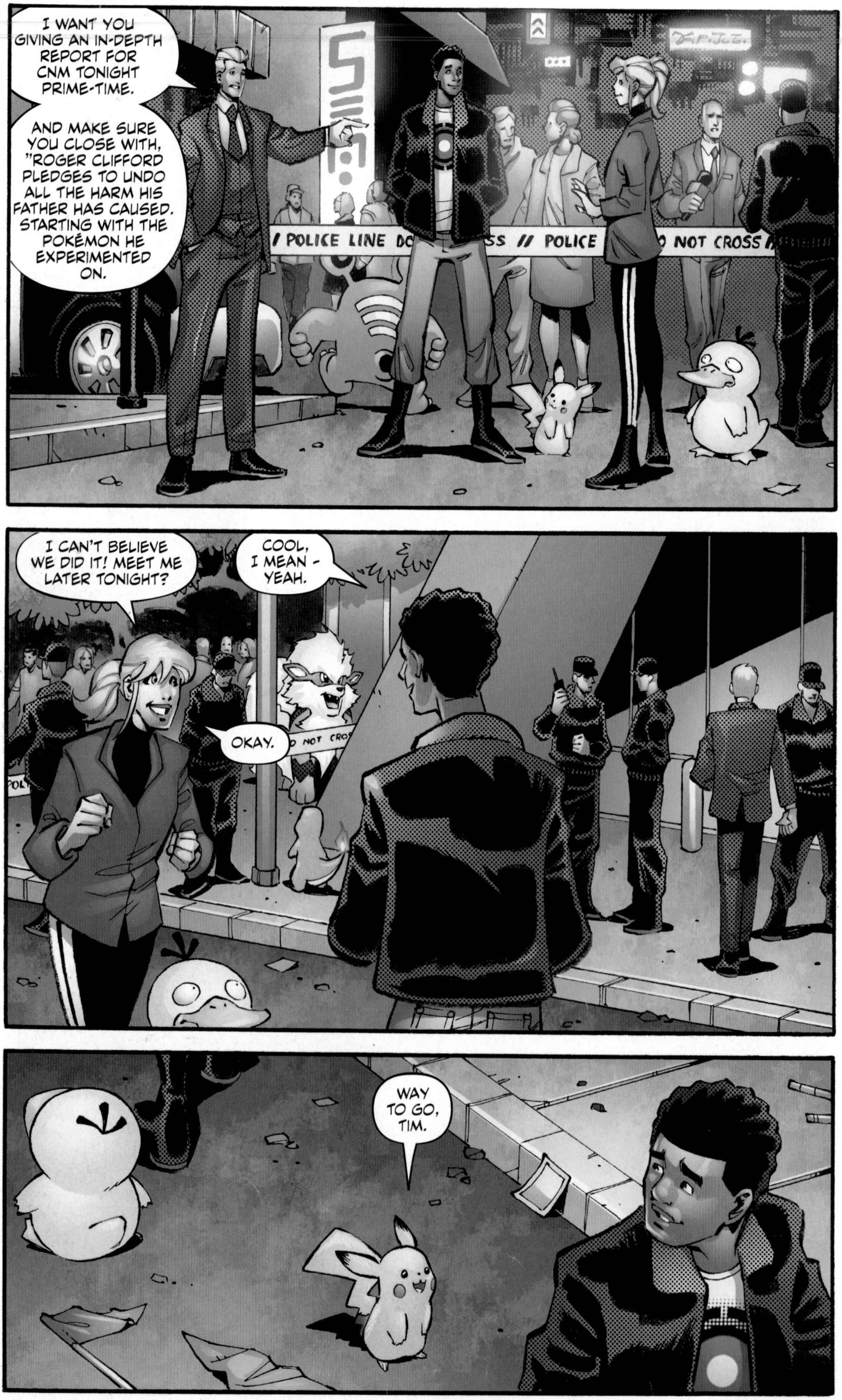
I WANT YOU GIVING AN IN-DEPTH REPORT FOR CNM TONIGHT PRIME-TIME.
AND MAKE SURE YOU CLOSE WITH, "ROGER CLIFFORD PLEDGES TO UNDO ALL THE HARM HIS FATHER HAS CAUSED. STARTING WITH THE POKÉMON HE EXPERIMENTED ON.
/ POLICE LINE DO
SS // POLICE
O NOT CROSS
I CAN'T BELIEVE WE DID IT! MEET ME LATER TONIGHT?
COOL, I MEAN - YEAH.
OKAY.
O NOT CROS
WAY TO GO, TIM.

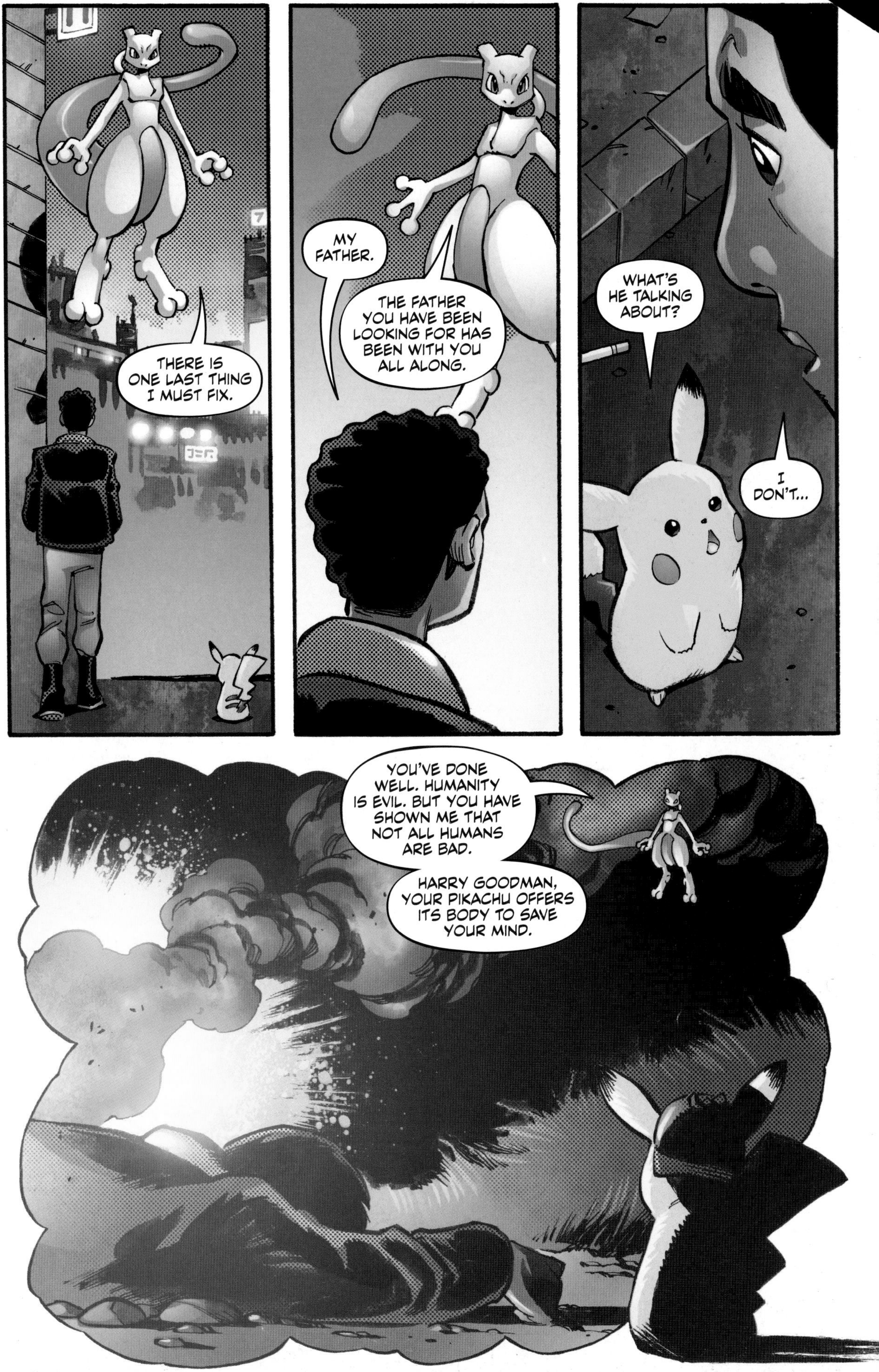
THERE IS ONE LAST THING I MUST FIX.
MY FATHER.
THE FATHER YOU HAVE BEEN LOOKING FOR HAS BEEN WITH YOU ALL ALONG.
WHAT'S HE TALKING ABOUT?
I DON'T...
YOU'VE DONE WELL. HUMANITY IS EVIL. BUT YOU HAVE SHOWN ME THAT NOT ALL HUMANS ARE BAD.
HARRY GOODMAN, YOUR PIKACHU OFFERS ITS BODY TO SAVE YOUR MIND.

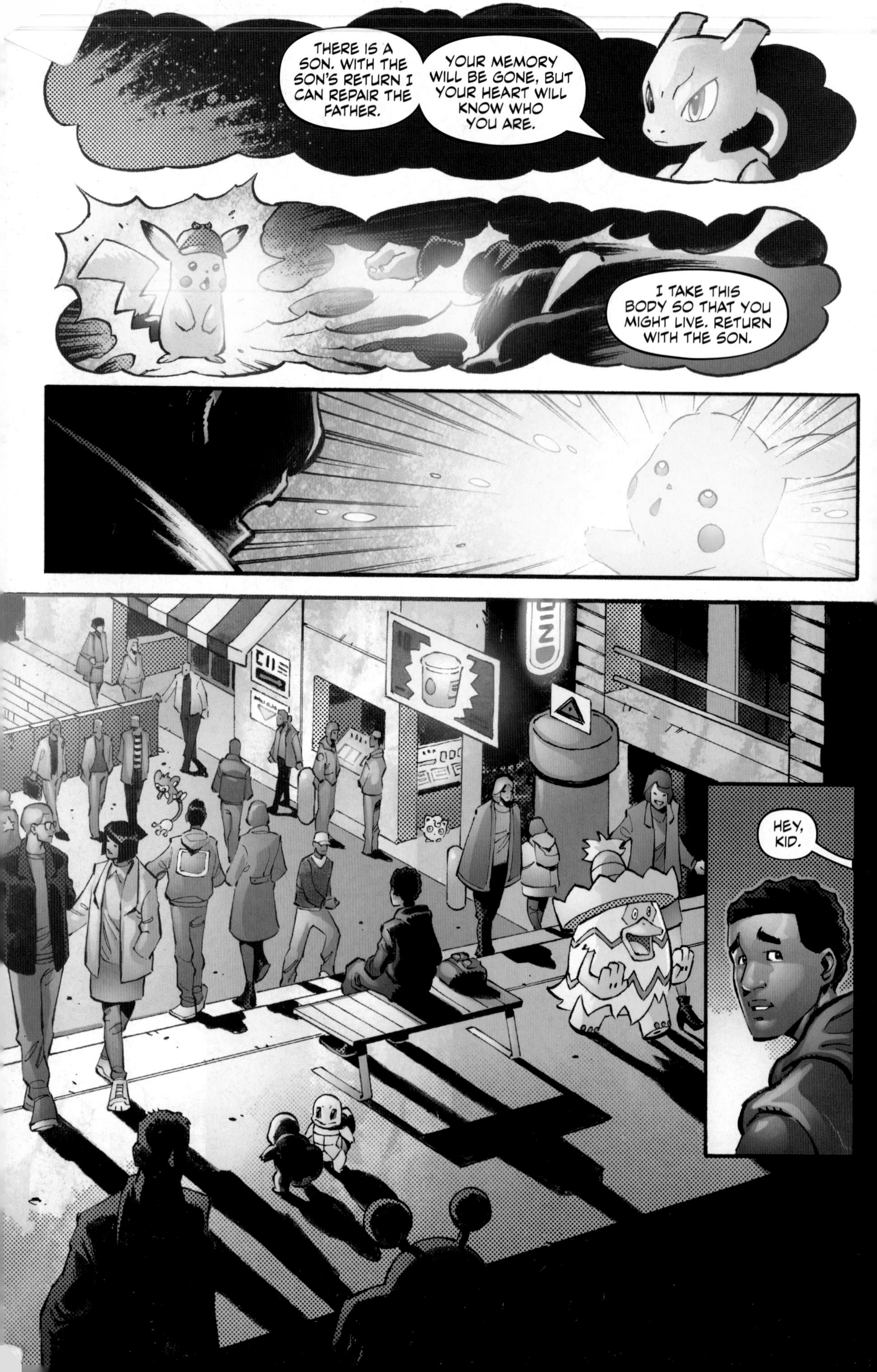
THERE IS A SON. WITH THE SON'S RETURN I CAN REPAIR THE FATHER.
YOUR MEMORY WILL BE GONE, BUT YOUR HEART WILL KNOW WHO YOU ARE.
I TAKE THIS BODY SO THAT YOU MIGHT LIVE. RETURN WITH THE SON.
HEY, KID.

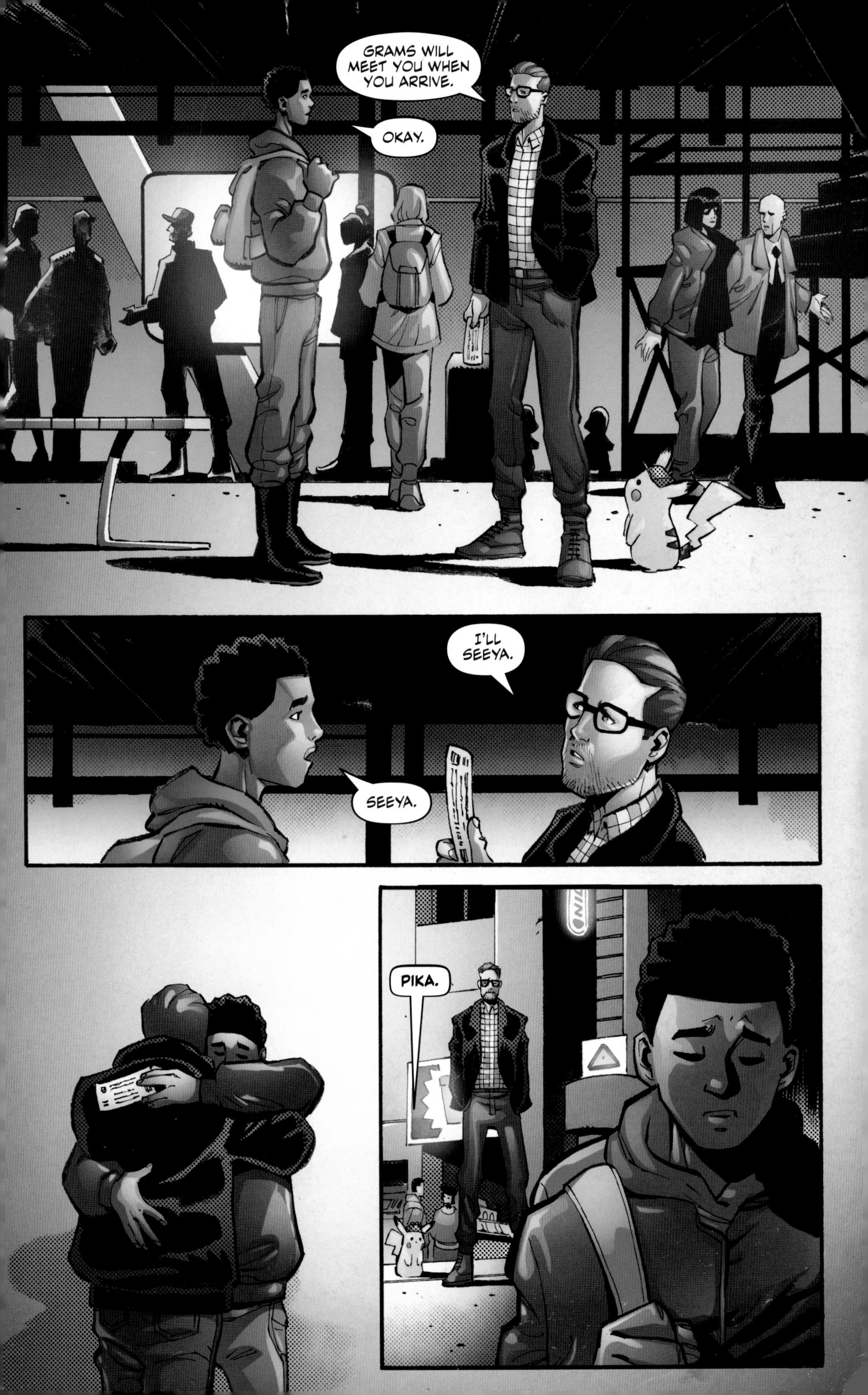
GRAMS WILL MEET YOU WHEN YOU ARRIVE.
OKAY.
I'LL SEEYA.
SEEYA.
PIKA.

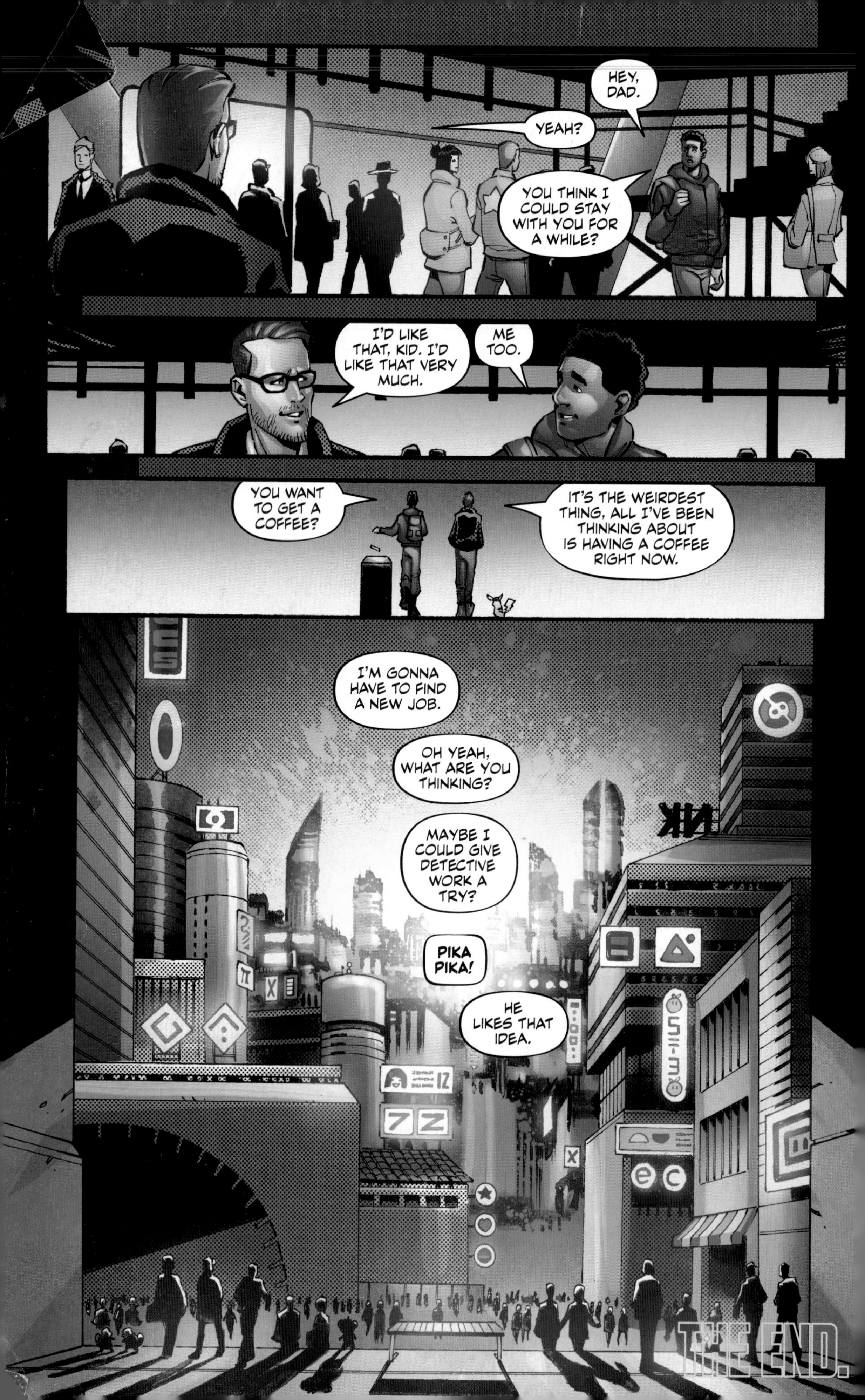
HEY, DAD.
YEAH?
YOU THINK I COULD STAY WITH YOU FOR A WHILE?
I'D LIKE THAT, KID. I'D LIKE THAT VERY MUCH.
ME TOO.
YOU WANT TO GET A COFFEE?
IT'S THE WEIRDEST THING, ALL I'VE BEEN THINKING ABOUT IS HAVING A COFFEE RIGHT NOW.
I'M GONNA HAVE TO FIND A NEW JOB.
OH YEAH, WHAT ARE YOU THINKING?
MAYBE I COULD GIVE DETECTIVE WORK A TRY?
PIKA PIKA!
HE LIKES THAT IDEA.
THE END.

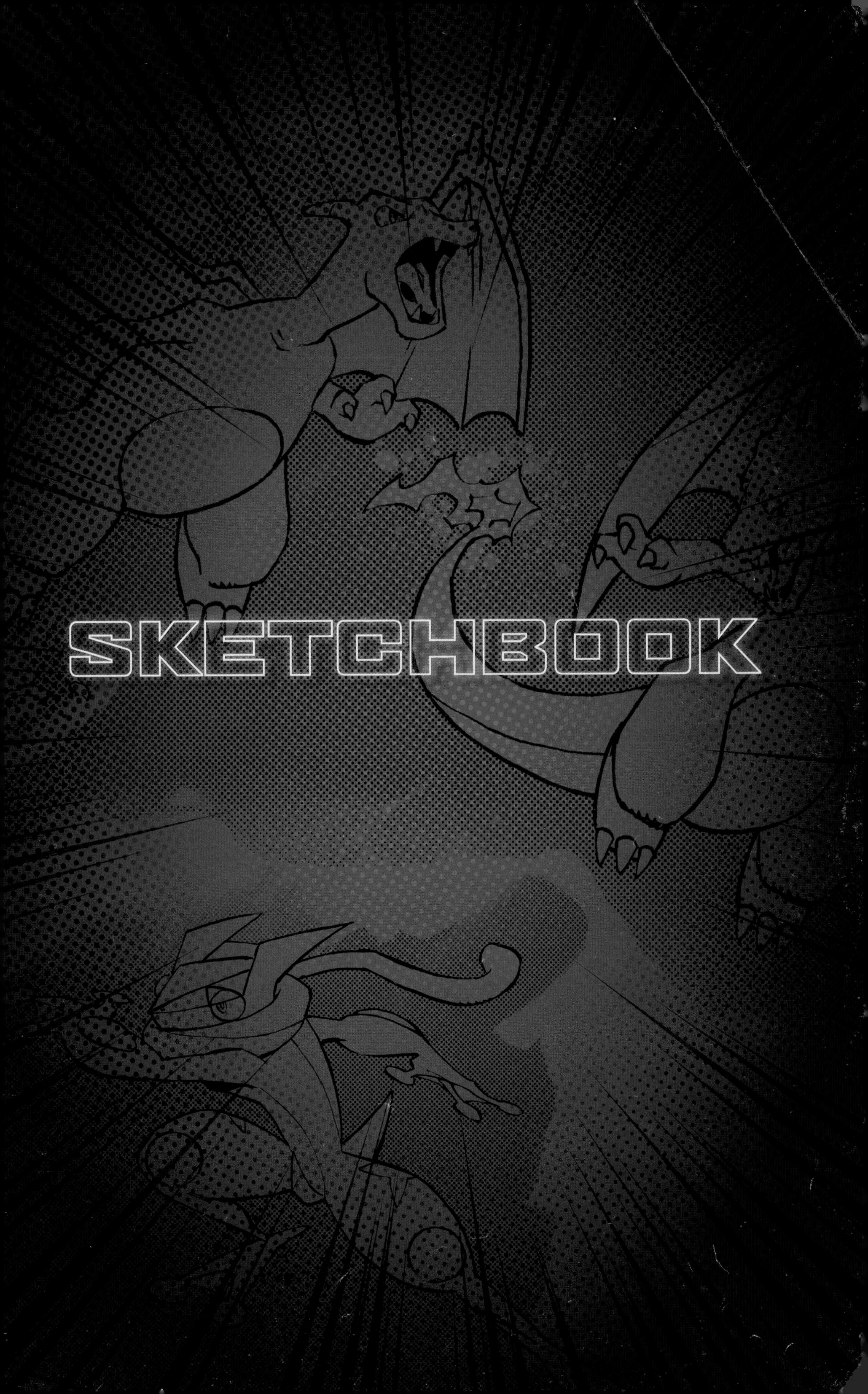
SKETCHBOOK

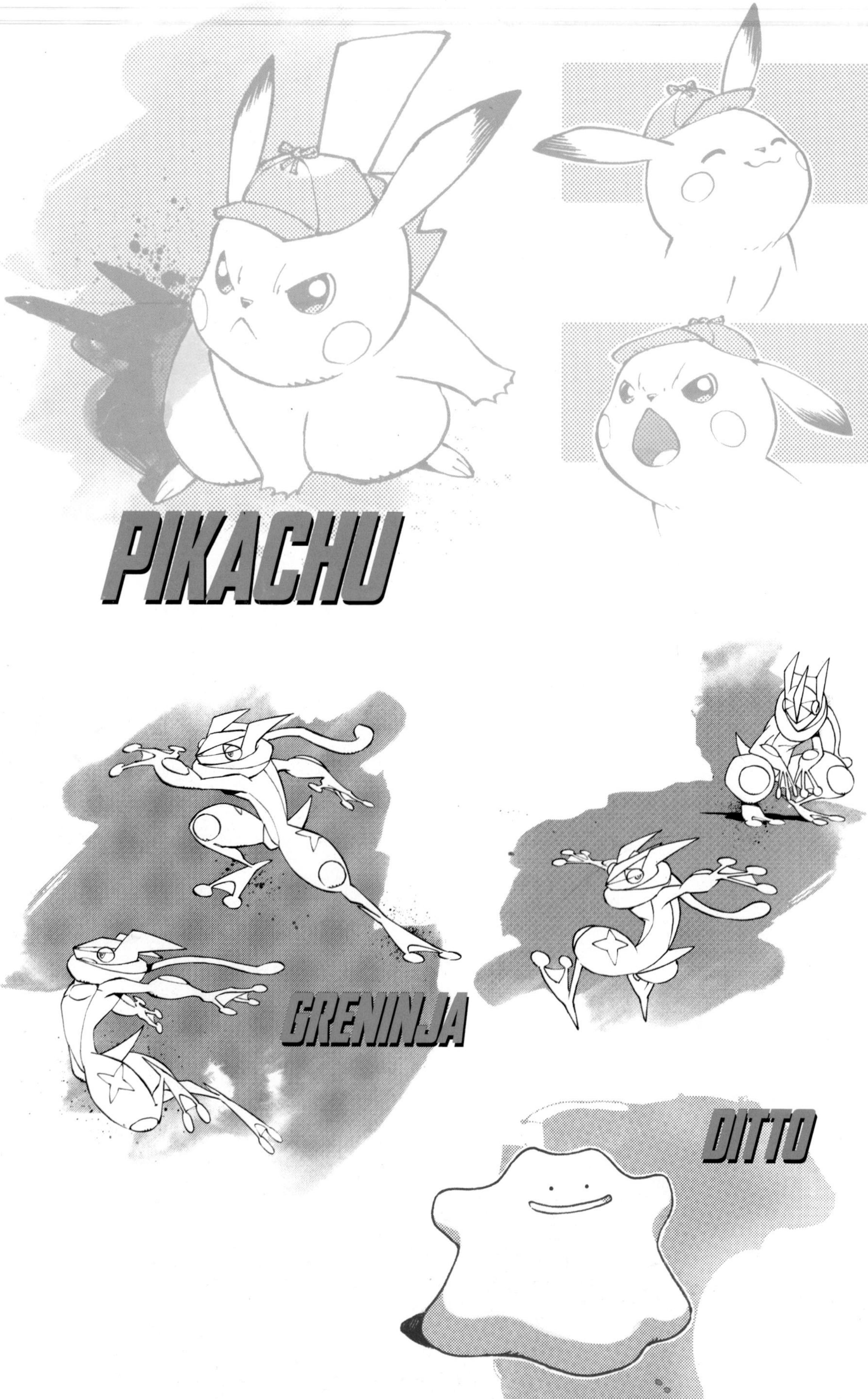
PIKACHU
GRENINJA
DITTO

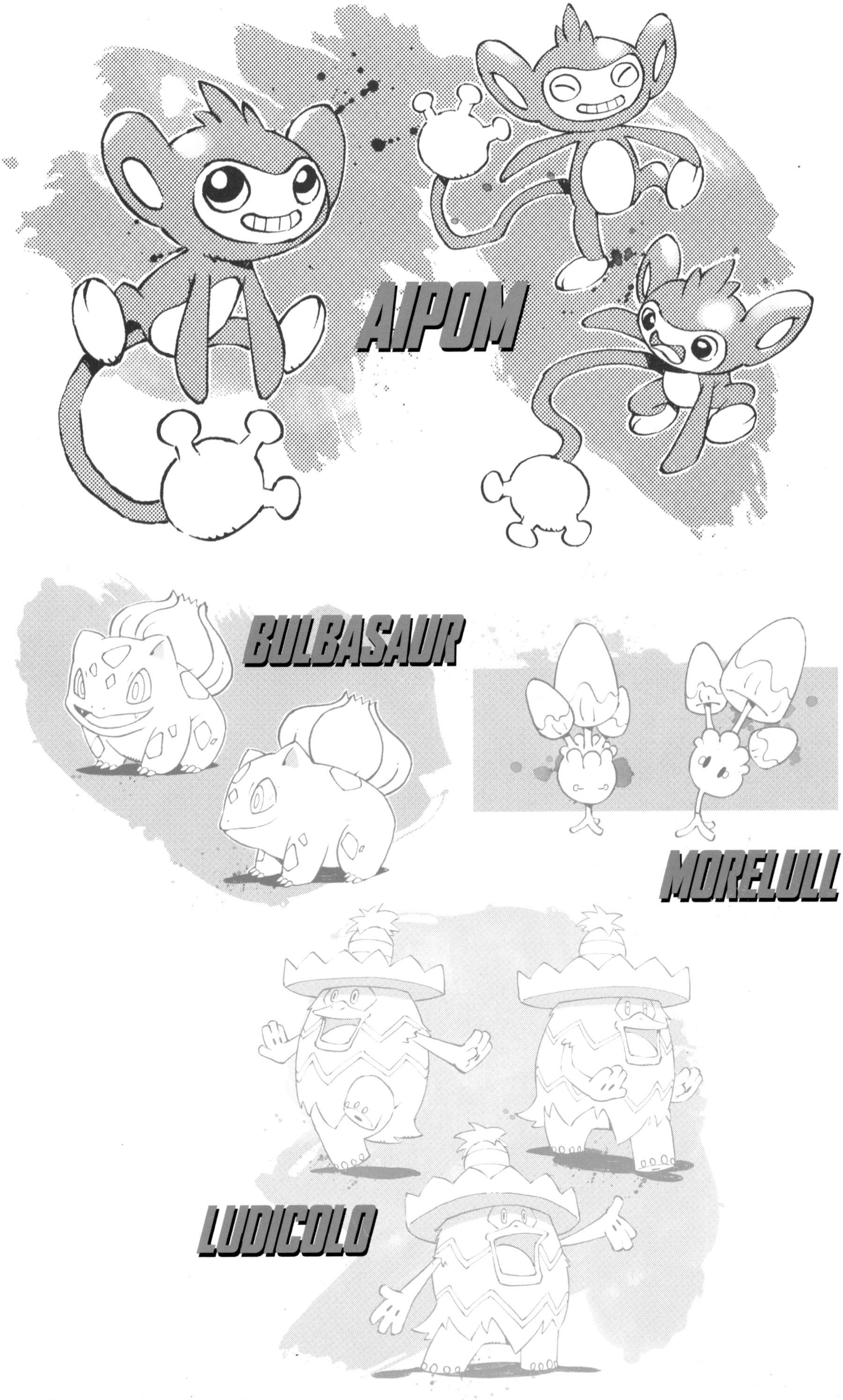
AIPOM
BULBASAUR
MORELULL
LUDICOLO

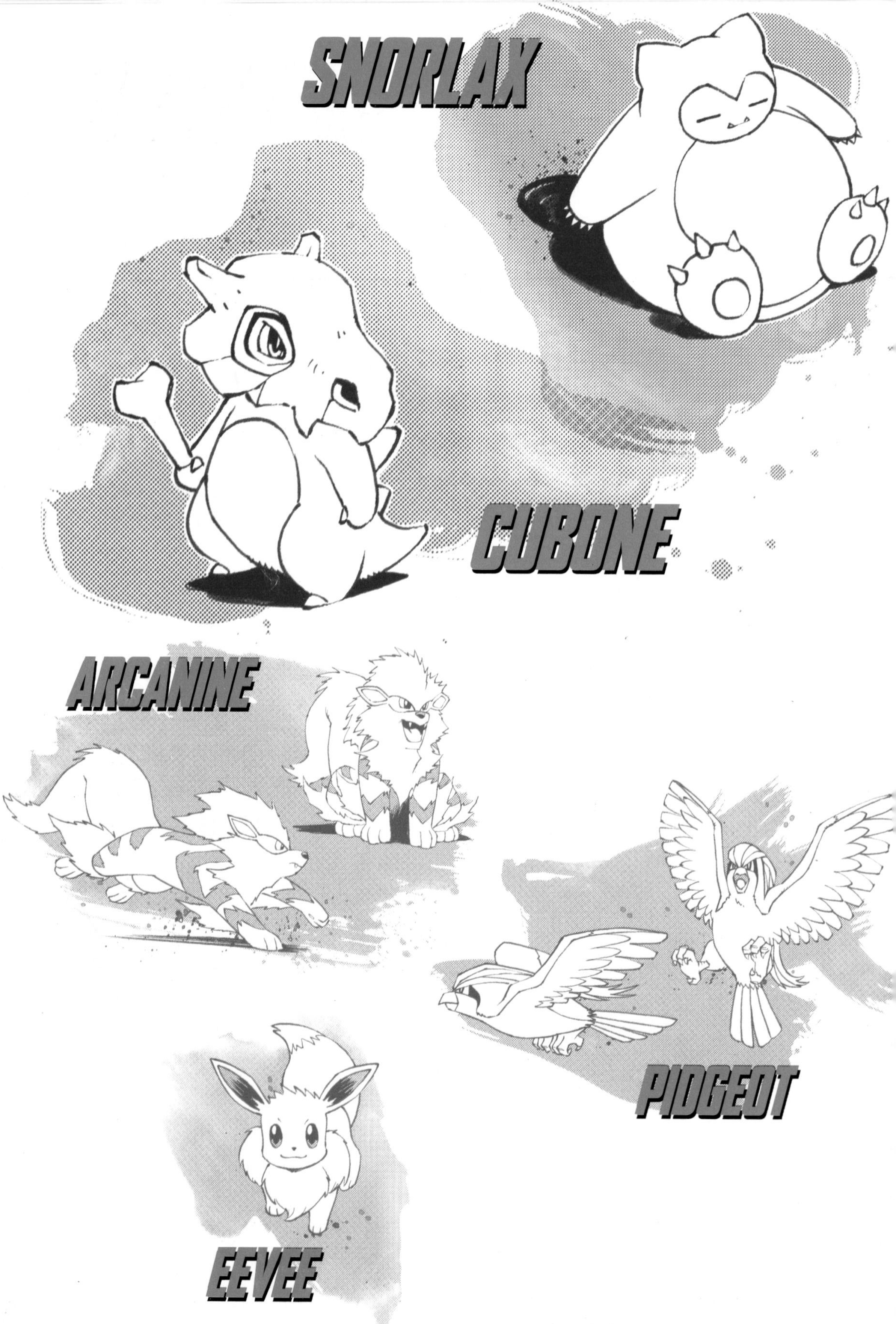
SNORLAX
CUBONE
ARCANINE
PIDGEOT
EEVEE

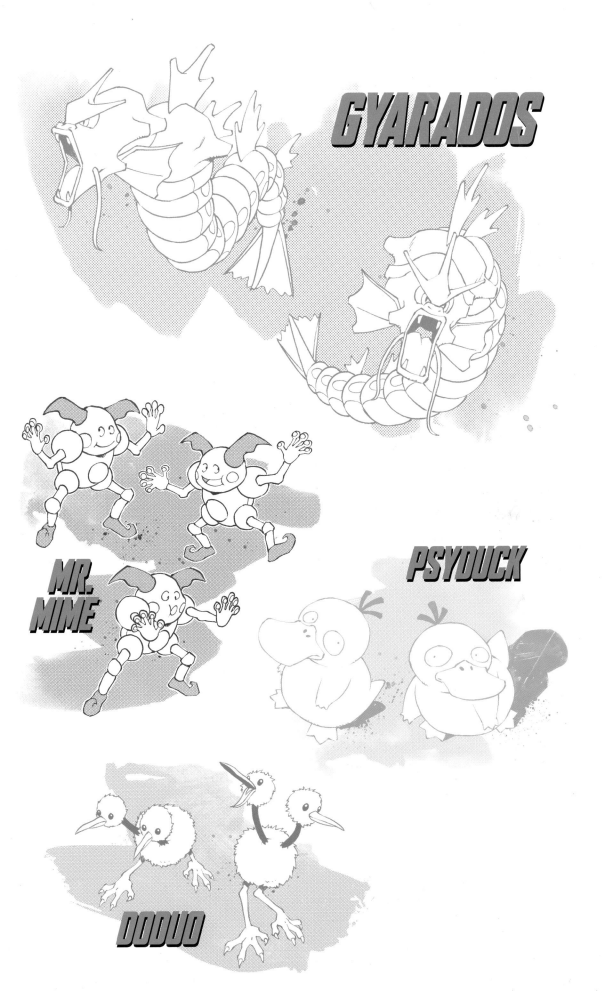

GYARADOS

MR. MIME

PSYDUCK

DODUO

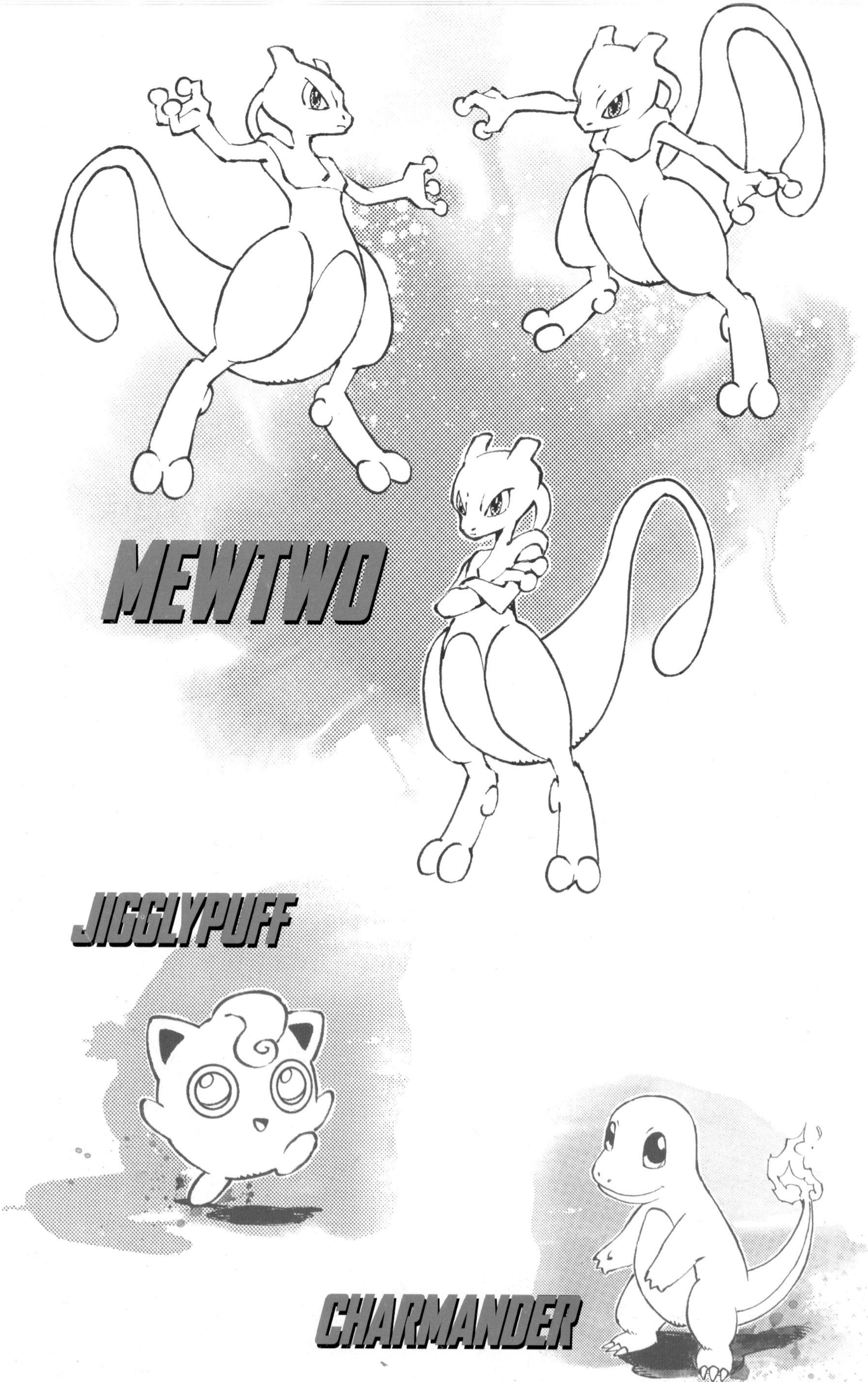
MEWTWO
JIGGLYPUFF
CHARMANDER

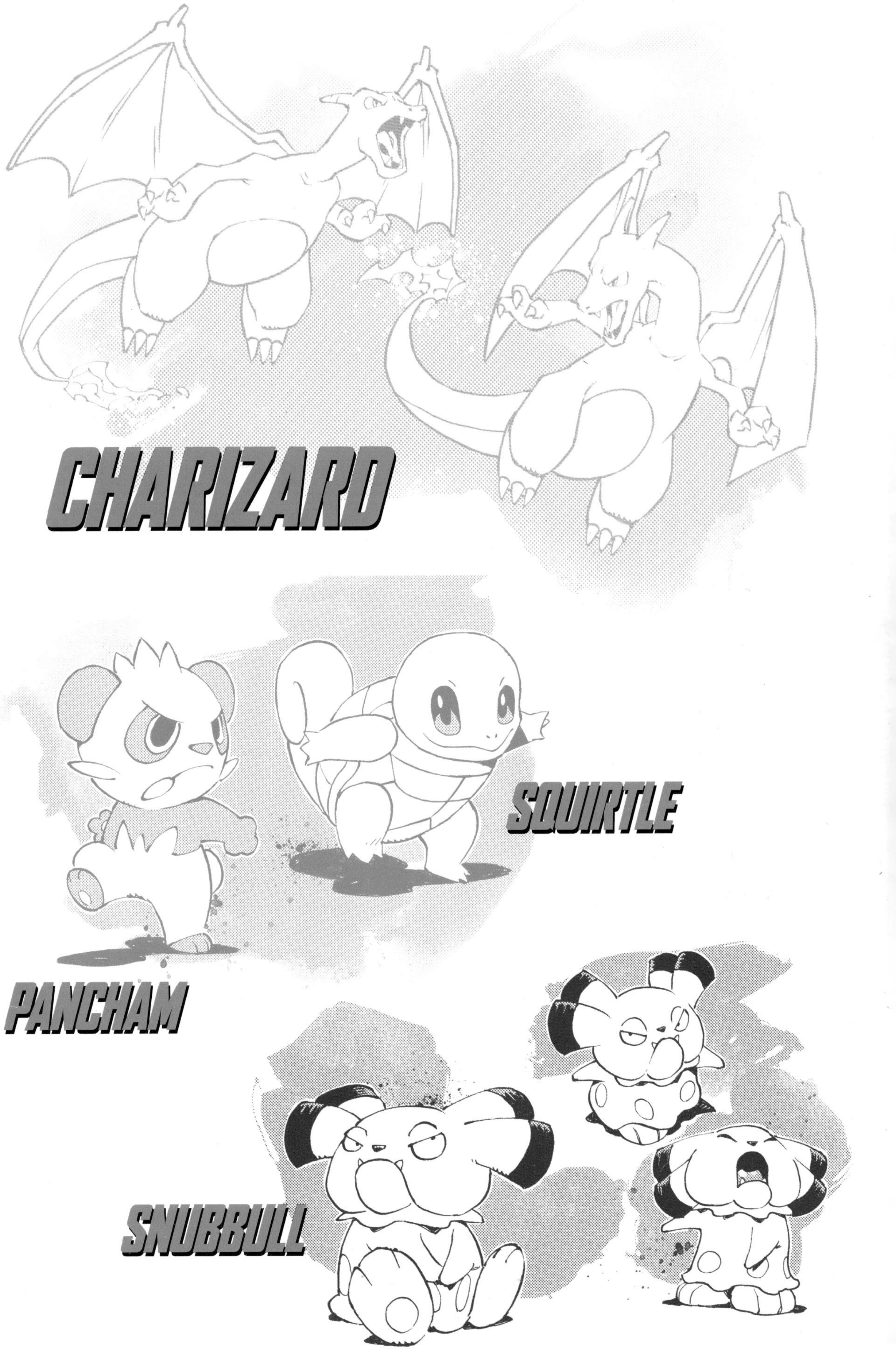
CHARIZARD
SQUIRTLE
PANCHAM
SNUBBULL

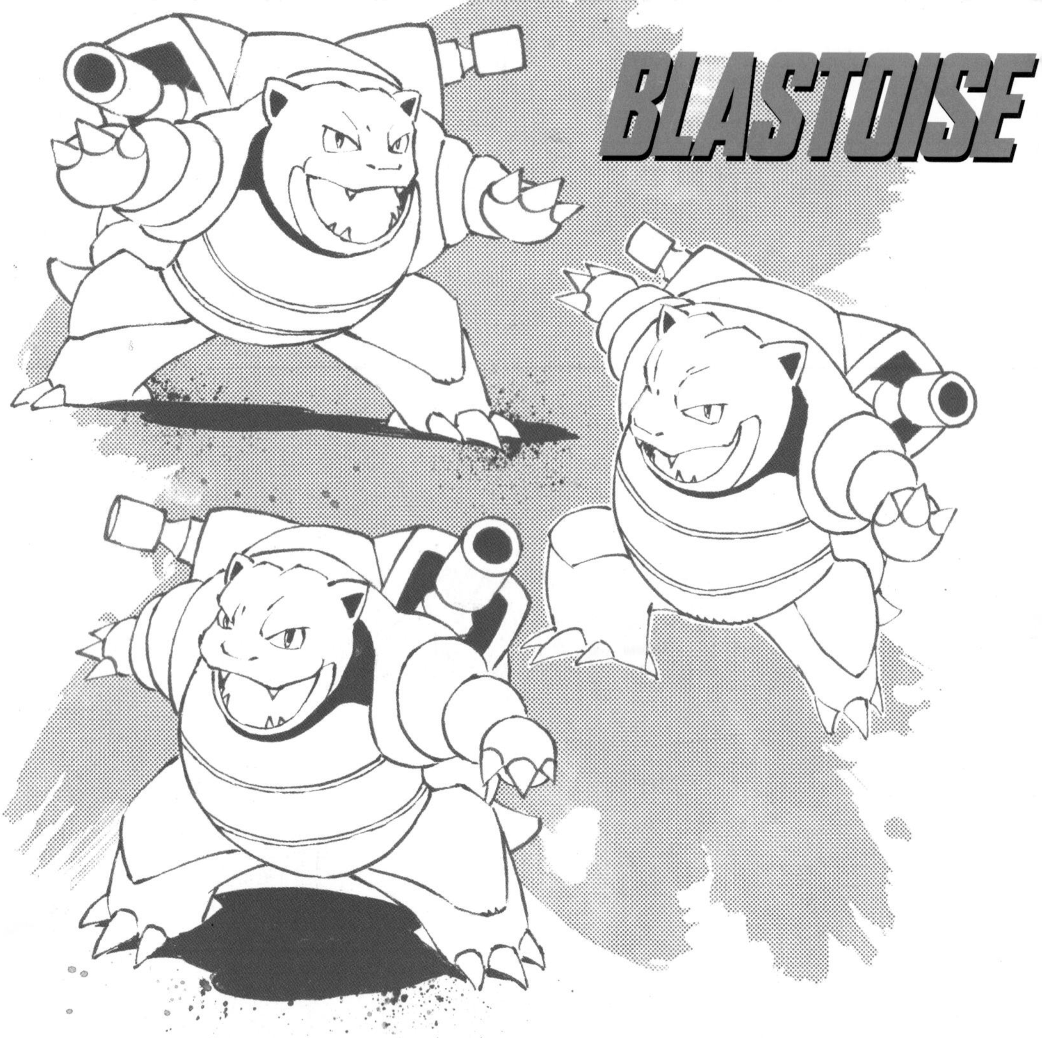
BLASTOISE

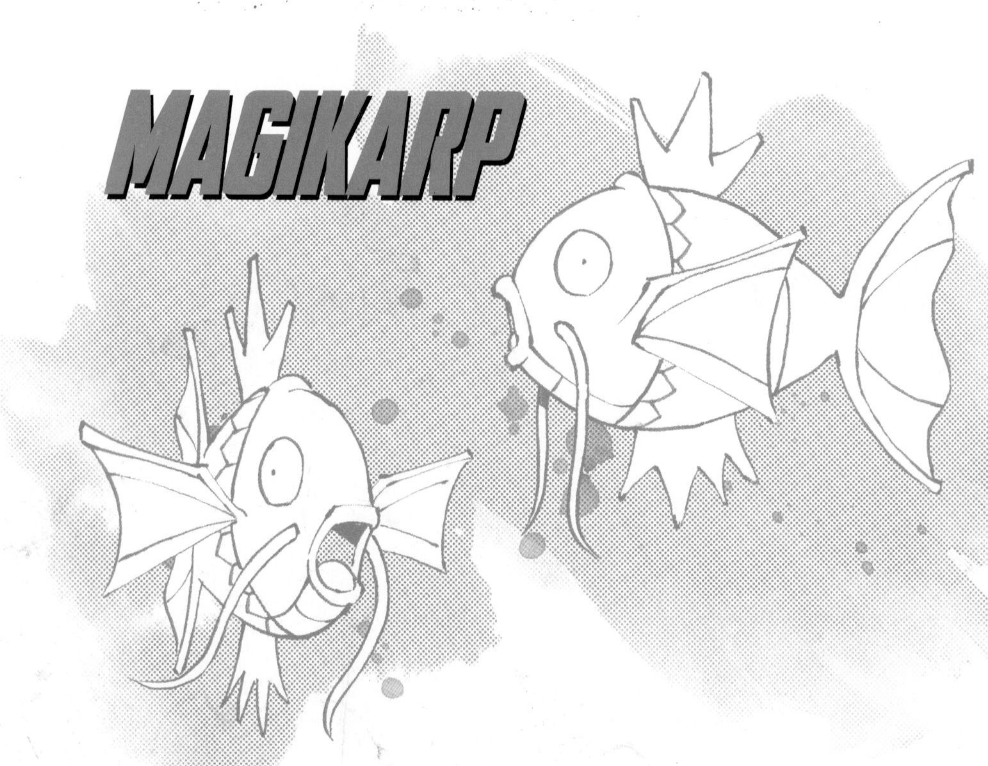
MAGIKARP

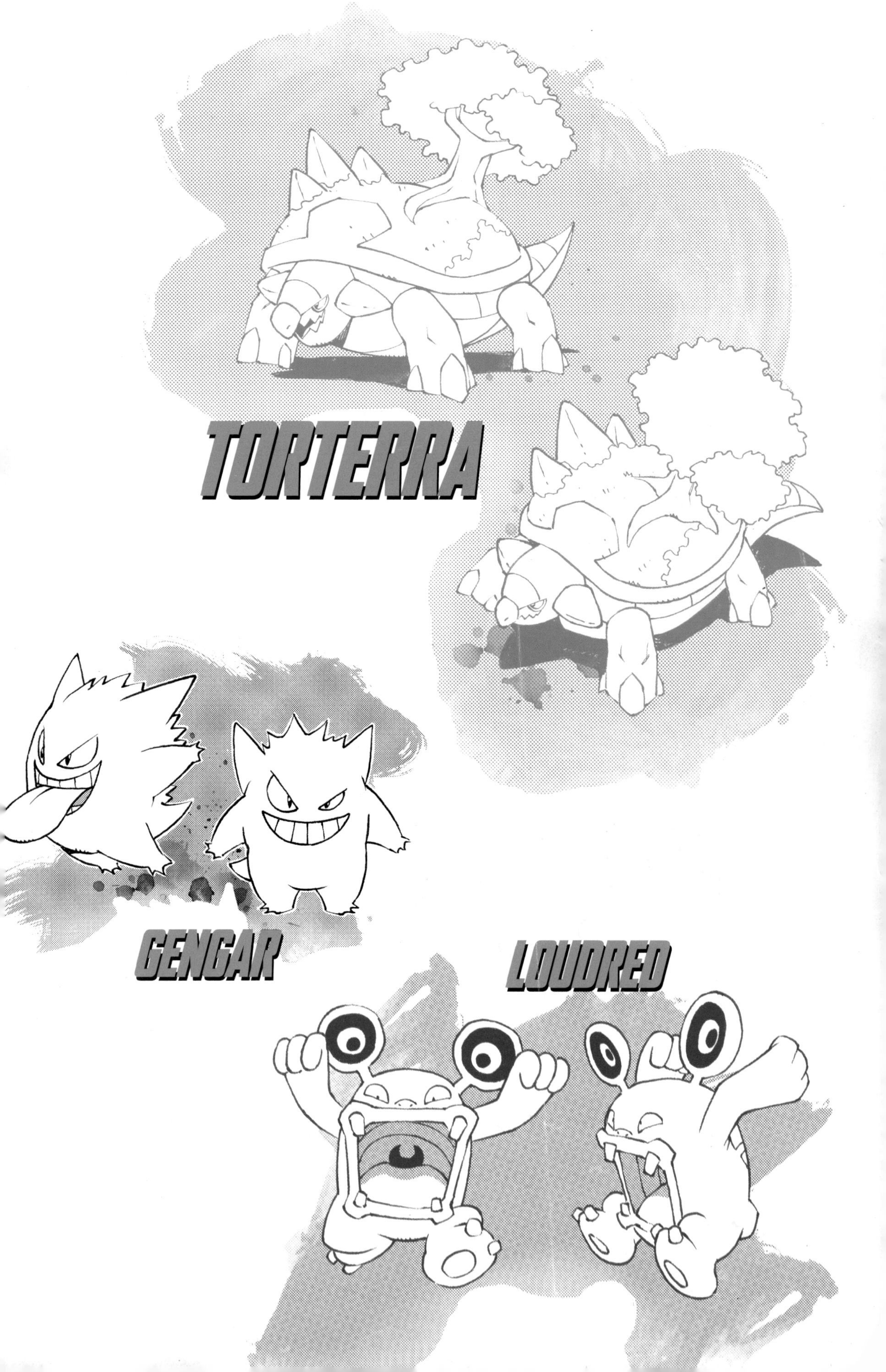
TORTERRA
GENGAR
LOUDRED

Brian BUCCELLATO

is a New York Times best-selling writer best-known for his work on FLASH and INJUSTICE for DC Comics. Brian started in comics as a colorist for the Marvel/DC crossover PUNISHER/BATMAN, and went on to color for all the major publishers, including work on THE UNCANNY X-MEN, SUPERMAN and THE FLASH. He began writing as part of The Story Company, where he collaborated on a number of screenplays. Buccellato started his comic writing career at Top Cow with THE DARKNESS before teaming with Francis Manapul to co-write THE FLASH and DETECTIVE COMICS at DC. He is the creator of FOSTER, SONS OF THE DEVIL and co-creator of CANNIBAL for Image Comics. His most recent work includes LOWLIFES from IDW, and LOST IN SPACE for Legendary. He currently lives in West Hollywood with a very small cat and dog

Nelson DANIEL

has worked for over 15 years in films and commercials as an art director, production designer, storyboard and concepts artist for films like AFTERSHOCK and Eli Roth's GREEN INFERNO, Robert Rodriguez's MACHETE among others. Nelson lives in Chile, where he has published the graphic novel LUCCA. His latest graphic novels, 1899 and 1959 will be published in Europe this year. He also did all art and colors on THE CAPE: 1969, monthly series JUDGE DREDD, DUNGEONS AND DRAGONS, CLUE, and the Stephen King/ Joe Hill collaboration ROAD RAGE, in addition to the single issues of GHOSTBUSTERS, GI JOE, TEENAGE MUTANT NINJA TURTLES and more. Nelson has also worked as colorist for Marvel and IDW on series such as THE CAPE, WILD BLUE YONDER and the 2015 Eisner Award-winning best limited series, LITTLE NEMO: RETURN TO SLUMBERLAND, where he was also nominated for best colorist.

Peter PANTAZIS

is a 20 year veteran of the comic industry, and color artist of titles such as DC's SUPERMAN, JUSTICE LEAGUE, BATMAN, BLUE BEETLE and ASTRO CITY, and Marvel's: NEW X-MEN,SPIDERMAN/FANTASTIC FOUR, X-CALIBUR, PARADISE X, IMAGES: POWERS, EXORSISTERS and many more. Pete is extremely thrilled to be working with Legendary to bring DETECTIVE PIKACHU to life in graphic novel form.